Korean War
Biographies

Korean War
Biographies

Sonia G. Benson
Gerda-Ann Raffaelle, Editor

GALE GROUP

THOMSON LEARNING

oit • New York • San Diego • San Francisco
on • New Haven, Conn. • Waterville, Maine
London • Munich

Korean War: Biographies

Sonia G. Benson

Staff

Gerda-Ann Raffaelle, *U•X•L Editor*
Carol DeKane Nagel, *U•X•L Managing Editor*
Thomas L. Romig, *U•X•L Publisher*

Robyn V. Young, *Project Manager, Imaging and Multimedia Content*
Robert Duncan, *Senior Imaging Specialist*
Kim Davis, *Permissions Associate, Text*
Tracey Rowens, *Senior Art Director, Cover Design*
Pamela A. E. Galbreath, *Senior Art Director, Page Design*

LM Design, *Typesetter*

Rita Wimberley, *Senior Buyer*
Evi Seoud, *Assistant Manager, Composition Purchasing and Electronic Prepress*

Front cover photograph of Douglas MacArthur and others reproduced by permission of Double Delta Industries, Inc. Back cover photograph of Anna Rosenberg reproduced by permission of AP/Wide World Photos, Inc.

Library of Congress Cataloging-in-Publication Data

Benson, Sonia.
  Korean War : biographies / Sonia G. Benson ; Gerda-Ann Raffaelle, editor.
    p. cm.
  Includes bibliographical references and index.
  Summary: Presents biographies of twenty-six men and women who participated in or were affected by the Korean War, including politicians, military leaders, journalists, and nurses.
  ISBN 0-7876-5692-5 (hc. : alk. paper)
  1. Korean War, 1950–1953—Biography—Juvenile literature. 2. Korea (South)—Biography—Juvenile literature. 3. United States—Biography—Juvenile literature. [1. Korean War, 1950–1953—Biography.] I. Raffaelle, Gerda-Ann. II. Title.

DS918.A553 B46 2001
951.904'2'0922–dc21
[B]   2001044241

Contents

Reader's Guide

A long with being the "forgotten war" that no one wants to think about and the "wrong war" that the world powers probably should have avoided, the Korean War was a war that lacked definition. It had no exact beginning or end. The traditional dates are 1950 to 1953, from the North Koreans' invasion of South Korea to the signing of the armistice. Many historians, however, place the beginning of the war in 1945, when the United States and the Soviet Union began their occupations of the country, splitting it in two in a way that the Koreans had never imagined. Though the fighting ended in 1953, the country is still divided: many Koreans have not seen nor heard from family and loved ones—mother, father, sister, husband, friend, cousin—nor have they been allowed to return to their homeland for fifty years. For them, the war is not over.

The Korean War was neither civil war nor foreign conquest. Although the initial armed conflict was between the communist government of North Korea and the Westernized dictatorship in South Korea, these two opposing factions were created and supported by outsiders. In effect, Korea became a playing field for the cold war powers, so much so that many histories of the war written in the United States barely mention the Korean people and their struggles at all. But an estimated two million Korean civilians died during the war, leaving the survivors to rebuild a thoroughly decimated country.

Korean War: Biographies presents the life stories of twenty-five people who played pivotal roles in the Korean War, from the leaders of the world powers who created the situation that led to war to the leaders of Korea who found themselves on either side of a demarcation line despite their wanting the same thing: a unified country.

Format

The twenty-five entries in *Korean War: Biographies* are arranged alphabetically. Each opens with a portrait of the individual featured, birth and death information, and a quote by or about that person. Accompanying several biographies are sidebar boxes that highlight people and information of special interest. Each entry offers a list of additional sources students can refer to for more information, including sources used in writing the biography. Fifty black-and-white photographs help illustrate the material covered in the text. The volume begins with a timeline of important events in the Korean War and a "Words to Know" section that introduces students to difficult or unfamiliar terms. It concludes with a subject index so students can easily find the people, places, and events discussed throughout *Korean War: Biographies*.

Related Source

Korean War: Almanac and Primary Sources explores the Korean War through thirteen chapters and twelve documents. The Almanac chapters provide a solid overview of the war, from its underlying causes to its major battles through its drawn-out peace process. The twelve primary source documents include excerpted speeches, memoirs, oral histories, war correspondents' reports, and government documents pertaining to the war. This volume contains ninety maps and photographs, numerous sidebar boxes, a timeline of events, a glossary, lists of sources for further study, and a subject index.

Comments and Suggestions

We welcome your comments on this work as well as your suggestions for individuals to be featured in future editions of *Korean War: Biographies*. Please write: Editors, *Korean War: Biographies*, U•X•L, 27500 Drake Rd., Farmington Hills, MI 48331-3535; call toll-free: 1–800–877–4253; fax: 248–414–5043; or send e-mail via www.galegroup.com.

Korean War Timeline

1905 Japan declares Korea its protectorate.

1907 Widespread rebellion against Japanese rule rages through Korea. The Japanese brutally repress the Korean rebels, killing thousands.

1910 Japan annexes Korea, beginning a thirty-five-year colonial rule.

March 1, 1919 Protestors against Japanese rule read a Proclamation of Independence in Seoul, the capital of Korea, initiating a massive nationwide protest, later known as the March First Movement. The Japanese respond with deadly force.

1919 The first Korean Communist Party is formed in Siberia, a region in the Soviet Union.

1919 The Korean Provisional Government is formed in Shanghai, China; Korean independence leader **Syngman Rhee**, residing in the United States, is named its president.

1931 Japan invades Manchuria, China, extending its industrial empire from Korea into Manchuria.

1937 The Japanese enter full-scale war with China.

1941 A half million Korean men are forced to serve in the Japanese military in World War II.

August 6, 1945 The United States drops an atomic bomb on Hiroshima, Japan. Three days later it drops another on Nagasaki, Japan.

August 8, 1945 The Soviet Union enters the Pacific theater of World War II, assembling its troops in Manchuria and preparing to march into Korea.

August 10, 1945 Two U.S. officials select the 38th parallel as the dividing line across Korea. The United States then issues an order stating that Americans will accept the Japanese surrender to the south of the 38th parallel and Soviets will receive the surrender to the north of it.

August 15, 1945 As Japan surrenders, Korean leaders headed by **Yö Un-hyöng** and **Pak Hön-yöng** begin to prepare for an interim government, forming the Committee for the Preparation of Korean Independence (CPKI). By the end of the month, 145 branches of the CPKI, called "People's Committees," set up as local governments throughout the country.

September 5, 1945 U.S. troops arrive in Korea south of the 38th parallel, establishing the U.S. military government.

September 6, 1945 The CPKI elects fifty-five leaders to head the new Korean People's Republic (KPR), hoping to create an independent Korean government. The U.S. military government refuses to recognize the KPR.

October 1945 Exiled Korean leader Syngman Rhee arrives in Seoul on the plane used by General **Douglas MacArthur**, commander of the U.S. forces in the Far East.

1946–47 The Soviet Union and the United States try to create a joint trusteeship in Korea, but talks fail.

September 1947 The United States passes the matter of Korea to the United Nations (UN).

May 1948 Members of the United Nations Temporary Commission on Korea (UNTCOK) arrive in Seoul to supervise elections in Korea. The North Koreans refuse to allow them north of the 38th parallel.

May 10, 1948 The Republic of Korea's first National Assembly is elected without participation of the north.

August 15, 1948 Rhee is inaugurated as president of the Republic of Korea (ROK or South Korea).

September 9, 1948 The Democratic People's Republic of Korea (DPRK or North Korea) is created; **Kim Il Sung** is elected its premier.

December 1948 The Soviet Union withdraws its troops from North Korea.

1948–49 Guerrilla resistance to the rule of Rhee in the southern provinces of the Republic of Korea rages; a year of brutal police action follows.

1949 The Soviets successfully test their first atomic bomb.

January 1949 **Dean Acheson** is appointed U.S. Secretary of State; under him, the cold war policy of containment flourishes.

August 1949 General **Omar N. Bradley** is named the first permanent chairman of the Joint Chiefs of Staff, serving as a top military advisor to two presidents, **Harry S. Truman** and **Dwight D. Eisenhower**, through the course of the war.

October 1, 1949 Chinese leader **Mao Zedong** proclaims the establishment of the People's Republic of China, having driven Chinese Nationalist leader **Chiang Kai-shek** and his forces to the island of Taiwan (formerly Formosa).

December 1949 The United States withdraws its troops from Korea.

1949–50 Skirmishes periodically erupt across the 38th parallel, initiated by both the South and North Korean armies.

February 1950 At a conference in Wheeling, West Virginia, Senator **Joseph McCarthy** announces that there are communists working in the U.S. State Department.

June 25, 1950 Ninety thousand North Korean People's Army troops cross the 38th parallel, attacking the ROK Army at five key locations.

June 25, 1950 The UN Security Council passes a U.S.-proposed resolution condemning North Korea's "armed attack on the Republic of Korea" and calling for "the immediate cessation of hostilities" and withdrawal of NKPA troops to the 38th parallel.

June 26, 1950 U.S. ambassador to the Republic of Korea **John J. Muccio** organizes the evacuation of the families of Americans stationed in Korea as well as all American embassy workers.

June 27, 1950 Seoul falls to the North Koreans.

June 27, 1950 The United Nations passes a resolution that its members are to "furnish such assistance to the Republic of Korea as may be necessary to repel the armed attack and to restore international peace and security to the area."

June 30, 1950 Truman authorizes MacArthur to use ground forces in Korea. He also approves a naval blockade of North Korea. The president does not consult with Congress and calls this a "police action under the United Nations," rather than declaring war.

July 5, 1950 Task Force Smith, a small U.S. unit of 406 men—the first to fight in Korea—is shattered by the North Koreans at Osan.

July 10, 1950 The UN Security Council agrees to create a unified Korean command with MacArthur serving as commander in chief of the UN forces. Rhee places the Republic of Korea Army in the service of MacArthur.

July 14–16, 1950 North Koreans shatter two regiments of General **William F. Dean**'s Twenty-fourth Division at the Kum River.

July 19, 1950 The city of Taejon falls to the North Koreans.

July 26–29, 1950 U.S. soldiers kill an estimated three hundred unarmed South Korean civilians at the No Gun Ri Bridge.

August 1950 The People's Republic of China, alarmed with U.S. intervention in Korea, begins to move troops into Manchuria.

August 1950 The North Korean Army continuously attacks UN defenses of the city of Taegu, which is the temporary capital of the Republic of Korea.

August 1, 1950 Soviet delegate to the UN Security Council **Jacob A. Malik** introduces a resolution to invite representatives of the People's Republic of China and both Koreas to the Security Council to discuss the war. The resolution is defeated after debate.

August 1–3, 1950 UN forces in Korea are forced to retreat to the Pusan Perimeter in the south of the peninsula.

August 5, 1950 North Koreans successfully attack at the Naktong Bulge, penetrating the Pusan Perimeter defense.

August 17, 1950 The U.S. Marines strike the enemy at the Naktong Bulge and shatter them.

September 15, 1950 MacArthur leads the newly created X Corps in a massive and highly successful amphibious assault on the port city of Inchon.

September 23, 1950 General **Walton H. "Johnnie" Walker** leads the Eighth Army's breakout from the Pusan Perimeter and drives north to meet the X Corps.

September 24, 1950 China cables the United Nations to protest the strafing of sites in Manchuria by U.S. aircraft.

September 27, 1950 UN forces recapture Seoul.

September 30, 1950 ROK troops cross the 38th parallel, followed by other UN units.

October 14–18, 1950 Communist Chinese Forces (CCF) Commander **Peng Dehuai** moves 180,000 troops from Manchuria into North Korea.

October 15, 1950 Truman and MacArthur meet at Wake Island.

October 19–20, 1950 UN forces capture the already abandoned capital of North Korea, Pyongyang, and continue north toward the Korea-China border.

October 26–31, 1950 Chinese troops attack UN forces in several places near China's border with North Korea.

November 1, 1950 China launches the first Chinese offensive against the UN forces. Walker orders a retreat for the Eighth Army.

November 6–7, 1950 The Chinese troops mysteriously withdraw into the mountains, even though they are winning the battles.

Mid-November 1950 The X Corps advances to the Chosin (Changjin) Reservoir, separated from the Eighth Army.

November 24, 1950 The Eighth Army advances toward the Yalu River at the North Korea-China border.

November 25, 1950 CCF forcefully attack the Eighth Army, beginning the second Chinese offensive.

November 27, 1950 The Chinese strike at seven different fronts in Chosin, particularly targeting the well-trained marines under the command of General **Oliver P. Smith.**

November 28, 1950 The Eighth Army begins its withdrawal.

November 28–December 5, 1950 The X Corps retreats from the Chosin Reservoir to Hagaru in some of the worst fighting in the Korean War.

December 3, 1950 MacArthur orders a withdrawal of all UN forces to the 38th parallel. ROK General **Paik Sun Yup** recalled that on that day the South Korean army's "dream of national reunification by force was dashed forever."

December 11, 1950 105,000 UN troops and nearly 100,000 Korean civilians begin a two-week evacuation from Hungnam, North Korea.

December 23, 1950 Eighth Army commander Walker dies in a jeep accident.

December 26, 1950 Lieutenant General **Matthew B. Ridgway**, appointed to replace Walker as the commander of the Eighth Army, arrives in Korea.

1951 *New York Herald Tribune* correspondent **Marguerite Higgins** wins a Pulitzer Prize for the reports she filed on the Korean War.

January 1, 1951 The Chinese launch their third offensive, pushing UN forces fifty miles south of the 38th parallel.

January 4, 1951 Seoul is recaptured by the enemy.

January 15–February 11, 1951 Ridgway sends out patrols to find the enemy. They cover significant distance without resistance.

February 1951 Preparations for a prison camp begin on an island called Koje-do in South Korea.

February 11, 1951 The Chinese counterattack Ridgway's patrols in the battle at Chipyong-ni, but the UN forces stand, killing many Chinese.

March 14 15, 1951 Seoul is back in UN control; the Eighth Army is again approaching the 38th parallel.

April 11, 1951 MacArthur is relieved of command; Ridgway replaces him as commander of the UN forces; General **James A. Van Fleet** succeeds Ridgway as commander of the Eighth Army.

April 21, 1951 UN forces enter a three-day battle with the Chinese and North Koreans; UN forces are victorious.

May 1951 CCF continues to strike at UN forces, but without much success.

June 1951 Chinese and UN forces dig in across from each other at the crater known as the Punchbowl, beginning two years of stationary trench warfare.

June 23, 1951 After meeting with American diplomat George F. Kennan, Soviet ambassador Malik broadcasts a message on UN radio, stating that the Soviet people believe a cease-fire and an armistice can be arranged.

July 10, 1951 The first armistice meeting convenes.

July 16, 1951 Rhee and other Korean officials declare their unwillingness to accept a cease-fire while Korea remains divided.

August 1951 The Communists call off the armistice talks because, they claim, UN aircraft were bombing neutral zones.

August 1951 Assistant Secretary of Defense **Anna Rosenberg** establishes the Defense Advisory Committee on Women in the Service to recruit women into military service and improve the working conditions of those already enlisted.

September 13–26, 1951 A violent battle is fought at Heartbreak Ridge, in which many die on both sides and little ground is exchanged. This is typical of the fighting during the armistice talks.

October 1951 Armistice meetings resume at Punmanjom, a small village near the 38th parallel.

November 23, 1951 In the armistice negotiations, a new demarcation line is established at the front, with a demilitarized zone that stretches out two kilometers on each side of the line.

January 1952 The two sides at the armistice talks enter a long and difficult stalemate over the issue of repatriating prisoners of war who do not wish to return to their country.

February–March 1952 The Communists accuse the United States of engaging in biological warfare.

May 1952 Mark W. Clark replaces Ridgway as commander of the Far East Forces and the UN command.

May 7, 1952 Inmates at the United Nations' Koje-do prisoner of war camp kidnap the camp commander and begin making demands. The acting commander yields to the prisoners' requests.

March 5, 1953 Soviet Premier **Joseph Stalin** dies and is replaced by Georgy M. Malenkov, who soon broadcasts a speech expressing the Soviet Union's desire for peace in Asia.

April 20–May 3, 1953 The first exchanges of Korean War POWs begins with "Little Switch," a transfer of sick and wounded prisoners.

June 18, 1953 As truce negotiations near completion, Rhee secretly orders the release of about twenty-five thousand North Korean POWs who did not wish to be repatriated, effectively sabotaging the armistice agreements.

July 11, 1953 With promises of enormous economic aid and the continued presence of U.S. troops to provide security in South Korea, Rhee agrees not to obstruct the armistice.

July 27, 1953 The armistice agreement is signed by both sides. At ten o'clock P.M. the fighting stops.

August 5–September 6, 1953 "Operation Big Switch," the exchange of all POWs between the opposing sides, takes place.

1954 The Geneva Conference raises the issue of the unification of Korea; discussions continue for two months without progress.

Words to Know

A

airborne unit: a military unit that moves the troops into a combat area by aircraft, often using parachutes.

amphibious assault: an invasion that uses the coordinated efforts of land, sea, and air forces.

annex: to take over a nation that was independent, making it a dependent part of another nation.

annihilate: to destroy or kill.

armistice: talks between opposing forces in which they agree to a truce or suspension of hostilities.

atomic bomb: a powerful bomb created by splitting the nuclei of a heavy chemical, such as plutonium or uranium, in a rapid chain reaction, resulting in a violent and destructive shock wave as well as radiation.

autocrat: a person who rules with unlimited authority.

B

bayonet: a steel blade attached to the end of a rifle or other firearm, used as a sword or knife in hand-to-hand combat.

biological warfare: the act of spreading disease germs or other living organisms through enemy territory, using the germs as a weapon with which to kill or disable the enemy.

boycott: a refusal to participate in something (purchasing from a store, working, attending meetings of an organization) until stated conditions are met.

bug-out: to panic and run away from a battle in confusion; a disorderly retreat without permission.

bunker: a reinforced underground room dug into a battle area for protection against enemy gunfire and bombs.

bureaucrat: a person working in the administration of a government or organization in a nonelective function.

C

censure: an official scolding.

China Lobby: a group of Americans during the late 1940s and early 1950s who fervently supported Chinese Nationalist leader Chiang Kai-shek in his struggles against the Communist Chinese, and who held a romanticized and sometime patronizing view of the Chinese people and their relations with Americans.

coalition government: a temporary government formed by combining all the different parties and interests in order to take a joint action.

cold war: the struggle for power, authority, and prestige between the communist Soviet Union and the capitalist Western powers of Europe and the United States from 1945 until 1991.

collaborator: someone who cooperates with, or helps out, enemies to his or her own nation.

collective farm: a farm under government control, in which the government dictates what will be grown, how much of it, and what the farmworkers will be paid for their work.

colonial domination: a repressive rule imposed upon one nation by another, more powerful, nation.

communism: an economic theory that does not include the concept of private property; instead, the public (usually represented by the government) owns the goods and the means to produce them in common.

concentration camp: a camp where groups of people, such as prisoners of war, political prisoners, or refugees, are confined.

concessions: things that are given up and granted to the other side in an argument or conflict.

constabulary: a police force separate from the regular army but organized in the same manner as the army.

constitutional government: a ruling body of a nation that is regulated by the nation's constitution, which sets out the laws of the land, the responsibilities of the government, and certain rights of the people.

containment: a policy or process of keeping an enemy power, such as the Soviet Union, from expanding its empire outside its own borders.

cooperative farm: a farm owned and run by the farmworkers who use its goods or sell them for profit.

czar: a Russian ruler who exercises unlimited power over the people.

D

demobilization: bringing the soldiers home.

desegregation: eliminating separation of people because of race or other factors.

diplomat: a professional representative of a nation who helps handle affairs and conduct negotiations between nations.

dissent: disagreement or difference of opinion.

division (or infantry division): a self-sufficient unit, usually about 15,000 to 16,000 strong, under the command of a major general.

dynasties: periods in China's history in which one particular family ruled, sometimes for centuries.

E

evacuate: to remove people from a dangerous area or a military zone.

exile: forced or voluntary absence from one's home country.

G

gender bias: sexual stereotyping; assuming someone will only perform certain functions because of his or her gender.

GI: someone who is or has been enlisted in the U.S. Army.

Great Depression: a decrease in economic activity and time of high unemployment that started with the stock market crash in 1929 and whose effects were felt throughout the 1930s.

grenade: a small explosive weapon that can be thrown, usually with a pin that is pulled to activate it and a spring-loaded safety lever that is held down until the user wants to throw the grenade; once the safety lever is released, the grenade will explode in seconds.

guerrilla warfare: an irregular form of combat; in Korea it usually involved small groups of warriors who hid in mountains, enlisted the help of the local population, and used ambushes and surprise attacks to harass or even destroy much larger armies.

Gulag: a network of labor camps in Russia for people accused of committing crimes against the state.

H

hydrogen bomb: a very powerful bomb created by the fusion of light nuclei, such as hydrogen atoms, to form helium nuclei, which causes a sudden release of atomic energy.

I

industrialization: causing a place to become more devoted to industry, the manufacture or refinement of products in a systemized manner and usually by many people in one place, as a factory or plant.

infiltrate: to enter into enemy lines by passing through gaps in its defense.

integration: the act of bringing all the groups of individuals within an organization into the whole as equals; the elimination of separate facilities and structures for different racial groups.

intelligence (military): information about the enemy.

interim government: a government formed after the ruling government in a nation is eliminated; when necessary, an interim government fills in until a permanent one can be established.

interrogation: a systematic questioning; for prisoners of war, an attempt by the enemy to get information from them about their own army.

intervention: the act of a third party who steps into an ongoing conflict in the attempt to interfere in its outcome or stop it altogether.

isolationism: the view that a country should take care of its problems at home and not interfere in conflicts in other countries.

J

Joint Chiefs of Staff: an agency within the Department of Defense serving to advise the president and the secretary of defense on matters of war. The Joint Chiefs of Staff consists of a chairman, a vice chairman, the chief of staff of the army, the chief of naval operations, the chief of staff of the air force, and the commandant of the marine corps.

L

leftist: advocating change and reform, usually in the interest of gaining greater freedoms and equality for average citizens and the poor; some leftist groups aspire to overthrow the government; others seek to change from within.

leniency: forgiving; kind and tolerant.

limited warfare: warfare with an objective other than the enemy's complete destruction, as in holding a defensive line during negotiations.

M

martial law: suspension of civil rights during a time of state or national emergency.

Marxism: the belief, originating with German political philosopher Karl Marx, that a revolution by the working class would eventually lead to a classless society.

military preparedness: being ready to fight in a war, in terms of personnel, training, equipment, arms, transportation, and other factors.

mobilization: assembling soldiers to serve in the war.

moderate: of neither one extreme nor the other; having political beliefs that are not extreme.

mop up: the clearing of an area of all enemy troops or resistance.

morale: the way that a person or a group of people feels about the job they are doing or the mission they are working on.

motivate: to give someone a desire or need to do something; to make a person or a group want to excel at something.

multinational trusteeship: government by the joint rule of several countries that have committed to act in what they deem to be the country's best interest.

N

National Guard: a military defense force recruited by the states, but equipped by the federal government.

nationalism: belief that one's nation is superior in all ways.

Nationalists (Chinese): the ruling party led by Chiang Kai-shek in China from the 1920s until 1949, when the Nationalists were defeated by the Communists in the Chinese Civil War and forced to withdraw to the island of Taiwan.

NATO: the acronym for the North Atlantic Treaty Organization, an alliance of nations in Europe and North America with shores on the Atlantic Ocean, formed in 1949 primarily to counter the threat of Soviet and communist expansion.

nuclear buildup: the creation and maintenance of a reserve of atomic weapons.

O

occupation: taking over a state or nation and ruling it by a foreign military force.

ostracize: to exclude from the rest of the group.

P

paranoia: a condition in which someone feels obsessive suspicion and has delusions that others are bent on doing him or her harm.

profiteering: making a lot of money out of a crisis situation; finding a way to profit from a national emergency, when others are suffering.

protectorate: a dependent nation subject to the control of a more powerful nation, but not officially a part of the more powerful nation.

Provisional Korean Government: a government in exile, formed in Shanghai, China, during Japanese rule of Korea (1910–45), that elected leaders and fought for the cause of an independent Korea, but had no actual power within occupied Korea.

puppet: someone who seems to be acting on his or her own, but is in fact controlled by someone or something else.

purges: a method of removing or eliminating unwanted elements or members from an organization.

R

regiment: a military unit composed of three battalions.

rejuvenate: to restore something or someone to the way it once was; to make youthful.

reprisal: violence or other use of force by one side in a conflict in retaliation for something bad that was done by the other side; a system of getting even for harm done.

reserve army: a branch of the army that organizes units that are not active, but keep up training on a part-time basis to be prepared should they be called into active duty during war or an emergency.

resolution: the formal statement of an organization's intentions or opinions on an issue, usually reached by vote or general agreement.

reunification: the process of bringing back together the separate parts of something that was once a single unit; in Korea, this usually refers to the dream of a single Korea ruled under one government, no longer divided into two nations at the demarcation line.

rightist: a person who advocates maintaining tradition and the status quo and generally supports a strong and authoritarian government by the elite.

S

sabotage: deliberate destructive acts designed to undermine a person, organization, or army.

satellite: a state or nation that is controlled by a stronger nation.

segregation: the separation of different groups of individuals within an organization or society.

serf: member of a servant class who works the soil.

socialism: a system in which there is no private property, and business and industry are owned by the workers.

Soviet bloc: The Soviet Union and all the nations within the Soviet empire during the second half of the twentieth century.

stalemate: deadlock; the state in which the efforts of each party in a conflict cancels out the efforts of the other party so that no one makes any headway.

subversive: tending toward the destruction or overthrow of an institution or government from within.

suffrage: the right to vote.

suicide mission: an activity taken on with the knowledge that carrying it out will mean one's own death.

T

38th parallel: the 38th degree of north latitude as it bisects the Korean Peninsula, chosen by Americans as the dividing line between what was to be Soviet-occupied North Korea and U.S.-occupied South Korea in 1945.

trench warfare: combat in which enemies dig into ditches facing each other across the battlefield; the ditches then serve as defensive positions. Trench warfare is usually associated with World War I (1914–18).

U

unification: the process of bringing together the separate parts of something to form a single unit; in Korea, the hoped-for act of bringing North and South Korea together under a single government.

unilateral: acting alone, on one's own part and in one's own interests, without reference to others.

United Nations: an international organization founded in 1945 comprised of member nations whose goal is to promote international peace and good relations among nations.

unlimited war: a military conflict in which a combatant nation uses every means within its power to pursue the goal of completely defeating the enemy.

W

war correspondent: someone who provides news stories to a newspaper or television or radio news program from the battlefront or on location in a war.

warlord: a leader with his own military whose powers are usually limited to a small area that, in most cases, he took by force.

Western nations: the noncommunist nations of Europe and America.

witch-hunt: an extreme form of seeking out and harassing people whose views are for some reason against the standard.

Z

zealot: fanatic; someone who pursues his or her objectives with extreme passion and eagerness.

Korean War
Biographies

Dean Acheson

Born April 11, 1893
Middletown, Connecticut
Died October 12, 1971
Sandy Spring, Maryland

American diplomat, lawyer, and author

In his twelve-year career with the U.S. State Department, including four years as secretary of state under President **Harry S. Truman** (1884–1973; see entry), Dean Acheson became one of the most influential individuals in the entire history of American foreign relations. He believed that the top concern of American foreign policy was to stop the Soviet Union in what he saw as an attempt to conquer the world. Acheson also held that the Soviets could be controlled only through the use of power, not negotiation. All of his major policies and programs were based on the principal that the United States should actively support any and all countries that were in any way threatened by Soviet communism, through economic aid, arms, and politics, in an effort to stop—or contain—the spread of communism. (The United States felt threatened by the Soviet Union because it was a communist country. Communism is a set of political beliefs that advocates the elimination of private property. Under it, goods are owned by the community as a whole rather than by specific individuals and are available to all as needed. It greatly differs from the American capitalist economic system, in

"I sought to meet the Soviet menace and help create some order out of the chaos of the world. I was seeking stability and never had much use for revolution."

Portrait reproduced by permission of AP/Wide World Photos.

1

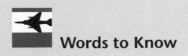

Words to Know

armistice: talks between opposing forces in which they agree to a truce or suspension of hostilities.

atomic bomb: a powerful bomb created by splitting the nuclei of a heavy chemical, such as plutonium or uranium, in a rapid chain reaction, resulting in a violent and destructive shock wave as well as radiation.

China Lobby: a group of Americans during the late 1940s and early 1950s who fervently supported Chinese Nationalist leader Chiang Kai-shek in his struggles against the Communist Chinese, and who held a romanticized and sometime patronizing view of the Chinese people and their relations with Americans.

cold war: the struggle for power, authority, and prestige between the communist Soviet Union and the capitalist Western powers of Europe and the United States from 1945 until 1991.

Communism: a system of government in which one party (usually the Communist Party) controls all property and goods and the means to produce and distribute them.

hydrogen bomb: a very powerful bomb created by the fusion of light nuclei, such as hydrogen atoms, to form helium nuclei, which causes a sudden release of atomic energy.

intervention: the act of a third party who steps into an ongoing conflict in the attempt to interfere in its outcome or stop it altogether.

isolationist: someone who holds the view that a country should take care of its problems at home and not interfere in conflicts in other countries.

military preparedness: being ready to fight in a war, in terms of personnel, training, equipment, arms, transportation, and other factors.

Nationalists (Chinese): the ruling party led by Chiang Kai-shek in China from the 1920s until 1949, when the Nationalists were defeated by the Communists in the Chinese Civil War and forced to withdraw to the island of Taiwan (formerly Formosa).

NATO: the acronym for the North Atlantic Treaty Organization, an alliance of nations in Europe and North America with shores on the Atlantic Ocean, formed in 1949 primarily to counter the threat of Soviet and communist expansion.

nuclear buildup: the creation and maintenance of a reserve of atomic weapons.

which individuals own property.) In the years after World War II (1939–45), Acheson developed groundbreaking policies and proposals for massive economic aid programs for foreign countries and he played a central role in the Korean War (1950–53).

Tall, elegantly dressed, and sporting a bushy mustache and eyebrows and thick wavy hair, Acheson made an impressive public figure. A brilliant speaker and writer, he was perhaps best known for his sharp wit on a wide range of subjects, and he never minced words about what he thought. During his career he was labeled a communist sympathizer by certain Republicans, while at the same time some liberals accused him of heating up the cold war—a period of political anxiety and military rivalry between the United States and the Soviet Union that stopped short of full-scale war—by his unwillingness to negotiate with the communists. But Acheson was highly respected by many American leaders of both major parties, and by none more than Truman, who called him one of the "greatest Secretaries of State this country had." With the support of Truman, Acheson was one of the principal architects of the basic foreign policies that guided the United States throughout the decades of the cold war.

From prep school to Harvard Law

Dean Gooderham Acheson was born in Middletown, Connecticut, the son of Edward Campion Acheson, the Episcopal bishop of Connecticut, and Eleanor Gertrude Gooderham. His father had been born in England, and then served briefly in the British army in Canada before entering the ministry and settling in New England. His mother was a member of a prominent Toronto family in the whiskey distillery business. Acheson graduated in 1911 from Groton School, an exclusive preparatory school where he had not been very interested in studies or sports. At Yale University, Acheson still was not a great student, finding the social life more amusing than studying. Then, in 1915 Acheson went on to Harvard Law School. There he took his studies very seriously, working with some of the great legal minds of the time. On May 5, 1917, he married Alice Stanley, a painter. They would have a son and two daughters.

Acheson graduated from Harvard Law in 1918 and entered a brief service in the U.S. Navy during World War I (1914–18). Then he went to Washington, D.C., for a two-year clerkship with Supreme Court Justice Louis D. Brandeis (1856–1941). Brandeis was a tremendous influence on the young lawyer, teaching him to be realistic in his application of the law, that ideals were fine, but it was necessary to find practical ways to fulfill them. In 1921, Acheson entered the firm of Covington and Burling in Washington. He quickly proved himself to be a very talented attorney, becoming a partner of the firm within five years.

In FDR's State Department

In the late 1920s, Acheson became outspoken in his criticism of the Republican party's isolationist policies, those designed to avoid alliances with other countries that might involve the United States in armed conflict. Believing the United States should defend freedom throughout the world from a position of power, he supported Democratic candidate Franklin D. Roosevelt (1882–1945) in the 1932 presidential campaign. In May 1933, Acheson joined President Roosevelt's administration as undersecretary of the Treasury. He had been in office only six months when he resigned because he disagreed with the president's policy in regard to the gold standard. He returned to his law practice.

When World War II broke out in Europe in 1939, Acheson was again a champion of military preparedness and a foe of isolationism. In January 1941, Roosevelt brought Acheson back into government as assistant secretary of state for economic affairs. For the next four years he dealt with both wartime economic measures and postwar planning. He played a major role in creating the International Monetary Fund and the International Bank for Reconstruction and Development (better known as the World Bank), the basic institutions of a new international economic system.

Early days with Truman

When Roosevelt died in 1945, Harry S. Truman became president. He appointed James F. Byrnes (1879–1972) as secretary of state; Acheson was promoted to undersecretary of state. He also served in that capacity under Byrnes's successor, George C. Marshall (1880–1959), until June 30, 1947. During this period, when the hostilities that became known as the cold war between the Soviet Union and the West began, Byrnes or Marshall were frequently out of the country. Truman began to rely heavily on Acheson for advice on American foreign policy. Acheson directed much of the day-to-day activity of the Department of State, although as a lower and relatively unknown official, he frequently did not get credit for his work.

The Truman Doctrine

Acheson hoped that the United States and the Soviet Union would cooperate with each other after World War II. By 1946, it was apparent to him that Soviet premier **Joseph Stalin** (1879–1953; see entry) was attempting to expand Russia's spheres of control, particularly in Iran and Turkey. Acheson warned Truman about the dangers of leaving these areas open to the Soviets. Truman responded to Acheson's warnings by sending naval units to the Mediterranean. In Greece, communists were engaged in a civil war to topple the existing government. A democratic Greece was not vital to American security, but Acheson feared that the fall of Greece would set off a chain reaction, leading to communism prevailing in Turkey, Iran, and perhaps even Italy and France. He therefore convinced Truman of the need to provide economic aid to Greece and Turkey. On March 12, 1947, when Truman went before Congress to request the aid, he outlined his new policy, which became known as the Truman Doctrine. The doctrine was dedicated to containing the spread of communism. Truman's speech, which was largely borrowed from Acheson's report, set the guidelines for U.S. foreign policy for much of the cold war.

Marshall Plan

In 1947, Europe was still suffering greatly from the devastation of World War II. Acheson recommended a massive American economic aid package to the hard-pressed European nations. In May 1947, he gave a speech outlining the importance to the United States of the continued freedom and democracy of Europe. These ideas became the basis of the Marshall Plan, named for Acheson's boss, Secretary of State George C. Marshall. Put into effect in June 1947, the $12 billion Marshall Plan restored European industry and agriculture, expanded trade, and thereby stabilized social conditions.

Secretary of state

In July 1947, Acheson resigned as undersecretary of state and returned to the practice of law, but not for long. In

Dean Acheson (standing left) conferring with Harry S. Truman (seated left), British Prime Minister Clement Attlee (seated right), and George C. Marshall in December 1950. *Reproduced by permission of Archive Photos, Inc.*

January 1949, he was nominated by President Truman as secretary of state and confirmed by the Senate to succeed Marshall, who had resigned for health reasons. The close daily collaboration between the sophisticated and haughty Acheson and the small-town president was the heart of foreign policy for the next four years.

To Acheson, the nation's fundamental international objective was to maintain sufficient power to stop the expansion of the Soviet Union. Acheson judged every action in terms of its importance in the struggle against the Soviet Union. That which strengthened the West (the United States and the western European nations) and weakened the Soviet Union was always to be sought, and its reverse avoided.

The first months of Acheson's secretaryship, from January to July 1949, were filled with accomplishment. His first major act was to negotiate the formation of the North Atlantic Treaty Organization (NATO), the first peacetime military alliance the United States had ever entered. The founding nations—the United States, Canada, Great Britain, France, Norway, Denmark, the Netherlands, Belgium, Luxembourg, and Italy—formed the alliance in the belief that a collective defense was the best way to protect Western Europe against Soviet attack. Greece, Turkey, West Germany, Spain, and Portugal were later to join the alliance, and at the end of the twentieth century the Czech Republic, Poland, and Hungary joined as well.

Acheson completed the negotiation of the North Atlantic treaty and shepherded it through the Senate in the spring of 1949. By May, he had facilitated the creation of the Federal Republic of West Germany. After World War II, Germany had been split into four zones, with the western portions falling under the jurisdiction of the Western powers while the eastern portion fell under the influence of the Soviets. The Soviets, having failed to prevent the establishment of a pro-West West German government, then lifted a blockade they had placed on West Berlin, similarly divided but situated in what soon became East Germany (the German Democratic Republic). In the summer, Congress approved an expensive military aid program for the North Atlantic allies. Then came two shocks: the Soviet detonation of an atomic bomb in August 1949 and the triumph of the Communists against the Nationalists in the Chinese Civil War, formally marked by leader **Mao Zedong**'s (Mao Tse-tung; 1893–1976; see entry) proclamation of the People's Republic of China in October 1949.

A new look at Russia and China

Since the United States had been the only nation with the atomic bomb since the beginning of the cold war conflicts—the American military dropped two on Japan in August 1945 to hasten the end of World War II—Soviet nuclear capacity was an unwelcome change in the game plan. In response, Acheson argued for the development of the thermonuclear, or hydrogen, bomb. President Truman agreed in January 1950 and the work began. Acheson also arranged for a comprehensive study on the nature of the conflict with the Soviet Union. The result was a classified but widely leaked National Security Council memorandum, completed in April 1950. NSC 68 called for a three- to four-fold increase in military spending, intensified secret action against the communists, and an accelerated nuclear buildup. The report concluded that negotiating would not be effective in solving differences with the Soviet Union unless the Western nations had superior power.

When the Communists under Mao won the civil war in China, the Truman administration, and particularly Acheson, were accused of having sold out China, because they had withdrawn their support from Chinese Nationalist leader **Chiang Kai-shek** (1887–1975; see entry) when it became obvious that the Nationalists could not stay in power. (Chiang and the Nationalists lost popular support in China due to their own corruption and incompetence.) After the Communist victory in China, Acheson continued his effort to persuade congressional and other critics that events in China were determined by the Chinese, and specifically by the corruption and political blundering of the Chinese Nationalists, and not by

NSC 68 and the Cold War

At the time of the Korean War, the expansion of the Soviet Union and communism into Eastern Europe was of concern to many Americans. Prior to 1950, American policy was embodied in the Marshall Plan, in which the United States furnished enormous amounts of economic aid to countries, particularly in Europe, threatened by a communist overthrow. But this nonaggressive policy of containment, which was first brought to widespread public attention by the diplomat and Russian expert George F. Kennan (1904–), came into question late in 1949. At that time, the Soviets detonated their first atomic device and the Communist Chinese won their civil war against the Nationalists and established the People's Republic of China. In early 1950, China and the Soviet Union signed an alliance, and many were deeply concerned about the balance of world power.

On January 31, 1950, President Harry S. Truman requested an analysis of the Soviet threat, and soon one of the most provocative documents in foreign policy of the time was underway in Washington, D.C. National Security Memorandum No. 68 (NSC 68) was a top-level, top-secret government report on "United States Objectives and Programs for National Security." It was written by a joint state and defense department committee under the supervision of Paul Nitze, the director of the policy planning staff, and distributed to Truman and Secretary of State Dean Acheson and other top-level officials on April 14, 1950.

NSC 68 proclaimed that the Soviet Union "is animated by a new

anything the American government did or failed to do. Acheson went on to argue that China and the Soviet Union were natural enemies to each other, that the United States should stand aside and let that conflict develop, and not become China's enemy through a policy of intervention. He made this argument at the Press Club on January 1950.

Acheson's Press Club speech was remembered, however, for an incidental description of the American defense perimeter in the Pacific. He included Japan and the Philippines within the American lines of defense, but not South Korea. Acheson's critics would claim afterwards that this speech invited the North Korean attack of June 1950 that started the Korean War.

fanatic faith, antithetical [opposite] to our own, and seeks to impose its absolute authority over the rest of the world." Since the United States was the only world power to come out of World War II in a position to stop the Soviets, the memorandum continued, it must take responsibility to do so. And since the Soviets did not negotiate on the same terms as the Western noncommunist countries, only military force was proposed as the means to halt Soviet efforts. The report recommended a tremendous military buildup and an outrageously huge defense budget. It also urged a large increase in the creation of nuclear weapons. The NSC 68 put the cold war into new terms, saying "the cold war is in fact a real war in which the survival of the free world is at stake." The document stressed that the Soviets must not be allowed to take any more territory anywhere in the world, and that rather than containment, or holding Soviet expansion to the existing boundaries, the U.S. policy should be to roll back Soviet communism—that is, to actually take territory away. The report stated that any action that could stop the Soviets in their design to take over the world is reasonable: "covert [secret] or overt [out in the open], violent or non-violent."

Soon after the Korean War broke out on June 25, 1950, Truman made NSC 68 official (though still top-secret) U.S. policy.

Source: "NSC 68: United States Objectives and Programs for National Security, (April 14, 1950), A Report to the President Pursuant to the President's Directive of January 31, 1950." U.S. Department of State, Foreign Relations of the United States: 1950, Volume I. Also available online at http://www.fas.org/irp/offdocs/nsc-hst/nsc-68.htm (accessed on August 14, 2001).

The Korean War

The Korean War was the pivotal event of Acheson's four years as secretary of state. He reinforced Truman's determination that the North Korean aggression had to be turned back. Acheson handled the diplomatic side of that endeavor, arranging United Nations action (possible only because the Soviets happened to be absent) against the North Koreans and reassuring allies and gathering their support. After a terrible start for the Americans, by September 1950, U.S. military intervention had routed the North Korean army. Like the Joint Chiefs of Staff (the advisors to the president and the secretary of defense on matters of war), Acheson believed that all of Korea should be united by force. Acheson supported the crossing of the 38th parallel—the dividing line between North and South Korea—into North Korea by the UN forces under command of General **Douglas MacArthur** (1880–1964; see entry) and their drive north toward the border of China. Along with many others he had grossly underestimated the People's Republic of China. The Chinese struck in full force in November 1950, inflicting heavy casualties and throwing UN troops into a massive retreat.

After the devastating Chinese attack, Acheson struggled to stabilize American foreign policy. He reassured European allies fearful of the outbreak of nuclear war. As MacArthur had repeatedly disobeyed orders in publicly criticizing the president's foreign policy, Acheson supported Truman's decision to dismiss MacArthur as commander of Korean operations in April 1951. While he advocated strong military efforts to drive the Chinese back into North Korea, he began to prepare for an armistice (a truce or suspension of hostilities).

Other issues in the State Department

Acheson and Truman used the conflict in Korea to gather congressional support for the administration's cold war policies. Acheson pressed ahead with the political and military strengthening of NATO through the appointment of General **Dwight D. Eisenhower** (1890–1969; see entry) as its supreme commander, the stationing of additional American troops in Europe, assistance to the French in their war against the forces of nationalist leader Ho Chi Minh (1860–1969) in Indochina (Vietnam), and a peace treaty and defense agreement with Japan (signed in 1951). By February 1951, Truman and Acheson had reintroduced the selective service system (the draft), tripled defense-budget requests, doubled the number of U.S. air groups, increased the army by half to 3.5 million, raised the number of American divisions in Germany to six, and established American bases in Morocco, Libya, and Saudi Arabia. In March, the United States had completed development of a hydrogen bomb and secured a free-market trade system and American bases in Japan.

Private citizen Acheson

When Truman left office on January 20, 1953, Acheson left with him. His time in office was marked by controversy.

Despite his hard-line positions with the Soviet Union, he was often accused of being soft on communism. The China Lobby, a group made up mostly of Republican congressmen who had supported Chiang Kai-shek and the Nationalists in China, were most outspoken on the issue. One of Acheson's accusers was the Republican senator **Joseph McCarthy** (1908–1957; see entry) of Wisconsin, who repeatedly accused the State Department of harboring communists. Few secretaries of state have received so much criticism as Acheson. His superior manner was partly to blame. The open disdain he displayed for people and arguments he didn't like greatly angered his opponents.

Acheson was too committed to foreign policy to confine himself to the problems of corporate clients. In the final eighteen years of his life he wrote six books, scores of articles, and maintained an extensive exchange of letters with friends around the world. Three of the books were political commentary, three were memoirs, including his major work, *Present at the Creation: My Years in the State Department* (1969), which won a Pulitzer Prize in history in 1970.

With the inauguration of Democratic president John F. Kennedy (1917–1963) in 1961, Acheson's advice was once again welcome in the White House. In 1965, he urged President Lyndon B. Johnson (1908–1973) to press on to victory in the war in Vietnam. His message on every issue through 1967 was vintage cold war: be tough, be brave, and do not shrink from spending money or using military force. But when consulted by Johnson on Vietnam in 1968 after the Tet Offensive, in which the enemy Viet Cong surprised the United States in a major attack on several South Vietnamese cities, he abandoned his earlier stand. He believed that victory was no longer possible at acceptable cost, and that the United States should begin to pull out of the war. Acheson's abandonment of the traditional hard line was a significant element in Johnson's decision in March 1968 to seek a negotiated settlement of the war while renouncing his candidacy for reelection in November.

Acheson died suddenly of a stroke at the age of seventy-eight while working at his desk at his farm in Sandy Spring, Maryland.

Where to Learn More

Acheson, Dean. *Present at the Creation: My Years in the State Department.* New York: W. W. Norton, 1969.

Brinkley, Douglas. *Dean Acheson: The Cold War Years, 1953–1971.* New Haven, CT: Yale University Press, 1994.

Chace, James. *Acheson: The Secretary of State Who Created the American World.* Cambridge, MA: Harvard University Press, 1999.

McLellan, David S. *Dean Acheson: The State Department Years.* New York: Dodd, Mead, 1976.

McLellan, David S., and David C. Acheson, eds. *Among Friends: Personal Letters of Dean Acheson.* New York: Dodd, Mead, 1980.

Smith, Gaddis. *Dean Acheson.* New York: Cooper Square, 1972.

Web sites

"Books," *New York Times* Archives. Featured Subject: Dean Acheson. [Online] http://www.nytimes.com/books/98/08/23/specials/acheson.html (accessed on August 14, 2001).

1960 Civil disorder in the Republic of Korea arises from dissatisfaction with the corruption and violence within Rhee's government. At the age of eighty-five, Rhee is forced to resign and flee to Hawaii.

1994 Kim Il Sung dies, after being the absolute leader of Korea for forty-six years.

Omar N. Bradley

Born February 12, 1893
Clark, Missouri
Died April 8, 1981
New York, New York

American military leader and chairman
of the Joint Chiefs of Staff

The Korean War is "the wrong war, in the wrong place, at the wrong time, with the wrong enemy."

O mar N. Bradley was a five-star general of the U.S. Army whose career spanned two world wars and the Korean conflict. Known as the "GI's general," Bradley always identified with the common soldier and was unusually kind and mild-mannered while executing the most rigorous of commands. As commander of the Twelfth Army Group in Europe in World War II (1939–45), he proved to be one of the outstanding military leaders in that war. In the 1950s, Bradley made a transition to a very different kind of service and warfare. As the chairman of the Joint Chiefs of Staff during the Korean War (1950–53), he worked with the Truman administration in the troubling complexities of limited warfare in the age of cold war tensions between the United States and the Soviet Union and the atom bomb.

Early life

Omar Nelson Bradley was born in Clark, Missouri, on February 12, 1893. His father, John Smith Bradley, was a teacher, and his mother, Sarah Elizabeth Hubbard Bradley, was a homemaker. His mother's sister died while Bradley was

Portrait reproduced by permission of AP/Wide World Photos.

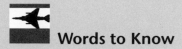

Words to Know

cold war: the struggle for power, authority, and prestige between the communist Soviet Union and the capitalist Western powers of Europe and the United States from 1945 until 1991.

GI: someone who is or has been enlisted in the U.S. Army.

Joint Chiefs of Staff: an agency within the Department of Defense serving to advise the president and the secretary of defense on matters of war. The Joint Chiefs of Staff consists of a chairman, a vice chairman, the chief of staff of the army, the chief of naval operations, the chief of staff of the air force, and the commandant of the marine corps.

limited warfare: warfare with an objective other than the enemy's complete destruction, as in holding a defensive line during negotiations.

United Nations: an international organization founded in 1945 comprised of member nations whose goal is to promote international peace and good relations among nations.

young, and although they had little money, his parents raised her two daughters as their own. Bradley's father died of pneumonia in January 1908. After his father's death, he moved with his mother to Moberly, where he graduated from high school. Although he had planned to become an attorney, he did not have the money for college. Instead, he won an appointment to West Point and entered that prestigious military academy in 1911. Bradley loved West Point. He was a good athlete and played on the varsity football and baseball teams. His was in an impressive class at West Point: one of his classmates was **Dwight D. Eisenhower** (1890–1969; see entry), who would go on to be a five-star general and win two terms as president of the United States.

Following his graduation in 1915, Bradley was assigned to duty at Fort Laughton near Seattle, Washington, and then in Douglas, Arizona. On December 28, 1916, Bradley married his high school sweetheart, Mary Quayle. In 1917, when the United States entered World War I, Bradley tried to get an assignment to a combat unit, but instead spent the war guarding copper mines in Montana.

Rising in the ranks

After the war, Bradley graduated from both the Infantry School at Fort Benning, Georgia, and the Army Command and General Staff School at Fort Leavenworth, Kansas. While at Benning, he drew the attention of the military and government leader George C. Marshall (1880–1959). Bradley then spent five years teaching, one year as an instructor in the Reserve Officers' Training Corps (ROTC) program at South

Dakota State University, and four years in the math department at West Point. While he was teaching at West Point, Mary gave birth to a daughter, Elizabeth, their only child. In 1934, Bradley graduated from the Army War College and served as assistant to Marshall following the latter's appointment as Chief of Staff in April 1939. As the United States became involved in World War II, Bradley was taking his place as an army commander. In his late forties when the United States entered the war, he was balding and wore glasses and was generally looked upon as an all around nice guy, not the usual tough guy who leads army units. In February 1941, he was promoted from lieutenant colonel to brigadier general. He became commandant of the Infantry School and was promoted to major general in February 1942. He was assigned to command the Eighty-second Infantry Division and later the Twenty-eighth Infantry Division.

Leader in World War II

Early in 1943, Bradley became General Dwight D. Eisenhower's personal representative in the field in North Africa. For a brief time he served as deputy commander of the United States II Corps under General George Patton (1885–1945). He assumed command of the II Corps when Patton took command of the Seventh Army in Sicily, Italy, again serving under Bradley. Patton, once an idol to Bradley, handled his men in combat in Italy in some ways that were troubling to Bradley. At this time, the larger-than-life Patton brought controversy to himself for his involvement in the infamous slapping incidents, in which he struck two enlisted men who were suffering from battle fatigue. When Sicily was safely in Allied hands, Bradley, rather than Patton, was chosen to command American forces in the next major operation of the war.

In the summer of 1943, Bradley was selected to command the First U.S. Army in the Normandy invasion and was designated commanding general of the First U.S. Army Group. Patton, who assumed command of the newly activated Third Army on August 1, 1944, reported to Bradley. Together they carried out Operation Cobra, leading to the eventual liberation of most of northern France. Bradley demonstrated remarkable ability as a strategist and battlefield manager. On August 1, 1944, he took command of the Twelfth Army Group, which eventually

Who's in Charge of U.S. Defense?

The Defense Department is based at the Pentagon, a huge five-sided building covering thirty-four acres in Arlington, Virginia, just across the Potomac River from Washington, D.C. The role of the Department of Defense is to coordinate and supervise all the different agencies and functions relating to national security and military affairs. It is divided into three sections: army, navy, and air force.

The secretary of defense supervises the entire U.S. military. This position is appointed by the president with the approval of the Senate. When the Korean War broke out in 1950, the secretary of defense was Louis Arthur Johnson (1891–1956). Johnson resigned his post in September 1950, and was replaced by former army chief of staff and former secretary of state George C. Marshall (1880–1959).

The secretary of defense oversees the Joint Chiefs of Staff. Omar Bradley, as the chairman of the Joint Chiefs of Staff, reported to Johnson and then Marshall, and presided over the chiefs of staff from the army and air force and the chief of naval operations. The other chiefs of staff when the Korean War broke out in 1950 were Chief of Naval Operations Admiral Forrest P. Sherman (1896-1951; died of a heart attack July 22, 1951, and was replaced by Admiral William M. Fechteler); Army Chief of Staff General J. Lawton Collins (1896–1987); and Air Force Chief of Staff General Hoyt Vandenberg (1899–1954).

---

comprised the First, Third, Ninth, and Fifteenth American armies, the largest body of American soldiers ever to serve under one field commander. In the spring of 1945, after his armies had broken the German winter attacks and pushed through to the Rhine River, Bradley was promoted to four-star general.

When the war ended in August 1945, Bradley became administrator of veterans affairs. In February 1948, he left what he called a challenging and rewarding career with the Veterans Administration to become chief of staff of the U.S. Army. Eighteen months later he became the first permanent chairman of the Joint Chiefs of Staff, a newly created agency within the Department of Defense charged with advising the president and the secretary of defense on matters of war, drawing up military plans and directing unified combat actions.

The Korean War

On June 25, 1950, the North Korean People's Army (NKPA) invaded South Korea with surprising force, driving the South Koreans into a rapid retreat. Within days, President **Harry S. Truman** (1884–1972; see entry) and his Departments of State and Defense and the Joint Chiefs of Staff made the decision to use U.S. troops to stop the attack. The decision was made on the assumption that the Soviet Union was behind the invasion and was attempting to expand its sphere of control into Korea. Shortly after the United States decided to intervene, the United Nations (UN) announced its support for South Korea.

Bradley's view that the United States was right to intervene in Korea while not seeking to expand the war in Asia represented a majority view within the military. Bradley's often quoted statement that an unlimited war in Asia would be "the wrong war, at the wrong place, at the wrong time, and with the wrong enemy," was a response to the position taken by Amer-

Omar N. Bradley (front seat, facing camera) arrives at X Corps airstrip in Korea in October 1951, accompanied by Matthew B. Ridgway (rear seat, facing camera) and others. *Reproduced by permission of AP/Wide World Photos.*

ican general **Douglas MacArthur** (1880–1964; see entry), then commander of UN forces in Korea, who believed that only an all-out war could present a victory against the communists. The Joint Chiefs had a difficult role to play with MacArthur throughout the first year of the war. "He always considered us a bunch of kids," Bradley said later at a seminar at Princeton University, as quoted in Joseph Goulden's *Korea: The Untold Story of the War*. "General MacArthur has always pretty much gone his own way." The Joint Chiefs may have allowed the military commander too much room for making his own policy. In the end, he was relieved of command because it was felt he could not be trusted to follow their orders or the orders of the president. Bradley had very mixed emotions when President Truman relieved MacArthur of his command in 1951, but the Joint Chiefs were in favor of his dismissal, and Bradley firmly supported the position of limited warfare in Korea.

Bradley had been appointed to the rank of General of the Army in September 1950, making him the fourth five-star general in the U.S. Army. After the Korean War ended in 1953, he resigned from full-time military service, after forty-three years of active service. He then pursued a business career, serving as chairman of the board of the Bulova Watch Company from 1958 to 1973. In 1965, Bradley's wife died, and for several months he suffered from severe depression. In September 1966, he married Kitty Buhler, a Hollywood screenwriter thirty years younger than Bradley. They remained together until his death in April 1981.

Bradley spent his last years in Texas. Upon his death, President Ronald Reagan said of Bradley, as quoted in *Newsweek:* "He was the GI's general because he was, always, a GI."

Where to Learn More

Blumenson, Martin. *Patton: The Man Behind the Legend, 1885–1945*. New York: William Morrow, 1985.

Bradley, Omar N. *A Soldier's Story*. New York: Henry Holt, 1951.

Bradley, Omar N., and Clay Blair. *A General's Life*. New York: Simon & Schuster, 1983.

Eisenhower, Dwight D. *Crusade in Europe*. Garden City, NJ: Doubleday, 1948.

Goulden, Joseph C. *Korea: The Untold Story of the War*. New York: Times Books, 1982.

Newsweek, April 20, 1981.

Pogue, Forrest C. *George C. Marshall.* 3 vols. New York: Viking Press, 1963–66.

United States Army in World War II: Mediterranean Theater of Operations. 3 vols. Washington, DC: Office of the Chief of Military History, Department of the Army, 1957–59.

United States Army in World War II: The European Theater of Operations. 7 vols. Washington, DC: Office of the Chief of Military History, Department of the Army, 1950–65.

Weigley, Russell F. *Eisenhower's Lieutenants: The Campaigns of France and Germany, 1944–1945.* Bloomington: Indiana University Press, 1981.

Chiang Kai-shek

Born October 30, 1887
Chikow, China
Died April 5, 1975
Taiwan

Chinese revolutionary, military leader, and politician

"If when I die, I am still a dictator, I will certainly go down into the oblivion of all dictators. If, on the other hand, I succeed in establishing a truly stable foundation for a democratic government, I will live forever in every home in China."

Portrait reproduced by permission of AP/Wide World Photos.

A fter the 250-year-old rule of the Manchu-Qing (Ch'ing) Dynasty came to an end in the early twentieth century, the country of China was fragmented and in the hands of hundreds of warlords, local military governors who wrested control of parts of the country since no central government was in power. At this time Chiang Kai-shek rose to leadership within the revolutionary army of Sun Yat-sen (1866–1925). After Sun's death, Chiang took over the army and brought about the unification of China's huge population under a single Chinese flag. He fostered the modernization of his nation and led the Chinese Republic during World War II (1939–45). After his defeat at the hands of China's Communists in 1949, he established a prosperous state on the island of Taiwan (formerly Formosa).

Early years

Chiang was born on October 30, 1887, in the tiny village of Chikow in the east coast province of Chekiang. His father, Chiang Su-an, was a moderately successful salt merchant who died when Chiang was eight. Raised by his mother,

Wang Tsai-yu, and his grandfather, Chiang spent the remainder of his childhood in poverty.

Chiang wanted to become a soldier, and knew that the best training would be in a Japanese military academy, so he went to Tokyo at the age of eighteen. There he became involved in revolutionary activities and met the Chinese Nationalist leader Sun Yat-sen. A typical revolutionary, young Chiang was extreme in his nationalism, the belief that one's nation is superior to all others in all ways. The Japanese academies would not admit radicals (people who don't conform to traditional views), so he was initially forced to attend a Chinese academy. Chiang was finally admitted to a military academy in Tokyo in 1907. After graduating in 1909, he served two years in the Japanese army.

Chaos throughout country

Chiang returned to China in 1911 after learning that Sun Yat-sen's revolution against the Manchus had begun. After the collapse of the Manchus in 1912, Sun formed a government, with Yüan Shikai (pronounced you-ahn shir-kie; 1859–1916), the commander of the northern forces, serving as its president. When Yüan died in 1916, chaos again reigned in China. Power in the country fell into the hands of some two hundred warlords, who controlled numerous regions. In 1918, Sun Yat-sen established a new government in Guangzhou (Kuang-chou or Canton; in southeast China) with Chiang as his personal military advisor. Sun began calling himself the "generalissimo." The majority of the warlords supported a rival government that had been set up in Beijing (Peking), in northeast China.

In early 1922, Sun broke with the warlord in Guangzhou who had been supporting him. The warlord then

Words to Know

Communism: a system of government in which one party (usually the Communist Party) controls all property and goods and the means to produce and distribute them.

dynasties: periods in China's history in which one particular family ruled, sometimes for centuries.

nationalism: belief that one's nation is superior in all ways.

profiteering: making a lot of money out of a crisis situation; finding a way to profit from a national emergency, when others are suffering.

warlord: a leader with his own military whose powers are usually limited to a small area that, in most cases, he took by force.

attacked Sun's presidential headquarters, hoping to kill him. Chiang helped Sun to safety on a gunboat, and the two men lived for fifty-six days on the boat in some very desperate circumstances. During their escape, they became very close.

Seeking support for Sun's revolutionary government, Chiang traveled to the Soviet Union in 1923 to study its military and social systems. He was not impressed with the Russians, but Sun welcomed their help. After Chiang returned to China, he became commandant of a new military academy at Whampoa (Huang-p'u), ten miles outside of Guangzhou. Although the academy was set up following a Soviet model, Chiang refused to embrace communism. Communism, a set of political beliefs that calls for the elimination of private property, is a system in which goods are owned by the community as a whole rather than by specific individuals and are available to all as needed.

Leads Northern Expedition to unify China

When Sun died in 1925, Chiang became one of three leaders of the Kuomintang (pronounced KWOE-min-TANG), the ruling party of the government, along with Wang Ching-wei (1883–1944) and Hu Han-min (1879–1936), leaders respectively of the Kuomintang left and right wings. (Leftists traditionally seek progress and reform, focusing on the needs of the common people, while rightists are more conservative, wanting to maintain business interests and strong, authoritative governments.) But in 1926, Chiang suddenly got rid of leading communists within the Kuomintang, such as the future Chairman of the Communist Party in China, **Mao Zedong** (Mao Tse-tung; 1893–1976; see entry), and he jailed others, including the future premier Zhou Enlai (Chou En-lai; 1898–1976). At the same time he forced Wang Ching-wei to retire. By these sudden and swift moves, Chiang had gained control of Sun's total movement, becoming the Kuomintang's chairman. But Chiang did not break with the communists completely. He needed them for his march north.

At this time, the Kuomintang controlled only two southern regions in China. Eager to defeat the powerful warlords and unify the country, Chiang began a military campaign called the Northern Expedition in 1926. As his Nationalist army defeated many warlord armies, they absorbed them into its own ranks. Within a year, the wealthy provinces of southern, central, and eastern China were under Nationalist control. On March 24, 1927, Chiang seized the eastern city of Nanking, which he then proclaimed as China's new capital. During the march, journalists bestowed upon him Sun's title of generalissimo, or "the gissimo" for short.

Under Sun, the Kuomintang had cooperated with the growing Communist Party in China, but Chiang reversed that policy. He ordered the execution of thousands of communists and forced those in the Kuomintang to resign. When Chiang's forces captured the city of Shanghai in 1927, Chiang called on a group of about one thousand armed civilians to attack the city's major trade unions. Chaos and terror followed, and thousands were killed. Chiang's "party purification" movement, aimed particularly at the communists, soon spread through other provinces. After capturing the warlord capital of Beijing in June 1928, his massive military campaign came to an end. He became the leader of the majority of China for the next twenty years, although he allowed some warlords to maintain their regional power.

Chiang institutes changes

Chiang then began modernizing China. Hospitals, high schools, universities, airports, and power stations were built throughout the country. Telephone lines were installed in remote regions and seventy-five thousand miles of road were laid. He balanced China's budget and stabilized its currency. Although the cities prospered, farming areas remained poor. Most crops were still harvested by hand. Lacking proper medical care, many farm children died.

Other problems abounded. Chiang's government was too small to provide adequate services to an impoverished population of four hundred million. Illiteracy was widespread and transportation was primitive. The warlords remained in power in the north. The ruling Kuomintang party was splintered into various factions. As the government fragmented, Chiang installed a disciplined military and secret police force that was personally loyal to him and intimidated Chiang's political opponents. In 1932, he made himself chief of the General Staff and chairman of the National Military Council, which gave him far broader political powers than were allowed in the constitution.

Japan invades China

In 1931, Japan seized Manchuria, an area of northeast China, but Chiang decided not to regain the region. He felt it necessary first to attack China's growing communist movement, which had proclaimed a Chinese Soviet republic in the southwest region of the country. Although the fighting was fierce and thousands of communists were killed, Chiang could not effectively crush the movement. In 1934, as a result of a major assault, he destroyed two-thirds of the communist forces. On October 16, 1934, one hundred thousand communists, led by Mao Zedong, began their famous Long March, traveling some five thousand miles amid daily battles. Chiang's mission to eliminate the communists was for good reason: while his support came from business people in the cities and landowners in the country, Mao was attracting the peasants and intellectuals.

The leaders of the Communist Party appealed to Chiang to stop the civil war and to fight with them against the Japanese, but he refused. In December 1936, while in Xi'an (Sian), the capital of Shanxi (Shensi) province, Chiang was kidnapped by the warlord Zhang Xueliang (Chang Hsueh-liang). Sympathetic to the communists, Zhang refused to release Chiang until he agreed to halt all attacks against the communists. Chiang agreed to a truce while China faced Japanese invasion and occupation.

Chinese and Japanese battle on the Marco Polo Bridge

On July 7, 1937, Chinese troops clashed with a Japanese force at the Marco Polo Bridge near Beijing, and the second Sino-Japanese War broke out. Whatever chance Chiang had of establishing a strong central government was gone. By the fall of 1938, he had lost all of eastern China. One million Japanese occupied eight provinces, including every harbor along the coastline. Because the Japanese controlled the most fertile farmland in the country, Chiang's Nationalist government seized the food of the poorer peasants, leaving five million Chinese to starve.

World War II

In 1941, the war in China had become part of World War II (1939–45), a worldwide engagement that pitted the

Allies (the United States, the British Commonwealth, the Soviet Union, and other European nations) against the Axis powers (Germany, Italy, and Japan, among others). The United States and England sent needed supplies to Chiang to help in his effort against Japan. Even with the additional aid, however, Chiang was not able to defeat the Japanese. At the end of the war in the Pacific, which came with the dropping of two atom bombs on Japan in August 1945, the Japanese were forced to surrender in China and Korea by the Allied powers.

Liberation from Japan did not bring peace to China, however. What little cooperation there had been between the Nationalists and the Communists during the war soon dissolved as both groups rushed in to claim the areas liberated from the Japanese. Civil war broke out again in 1946. The long war with Japan had weakened the Nationalist government. The Communists, under the leadership of Mao, made steady gains. By the end of 1947, they controlled most of Manchuria. By the end of 1948, they controlled the northern provinces.

Chiang's army had badly bungled its efforts against the communists. At the same time, his government was bungling the economy, with excessive taxation and profiteering (making money for oneself or friends at the expense of others), resulting in inflation and starvation. He was rapidly losing the support of the people of China and only added to this by continuing the civil war. Chiang's support had originally come from merchants and bankers. By the end of World War II, however, he was supported mainly by conservative landlords. During a protest demonstration in July 1948 Chiang's forces killed fourteen unarmed students in Beijing.

Flees country, rules in Taiwan

Unable to stop the communist forces in the south, Chiang and his government were forced to flee on December 10, 1949, to the island of Taiwan, one hundred miles off the east coast of China. Here he set up his Nationalist government. Six months later, the Korean War (1950–53) broke out. The United States retained its alliance with Chiang, recognizing his government in Taipai as the Republic of China. General **Douglas MacArthur** (1880–1964; see entry), commander of the United Nations forces in the Far East, even threatened to "unleash" Chiang's forces on the mainland, though this was only a threat.

Chiang Kai-shek (right) greets South Korean president Syngman Rhee upon Rhee's arrival in Taipai, Taiwan. *Reproduced by permission of AP/Wide World Photos.*

In the first days of the Korean War, the United States sent a navy fleet to the waters between Taiwan and mainland China with orders to prevent either the Nationalists or the Communists from returning to active combat. Chiang had a good-sized army with him at Taiwan and offered its use to the United Nations to repulse the communist North Koreans and later the Chinese who invaded South Korea. At first President **Harry S. Truman** (1884–1972) seriously considered taking Chiang up on this offer, but he was talked out of this by his Secretary of State **Dean Acheson** (1893–1971; see entries). The introduction of the Nationalists in the Korean War would have broadened the conflict to a multinational one. Other United Nations members were deeply opposed to it, for fear it would ignite another world war so soon after the last. Although many of the advocates of an all-out war in Korea argued for the use of Chiang's Nationalist troops in Korea, they were never deployed in the war. Taiwan was almost certainly saved from an attack from the mainland by the blockade imposed during the war.

Even though Chiang ruled as a virtual dictator (retaining the title of chairman of China's Military Affairs Commission, he became president in 1943; during the war years he held no fewer than eighty-two posts), the Taiwanese economy prospered under his control. Chiang promised to retake China from the Communists, but never did. In 1972, the United Nations recognized the Communist Party as the legal government of China, rejecting Taiwan's previous claim. Chiang died of a heart attack in Taiwan three years later, on April 5, 1975.

Where to Learn More

Chang, Chun-ming, ed. *Chiang Kai-shek, His Life and Times*. New York: St. John's University, 1981.

Ch'en, Chieh-ju. *Chiang Kai-shek's Secret Past: The Memoir of His Second Wife, Ch'en Chieh-ju*. Boulder, CO: Westview Press, 1993.

Crozier, Brian. *The Man Who Lost China: The First Full Biography of Chiang Kai-shek*. New York: Scribner, 1976.

Dolan, Sean. *Chiang Kai-shek*. New York: Chelsea House, 1988.

Payne, Robert. *Chiang Kai-shek*. New York: Weybright & Talley, 1969.

Mark W. Clark

Born May 1, 1896
Madison Barracks, New York
Died April 1984
Charleston, South Carolina

American military leader

Portrait reproduced by permission of AP/Wide World Photos.

M ark W. Clark was best known for his command of the U.S. Fifth Army in World War II (1939–45), which he led through Italy in some of the most difficult and decisive battles of the war. By the end of that conflict, he was considered one of the top generals in the United States armed forces. Clark came back into the spotlight in 1952 when he took command of the United Nations forces and the U.S. Army forces in the Far East, relieving **Matthew B. Ridgway** (1895–1993; see entry) during the Korean War (1950–53). In Korea, Clark faced many obstacles that he had never known before in war, particularly limited warfare, an uncooperative Korean president, and a prisoner-of-war camp takeover. The frustrated general saw the Korean War through to the end and was there to sign the armistice, but he never hesitated to express his disgust at being the first U.S. commander to agree to a truce without victory.

Heading for the military

Mark Wayne Clark was born in Madison Barracks, New York, on May 1, 1896. He was a third-generation soldier and his father was a career army officer. Although he had health problems throughout his youth, Clark was able to get an appointment to West Point, the U.S. military academy, at the age of seventeen with the help of his aunt, who was the mother of the noted military leader and statesman George C. Marshall (1880–1959). Clark continued to have health problems during his years at West Point and for a few years afterwards, which at first kept him from advancing or excelling in the military. During World War I (1914–18), however, he found a chance to prove himself as a captain in the Eleventh Infantry Division in France in 1917. He was wounded in action and awarded for his bravery.

During the next twenty years, Clark held a variety of posts and attended the Command and General Staff School at Fort Leavenworth, Kansas, and the Army War College. In August 1941, he was promoted to temporary brigadier general, at least in part because of his close associations with two top generals, his cousin George C. Marshall and **Dwight D. Eisenhower** (1890–1969; see entry). He served initially as assistant chief of staff for operations of general headquarters and rose quickly to chief of staff of army ground forces. In these positions he organized and trained the growing army to meet the demands being created by World War II (1939–45). He put a very rigorous training program into effect and was promoted to lieutenant general.

Words to Know

armistice: talks between opposing forces in which they agree to a truce or suspension of hostilities.

limited warfare: warfare with an objective other than the enemy's complete destruction, as in holding a defensive line during negotiations.

martial law: suspension of civil rights during a time of state or national emergency.

military preparedness: being ready to fight in a war, in terms of personnel, training, equipment, arms, transportation, and other factors.

stalemate: deadlock; the state in which the efforts of each party in a conflict cancels out the efforts of the other party so that no one makes any headway.

trench warfare: combat in which enemies dig into ditches facing each other across the battlefield; the ditches then serve as defensive positions. Trench warfare is usually associated with World War I (1914–18).

World War II

In 1942, Clark became deputy commander of the Allied forces in North Africa. (The Allies were the United States, the British Commonwealth, the Soviet Union, and some other European nations; they were fighting the Axis Powers, including Germany, Italy, and Japan.) In making his plans for a North African invasion, he made a secret submarine journey to the German-occupied territory of Algeria late in 1942. There he met with French officers and tried to convince them to help the Allies against the Germans in their invasion of North Africa. He even forced one French leader to denounce the Vichy government (the French government that collaborated with the Germans during the war; the Free French, on the other hand, supported the Allies). After his return, Clark made public his personal account of the rendezvous and became quite a sensation in the United States because of it.

In 1943 and 1944, Clark was in charge of the Fifth Army in Europe, a collection of American and British forces. Although Italy had surrendered before the Fifth Army landed there, the Germans were not giving up. Clark's forces landed with great difficulty at Salerno, in southwest Italy, on September 3, 1943, encountering heavy resistance. The army then conducted a grueling twenty-month campaign, traversing the entire length of the country. The Allies were greatly outnumbered by German troops that were better armed and equipped. The weather was terribly cold and the terrain was mountainous. Eventually, Clark's forces captured Naples and Rome and landed at Anzio. In the spring of 1945, they took Bologna, Genoa, Milan, Padua, and Venice. On May 2, 1945, the Germans in Italy surrendered.

A three-star general

After the tremendous successes in Italy, Clark took over the command of the Fifteenth Army and accepted the surrender of the Germans in Austria and Italy at the end of the war. His army then occupied southern Austria in an attempt to keep the Soviet Union from taking over there. (As World War II drew to a close, the Allies began to divide up territories that had been controlled by the soon-to-be-defeated enemies.) Clark served as the military governor of Austria until 1947.

Clark returned to the United States in 1947 as a three-star general and a leading American commander. He was by this time staunchly anti-Soviet and a champion of keeping

American forces in a state of military preparedness for war in order to stop the communist Soviet Union from expanding its spheres of control. (The Soviet Union existed as a unified country from 1922 to 1991. It was made up of fifteen republics, including Russia. Its form of government, communism, advocates the elimination of private property. It is a system in which goods are owned by the community as a whole rather than by specific individuals and are available to all as needed.) Tall, thin, and sharp-featured, Clark was not universally liked. Many found him arrogant, cold, and ambitious, and he was accused by some of looking out for his own interests and seeking publicity. But Clark also had many admirers, British Prime Minister Winston Churchill (1874–1965) and French President Charles DeGaulle (1890–1970) among them. He was well known for his efficiency and competence in organizing and training as well as for being tough and getting the job done. In 1949, he was appointed chief of the army's field forces.

Third supreme commander in Korean War

At the time the Korean War began in 1950, Clark was thinking about retiring, but U.S. President **Harry S. Truman** (1884–1972), seeing a need for his leadership, asked him to remain on active duty. In April 1951, Truman announced that he was firing General **Douglas MacArthur** (1880–1964), commander of the U.S. Army forces in the Far East and the supreme commander of the United Nations (UN) forces. **Matthew B. Ridgway** (1895–1993; see entries) took MacArthur's position. Soon after Ridgway took over, the truce talks with the North Koreans and the Chinese began (the UN forces—including the Americans—supported the anticommunist South Koreans), but the fighting continued for more than two years, with negotiations going off and on throughout. The fighting had been reduced to trench warfare, with enemies dug into position facing each other. Battles resulted in many casualties but not much advance. On April 30, 1952, Ridgway was appointed NATO commander in Europe and Mark Clark became supreme commander of the UN forces and the U.S. Army forces in the Far East. (NATO stands for North Atlantic Treaty Organization, an alliance of nations in Europe and North America formed in 1949 primarily to counter the threat of Soviet and communist expansion.)

Crisis in the POW camp

World War II had not prepared Clark for the kinds of problems that would face him in Korea. The first emergency he faced was in the UN prisoner of war (POW) camp at Koje-do, an island off the southern end of the Korean peninsula. When Clark arrived at his headquarters in Tokyo, Japan, on May 7, 1952, the North Korean and Chinese prisoners at Koje-do had just kidnapped the American general in charge of the camp. He soon learned some of the background to the crisis, particularly that the POWs in the camp had developed an internal government; that they received orders from Communist China and North Korea; and that some of the inmates had purposely allowed themselves to be taken captive so they could organize the prisoners from the inside. The prisoners had put the kidnapped general on trial for the deaths of nineteen inmates. They then presented the acting commandant of the camp with a list of demands. Without a go-ahead from his superiors, the acting commandant, urged on by the kidnapped commandant, met the prisoners' demands, giving them a statement saying that some North Korean and Chinese POWs had been killed by the American and South Korean guards and promising to correct the situation in the future.

Clark was furious that the prisoners' demands had been met. When an investigation by another general exonerated (cleared from wrong-doing) the two prison camp commandants, Clark would not stand for it. He recommended to the Joint Chiefs of Staff (the president's military advisors) that both generals be demoted in rank to colonels and that the investigating general be reprimanded for not taking action against them. Truman agreed, and Clark placed a hard-line general, supported with about fifteen thousand troops, in charge of the prison camp. After an initial uprising, the prison camp was brought under control by force. In this first incident, Clark was beginning to understand the difference in the kind of war being waged in Korea than what he had known in the world wars. He said in his memoirs, *From the Danube to the Yalu:* "I hadn't bothered to ask anyone in Washington about POWs, because my experience had been with old fashioned wars. . . . Never had I experienced a situation in which prisoners remained combatants and carried out orders smuggled out to them from the enemy High Command."

Syngman Rhee, ally or opponent?

When the United Nations decided to press for truce talks with the Chinese and North Koreans, it was evident that negotiations would settle the war with a Korea still divided near the 38th parallel and with the Chinese troops still in North Korea. (The 38th parallel—the 38th degree of north latitude as it bisects the Korean peninsula—was selected as the dividing line between North and South Korea in August 1945, at the end of World War II.) Peace talks were agreeable to most nations but not to the fiercely anticommunist South Korean president, **Syngman Rhee** (1875–1965; see entry). The United States decided to pursue the truce anyway, and present it as a done deal to Rhee.

Rhee's grip on his position in the Republic of Korea (ROK) was not strong. In the summer of 1952, the public elected a new National Assembly. The majority of these newly elected legislators did not support Rhee. Since the constitution specified that the National Assembly elect the president, it was clear that Rhee would not return to his position. He therefore demanded that the National Assembly change the constitution, so that he could be elected by popular vote. When it refused, Rhee declared martial law (law enforced by the military during emergencies) in the southern part of the peninsula and had his forces arrest some of the members of the assembly.

At first Clark found it best to put up with Rhee's dictatorial methods, but as the situation grew more and more tense, he believed Rhee was putting the entire military effort in Korea at risk. He and Eighth Army commander **James A. Van Fleet** (1892–1992; see entry) both tried to work with Rhee and talk reason into the old ruler. They both found him beyond rational discussion and even questioned his sanity. Clark eventually drew up a plan for a coup, with the UN forces taking over the government of the Republic of Korea. In July 1952, however, Rhee succeeded in persuading the National Assembly to change the constitution and lifted the martial law.

Trench warfare

In the spring of 1951, the UN forces and the North Korean/Chinese forces had entered a stalemate in which each side had dug into position across the demarcation line near the

38th parallel. Although the battles were violent and losses were high, there was no real advance in position after that time in the war. One side or the other would succeed only in gaining a hill or two. With negotiations between the two sides ongoing, there was a limit to how much damage to the enemy could be done. To Clark, the biggest limitation was the ban on fighting the Chinese on their own territory, at least by air. (UN forces had no authority to cross into China, and widespread international concern over the extent of American aggression in Korea ruled this out.) Clark wanted to bomb mainland China north of the Yalu River, which forms the border between North Korea and China. He developed elaborate plans to fight the Chinese with everything the UN forces could muster, including the use of Chiang Kai-shek's Nationalist army exiled in Taiwan (formerly Formosa). (**Chiang Kai-shek** [1887–1975; see entry] was the leader of the Chinese Nationalist government, which was driven to the island of Taiwan after being defeated by the Communist Chinese in 1949 following the Chinese Civil War.) Clark was told that his plan would widen the war and could not be put into effect. When his friend and close associate Dwight D. Eisenhower replaced Truman as president, Clark prepared another plan to bomb mainland China. To his dismay, Eisenhower, too, wanted to fight on a limited basis and end the war through the truce talks. In the meantime, however, Clark launched devastating air raid campaigns on North Korea.

Truce in Korea

In 1953, Clark negotiated with the Chinese and North Koreans to organize Operation Little Switch, in which sick and wounded prisoners were exchanged between the sides. After that the truce talks began again in earnest. Again, Rhee began to threaten to pull the ROK troops out of the fighting, swearing that he would never go along with the terms of a truce. As the truce became more assured, Clark worked hard to talk Rhee into cooperating, but made no progress, finding the ruler too emotional to listen. Then on June 18, 1953, Rhee ordered the release of twenty-seven thousand North Korean prisoners of war that did not want to go back to their country, just as their fate was being negotiated in the truce talks. It was clear that the UN was negotiating without any control over the primary party

to the truce: the Republic of Korea. U.S. diplomats then joined Clark's difficult task of persuading Rhee to accept the armistice arrangements and the end of warfare, promising massive aid in money, arms, training, and American troops. When Rhee finally agreed to go along with the truce, it was soon arranged. On July 27, 1953, Clark was one of the parties to sign the armistice. When asked for comment, he simply said, as quoted in Clay Blair's history, *The Forgotten War: America in Korea, 1950–1953:* "I cannot find it in me to exult in this hour."

Mark W. Clark signs the armistice bringing the Korean War to a close, July 27, 1953. *Reproduced by permission of AP/Wide World Photos.*

President of the Citadel

Clark retired from the army in October 1953 and took on the presidency of the Citadel, the private military college in Charleston, South Carolina. He held that position until 1960, and was president emeritus (honorary president after retirement) until 1965. Clark wrote two books of war memoirs, *Calculated Risk* in 1950 and *From the Danube to the Yalu* in 1954.

Clark died of cancer in South Carolina at the age of 87. Upon his death, President Ronald Reagan said of him, as quoted in his *Time* obituary: "We are free because of men like him. His professionalism and dedication will be the standard of every soldier who takes the oath to defend our nation."

Where to Learn More

Alexander, Bevin. *Korea: The First War We Lost.* New York: Hippocrene Books, 1986, revised edition, 2000.

Blair, Clay, *The Forgotten War: America in Korea, 1950–1953.* New York: Times Books, 1987.

Clark, Mark. *From the Danube to the Yalu.* New York: Harper Brothers, 1954.

Devine, Michael J. "Mark Wayne Clark." In *The Korean War: An Encyclopedia,* edited by Stanley Sandler. New York: Garland Publishing, 1995.

Goulden, Joseph C. *Korea: The Untold Story of the War.* New York: Times Books, 1982.

"The Last Commander Falls; Mark Wayne Clark: 1896–1984," *Time,* April 30, 1984, p. 68.

Paschall, Rod. *Witness to War: Korea.* New York: Perigree Book, 1995.

Webster's American Military Biographies. Springfield, MA: G. & C. Merriam Company, 1978.

William F. Dean

Born August 1, 1899
Carlyle, Illinois
Died August 24, 1981
Berkeley, California

American military leader

William F. Dean was one of the few U.S. officers in the Korean War (1950–53) who had been in that country prior to the war. As military governor in U.S.-occupied Korea from October 1947 until the South Koreans set up a constitutional government in August 1948, Dean had experienced firsthand some of the conflicts that had arisen due to the occupation of the country by Soviet and American forces. But by his own account, it was not until his three harrowing years of captivity as a prisoner of war (POW) that he reached an understanding of the Korean people and the issues before them in the war. Dean was the first commanding general to lead a division of American troops into battle in Korea. His remarkable twenty days at the battlefront and his three years of captivity as the highest ranking POW held by the North Koreans earned him a Medal of Honor and became the subject of his book *General Dean's Story* in 1954.

Rising in the ranks

William Frishe Dean was born in Carlyle, Illinois, in 1899, the son of Charles Watts Dean, a dentist, and Elizabeth

"I did see the face of the enemy close up, did have time to study his weaknesses and his remarkable strengths, not on the battlefield but far behind his lines."

Portrait reproduced by permission of AP/Wide World Photos.

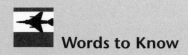

Words to Know

atomic bomb: a powerful bomb created by splitting the nuclei of a heavy chemical, such as plutonium or uranium, in a rapid chain reaction, resulting in a violent and destructive shock wave as well as radiation.

biological warfare: the act of spreading disease germs or other living organisms through enemy territory, using the germs as a weapon with which to kill or disable the enemy.

Communism: a system of government in which one party (usually the Communist Party) controls all property and goods and the means to produce and distribute them.

constitutional government: a ruling body of a nation that is regulated by the nation's constitution, which sets out the laws of the land, the responsibilities of the government, and certain rights of the people.

division (or infantry division): a self-sufficient unit, usually about 15,000 to 16,000 strong, under the command of a major general.

infiltrate: to enter into enemy lines by passing through gaps in its defense.

interrogation: a systematic questioning; for prisoners of war, an attempt by the enemy to get information from them about their own army.

leftists: people who advocate change and reform, usually in the interest of gaining greater freedoms and equality for average citizens and the poor; some leftist groups aspire to overthrow the government; others seek to change from within.

leniency: forgiveness; kindness and tolerance.

occupation: taking over a state or nation and ruling it by a foreign military force.

regiment: a military unit composed of three battalions.

reserve army: a branch of the army that organizes units that are not active, but keep up training on a part-time basis to be prepared should they be called into active duty during war or an emergency.

unification: the process of bringing together the separate parts of something to form a single unit; in Korea, the hoped-for act of bringing North and South Korea together under a single government.

Frishe Dean. He was a good student who loved to read and enjoyed outdoor activities. He graduated from high school as the class valedictorian. Dean wanted to go to West Point, the U.S. military academy, but did not get accepted; he went instead to the University of California at Berkeley. In 1918, he served in the Student's Army Training Corps. To pay his way through school, he worked as a police officer, a streetcar driver, and a cook. He was not a great student in college, and although he intended to pursue a law degree, he quickly realized he wasn't cut out for a legal career.

During college Dean had risen in the ranks of the reserve army (a branch of the army that organizes units that are not active, but keep up training on a part-time basis to be prepared should they be called into active duty during war or an emergency). In 1923, he took a commission in the regular army. Three years later he married Mildred Dern. They had a son and a daughter. Through the next seventeen years he served at a number of army posts, always working his way upward in the ranks. In 1940, he graduated from the Army War College and was promoted to major.

By 1942, Dean was a brigadier general. World War II (1939–45) was raging, and he wanted nothing more than to lead troops in combat. Because he was needed on staff duty in Washington, D.C., it wasn't until mid-1944 that he was appointed deputy commander of the Forty-fourth Infantry Division. He moved with it to the battlefront in France and became commanding general in December 1944.

World War II hero

In the months that followed, Dean's division faced the enemy in some of the deciding battles of the war in Europe and was responsible for victories that ended the occupation of Austria and caused the surrender of a German army division. His units captured thirty thousand prisoners in Germany and Austria. In July 1945, Dean brought his division back to the United States to high acclaim. Dean had personally shown remarkable heroism at the front and was awarded the Distinguished Service Cross, the Distinguished Service Medal, the Bronze Star Medal, and the Legion of Merit. He was promoted to major general.

Military governor of Korea

In 1947, Dean was appointed as the third military governor to serve in the three-year U.S. occupation of South Korea. The situation there was desperate when he came into the position. At the end of World War II, in August 1945, the Soviets were at the borders of Korea, which the Japanese had forcibly controlled it as if it were part of Japan since 1910. After the Americans dropped the atomic bombs on Japan and called for an end to the fighting, the Allies (the United States, the Soviet Union, the British Commonwealth, and other European nations) decided that the Americans would accept the Japanese surrender south of the 38th parallel and the Soviets would receive the surrender north of it (some American diplomats arbitrarily selected the 38th parallel—the 38th degree of north latitude—as the dividing line between northern and southern Korea).

When the American Military Government came in to accept the Japanese surrender in the south, the Koreans had already established a new government, which ruled by local branches of People's Committees. The People's Committees were reform-oriented, and leaned to the left, causing Americans to fear a communist takeover. ("Leftists" generally hold radical political views seeking change and reform, usually including more freedom, more equality, and better conditions for common people. Leftism may include communism, which is a kind of economic practice that eliminates private property, under which production of goods and the distribution of goods are owned by the state or the population as a whole. Communism is at odds with the American economic system, capitalism, in which individuals, rather than the state, own the property and businesses.) The Americans therefore kept intact the national police force that had been established by the hated (and vanquished) Japanese. The anticommunist Americans strove to eliminate the People's Committees, which, according to many accounts, represented the majority of Korean people. Many Korean people were angry and ready to rise up against the Americans.

As trouble arose, the military government imposed harsh ordinances that forbade saying anything against the U.S. occupation forces, and many Koreans were arrested for breaking the rules. Newspapers were not allowed to publish information or opinions that were contrary to the U.S. military government's wishes. One Korean paper was shut down.

Dean came into a messy situation that was already well in progress. By most accounts, he was a kind and fair man, six-feet tall with white hair and a healthy energy. He loved to take long daily walks. As a POW only three years later, Dean reflected on the way prisoners were treated in the South Korean prisons when he was in charge of them as military governor:

> I don't think that the treatment [in the South Korean prison] as a whole was bad, although some things possibly seemed worse to the Koreans than to me. . . . Prisons were overcrowded at that time, however, and I was very much disturbed when I found out how many people were being held for long periods without being brought to trial. In April of 1948 I had pardoned more than thirty-five hundred at one time because I found that some of them had been incarcerated for as long as eighteen months without trial, and charged only with talking against the government, or opposing rice collections. . . . We were only partially successful in raising the standards, and we never had enough U.S. personnel to be positive that all our orders were being carried out; but we were trying.

Violence during Dean's governorship

In 1947, when General Dean became military governor, a huge wave of uprisings prompted by the national police's campaign to eliminate the People's Committees had already been violently crushed. In April 1948, a major rebellion erupted on the island of Cheju (pronounced SHE-shoo). Tens of thousands of islanders were killed and entire villages were destroyed. A second rebellion broke out in the city of Yosu, and a third in the city of Taegu. U.S. troops helped suppress the uprisings.

In May 1948, the United Nations, at the request of the United States, supervised elections in Korea, with the idea that Korea would become independent after a leader was elected. (The UN was founded in 1945 by the Allies to maintain worldwide peace and to develop friendly relations among countries.) The elections took place, but amid great controversy. The northern Koreans and the Soviets claimed that the UN did not have the authority to determine the future of Korea and blocked its agents from entering the country to set up the elections. Southern Korean independence leader **Syngman Rhee** (1875–1965; see entry) urged going forward with the elections without the northern vote, a plan that clearly benefitted him. While a few agreed with Rhee, a large group of Korean leaders of all backgrounds strongly objected to the election, believing that an election in which only the south participated would doom any hope of the reunification of Korea. The election went on without the Koreans north of the 38th parallel, nonetheless, and a new government to rule over all of Korea, the Republic of Korea, with Rhee as its president, was established on August 15, 1948. Dean left with the military government, satisfied that the election had been legitimate and a tribute to the democratic process.

Twenty days

Dean spent the next few years in Japan. In 1949, he was made commanding general of the Twenty-fourth Infantry Division, headquartered in the town of Kokura, on the Japanese island of Kyushu. The Twenty-fourth Division consisted of three regiments, the Twenty-first, the Thirty-fourth, and the Nineteenth. In 1950, all three regiments added up to only 11,242 men, gravely down from the authorized war strength of 18,900. Equipment was in very short supply. The American troops were in Japan mainly for the purpose of occupation of the country after the war, and many of the troops had not been trained for combat. The Twenty-fourth Division was considered by the U.S. Army to be the least combat-ready of the four divisions in the Eighth Army.

Just a few days after the war broke out in Korea on June 25, 1950, Dean received orders to get his whole division to Korea as soon as possible. The North Koreans had crushed the Republic of Korea (ROK) Army and captured the capital city of Seoul. Dean needed to get his troops there to stop the North Korean southward advance. Dean quickly learned that the air transport could not handle great numbers of men. A small force of 406 men called Task Force Smith was chosen to proceed directly by air to Korea to begin delaying the North Korean Army. The rest of the division, with added men bringing it to a force of about 15,000 troops, was to cross over in ships.

Task Force Smith dug in near the Korean town of Osan early on the morning of July 5. Having been told that the North Koreans would turn and run if they saw an American uniform, the unit was totally unprepared for what was to come. They were hit by two regiments of well-trained North Korean soldiers and thirty-three tanks. They were hopelessly outnumbered and they had little ammunition that could penetrate the tanks, but they courageously faced the enemy.

Nearly half of the men of Task Force Smith were killed or injured on their first day of battle; the rest were forced to flee in disorder.

Dean had arrived in Korea on July 4 and established headquarters at Taejon, a city about one hundred miles south of Seoul. As news of the bloody defeat of Task Force Smith came in, he was deeply concerned. The rest of the Twenty-fourth Division arrived during that week. It was becoming clear that the enemy was far stronger than expected, and a plan was in place for support to arrive from the other divisions of the Eighth Army. But in the meantime it was Dean's task to delay the enemy with whatever troops he had. Dean set his units in the path of the advancing North Koreans to delay them, but the North Koreans continued to press southward, crushing unit after unit of the Twenty-fourth as well as the ROK divisions, which had rebuilt since the fall of Seoul.

The fall of Taejon

Dean's regiments were greatly weakened, having suffered great casualties. Soon the city of Taejon itself, a vital center for the war effort, was in jeopardy. North of Taejon was the Kum River, and Dean decided to concentrate all the forces of the Twenty-fourth Division there. But his forces weren't strong enough. From July 14 to 16, the North Koreans penetrated the Twenty-fourth on the south side of the river. Two of the three regiments were nearly shattered. No help was yet on the way, and Dean had to prepare his defense of the city of Taejon with what meager resources he had. His defense was set up by July 19, but no preparation under the circumstances could have sufficed.

At 3:00 in the morning on July 20, a North Korean division struck at Taejon. Dean was awakened by gun fire. North Korean tanks and hundreds of North Korean soldiers dressed in white robes had infiltrated the city and were opening fire on the American troops and the fleeing South Korean civilians. Dean's units were scattered and without proper communication. He watched as the enemy tanks razed buildings, slaughtering the troops inside.

By this time, Dean had been at or near the battlefront for more than two weeks and was thoroughly exhausted.

The Soviet tank in Taejon that William F. Dean knocked out with a bazooka on July 20, 1951.
Reproduced by permission of Double Delta Industries, Inc.

Throughout that day, in what seemed to some as odd behavior, Dean set out with an aide and fearlessly hunted on foot for enemy tanks that had come into the city. He finally got one, shooting it from close range with a bazooka. (He was awarded a Medal of Honor for this in 1951.) While he was hunting tanks, his units were besieged and awaited withdrawal instructions. When Dean finally called for retreat, his units were already gone, with the exception of one brave unit at a roadblock, holding off incoming North Koreans from three sides. When that unit retreated, the city was in North Korean hands. Dean had not yet gotten out.

By evening, the road out of Taejon was jammed with army vehicles. The city was on fire and the streets were littered with dead bodies. Dean finally got into a convoy heading out of the city, but his jeep took a wrong turn. After being forced into a ditch by enemy fire, Dean stumbled down a steep hill and was knocked unconscious. When he awoke, he was alone. He spent the next thirty-six days in the enemy-occupied area.

On the verge of starvation the whole time, he narrowly missed capture several times as he tried to find his way back to his men. In the end, he was turned over to the North Korean army by two South Korean civilians who received the equivalent of $5 for him.

The highest ranking prisoner of war

Dean was terribly ill in his first weeks as a POW. He had lost as much as sixty pounds and was too weak to walk more than a few steps. Because of his high rank, the North Koreans felt they had a negotiating asset, so he was not treated like other American POWs. He was placed in a room in a house with an adjoining room for guards and an interpreter and treated for his illness. As he began to recover, the North Koreans began daily interrogations, always with the goal of making Dean denounce the United States or the president or give them information. They threatened him with death and violence, but Dean did not budge. Sometimes the questioning would go on for days and nights, and Dean was not allowed sleep. He repeatedly asked to be placed with other POWs, but he never saw another American soldier in all the years of his captivity.

Early in his confinement, Dean tried to escape, but he was too weak and well guarded. When that proved unsuccessful, fearing that he might reveal army secrets if tortured, he attempted to kill himself. After failing at escape and suicide, the general carried on bravely, showing remarkable courage. One of the North Korean interpreters who was with him in prison admired him so much that he later wrote a long letter praising Dean to *Life* magazine.

Reflections as prisoner of war

Although as a prisoner of war Dean was subject to the worst the enemy had to offer, he came to view the North Korean people in more human terms than he had before being captured. His memoirs reflect his keen observation and growing understanding of the Korean people. "Perhaps I'm naturally naive," he wrote in *General Dean's Story*, "but the most important discovery to me was that the ordinary Communists who guarded me and lived with me really believed that they were following a route toward a better life for themselves and their children."

William F. Dean holds the *Stars and Stripes* issue celebrating his homecoming. *Reproduced by permission of Double Delta Industries, Inc.*

On reflection about the things he would change about the American presence in Korea, Dean concluded that the American military establishment had much to learn about respecting others. As he recounted in his memoirs:

> Through all the questioning and my many subsequent conversations with intelligent Koreans who had chosen communism after knowing something about our government in South Korea, ran one refrain: they resented being called "gooks," and the slighting references to their race and color more than any of our policies, ill advised or not. Again and again I was told that this man or that one had come north because he had decided he never could get along with people who called him a "gook," or worse, among themselves; because he resented American attentions to Korean women; or because he hated to see foreigners riding in his country in big automobiles while he and his family had to walk.

A visit from the outside

When the truce meetings began between the communist forces and the UN forces at Panmunjom in 1951, the

North Koreans decided to allow Wilfred Burchett, an Australian correspondent and a communist, to interview Dean and take pictures. Dean had been in prison for over a year and was very happy to have an English-speaking visitor. Their interview and conversation went on into the night. Burchett gave him a book to read (which he had not been allowed) and promised to write to Dean's wife. From that time on, Dean's imprisonment was not as harsh. He was given writing tools and was allowed to stand or lie down at will. Dean believed Burchett was responsible for his good treatment and admitted to liking Burchett a lot, although he remained very perplexed about his being a communist.

Nearly two years later, on September 3, 1953, Burchett appeared again with Chinese and North Korean photographers and reporters. The war was over and Dean was going home. He returned to the United States to a hero's welcome, which seemed to genuinely surprise him. He struck observers as humble but also as kind and understanding. He felt strongly that POWs who had "confessed" to war crimes while being "interrogated" by the enemy should be treated with leniency. He even testified at the trial of the most famous of these, a man who had confessed to involvement in the alleged U.S. biological warfare against the North Koreans. Dean also asked for leniency for the two South Koreans who had given him over to the enemy for $5.00.

Dean's captivity caused him to reflect about the cold war attitudes toward communism. (The cold war refers to the political tension and military rivalry that begun after World War II between the United States and the communist Soviet Union, which stopped short of full-scale war and persisted until the breakup of the Soviet Union in 1991.) Closely observing the North Koreans—seeing their character, needs, hopes, and fears—he was more sure than ever that communism was a dangerous and repressive force in their lives. He also saw that American arrogance was so disturbing to others that it could have the effect of pushing them away. He believed that all American soldiers and diplomats needed to be educated to their cause: "An army can be a show-window for democracy only if every man in it is convinced that he is fighting for a free world, for the kind of government he wants for himself, and that he personally represents the ideals that can make a world free. And every individual in that army must realize that his whole country is judged by his behavior, at home and abroad, and not by the ideals to which he gives lip service."

After the war

On January 1, 1954, Dean took a new post as deputy commander of the Sixth Army, Presidio of San Francisco, California. That same year he published *General Dean's Story,* which he dictated to William L. Worden. A contemporary review by Korean War historian S. L. A Marshall is quoted in an 1954 edition of *Current Biography:* "This is one of the warmest of books, though it treats of a bitterly cold ordeal. Its delightful humor, recurrent amid the recounting of excruciating personal experiences, is worthy of an exalted spirit capable of seeing all things in proportion in any circumstances." Less than two years later, General Dean began a long retirement devoted to his family and civic affairs in Berkeley, California. He died in Berkeley on August 24, 1981.

Where to Learn More

Dean, William F., as told to William L. Worden. *General Dean's Story.* New York: Viking Press, 1954.

"Dean, William F(rishe)." *Current Biography.* New York: H. W. Wilson, 1954.

"Dean, William Frishe." *Webster's American Military Biographies.* Springfield, MA: G. & C. Merriam Company, 1978.

Deane, Hugh. *The Korean War: 1945–1953.* San Francisco: China Books, 1999.

"Heroism of General Dean Is Revealed When Most Famous POW Is Set Free." *Life,* September 14, 1953.

Web sites

"Dean, William F." Congressional Medal of Honor Society. [Online] http://www.cmohs.org/medal/history_links/w_dean.htm (accessed on August 14, 2001).

Webb, William J. "The Korean War: The Outbreak" (army brochure). [Online] http://www.army.mil/cmh-pg/brochures/KW-Outbreak/outbreak.htm (accessed on August 14, 2001).

Dwight D. Eisenhower

Born October 14, 1890
Denison, Texas
Died March 28, 1969
Washington, D.C.

American president and military leader

Dwight D. Eisenhower was the commander of the Allied forces in Europe in World War II (1939–45), commander of the North Atlantic Treaty Organization (NATO) forces, and then the thirty-fourth president of the United States, serving two terms in office. He took office near the end of the Korean War (1950–53), inheriting from his predecessor, **Harry S. Truman** (1884–1972; see entry), a tangled truce process accompanied by violent battle near the 38th parallel, the dividing line between North and South Korea. Like Truman, Eisenhower carried out limited warfare in Korea and took a cautious approach to hostilities between the United States and the Soviet Union in the nuclear age. His foreign policy is generally considered as among the most successful of the cold war, the period between World War II and the breakup of the Soviet Union in 1991 in which the intense military rivalry between the United States and the Soviet Union approached but fell short of full-scale war.

A humble background

Long before Dwight Eisenhower's birth, his grandfather, Jacob Eisenhower, moved to Kansas from Pennsylva-

"All my life I have said what I meant, and meant what I said. No one will change that. All my life I had a deep and fundamental faith in my country, in its people, in its principles and in its spiritual value. No one will change that."

Portrait reproduced by permission of the Dwight D. Eisenhower Library.

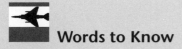

nia and bought farmland in Dickinson County. Although Jacob was very successful, his son David, Dwight's father, was not interested in farming. David attended college on the small campus of Lane University, where he met Dwight's mother, Ida Elizabeth Stover. The two were married in 1885. Both David and Ida were devout Christians. Jacob gave the newlyweds 160 acres of land and $2,000, but David mortgaged the land and joined with a partner in opening a general store in Hope, not far from Abilene. The store failed, and David moved to Denison, Texas, where he found work with a railroad. He sent for his wife and two sons and soon a third son, Dwight, was born. The family then moved back to Abilene, where David worked in a creamery. The family, which grew to include six boys, struggled to get by on David's small income.

Ida Eisenhower was a strong influence on her sons. She taught them that the only way to get what they wanted in life was to work for it. The boys attended public school, filling up the rest of their hours with work. They raised vegetables for the family meals and took outside jobs to help support the household. Their poverty was reflected in their school clothes. Dwight was the only boy in the fifth grade class picture wearing overalls. For a short time, he even had to wear his mother's shoes to school because the family could not afford new shoes for everyone. When the Eisenhower boys became the subjects of other children's teasing, Dwight became a pretty good fighter. Otherwise, his early life was not much different from that of a typical farm boy in Kansas. He found time to engage in sports and to play pranks on the neighbors, meanwhile earning average or better grades in school, working on the family's small farm plot, and selling some of the vegetables to neighbors.

Education

In high school, Eisenhower's great interest was sports. His football coaches considered the six-foot, 160-pound running back just an average player. But he loved the game and was popular with his teammates. Along with football, Eisenhower played baseball and was head of a new athletic association formed by the high school students to gain community support for the athletic program. He was an avid reader of history as well, and many thought he would become a history professor.

The Eisenhower boys all had hopes of improving their lot. Edgar (who would become a lawyer) and Dwight wanted to go on to college, but since there was not enough money, they developed a plan to take turns going to school; Dwight would work first and put Edgar through school and then Edgar would do the same for him. Dwight took a job working with his father at the Belle Springs Creamery. For a while, his hours were 6:00 P.M. to 6:00 A.M. seven days a week—an eighty-four-hour work week. Then one of his friends decided to become a naval officer and encouraged Dwight to join him in taking the exams. At that time examinations for the naval academy at Annapolis and the military academy at West Point were given at the same time. Although Eisenhower hoped for a career in the navy, the year off from school had made him too old to start at Annapolis.

West Point

Eisenhower was admitted to West Point in 1911. In those days, West Point cadets were very sternly disciplined. They were not allowed to have any money and were confined to the campus. Cadets received only one leave in four years, a two-week furlough after the second year. Eisenhower benefitted from the stern discipline at home, and adjusted to West Point easily. Football helped. By this time, Eisenhower had put on muscle and carried a strong and agile 175 pounds on his six-foot frame. He was an outstanding running back for West Point while managing to maintain above-average grades. In his second year, though, Eisenhower broke the same knee twice, ending his football career.

Without football, Eisenhower began to lose interest in West Point. He maintained his slightly above-average grades due mostly to his interest in history and English, but now he began to fill his hours playing cards and smoking, both forbidden by the academy. As a result, his last three years were spotted with demerits. He also reentered sports, first as a cheerleader, then as assistant coach of the freshman football players. His achievement at West Point was not spectacular—except that in his last year he managed to earn 100 demerits.

Marriage

Eisenhower's ranking at West Point did not merit any choice assignments in the regular army. After graduating, he was assigned to the infantry as a second lieutenant and sent to Fort Sam Houston in Texas. He met Mamie Doud at a party in San Antonio and soon fell in love. They were wed on July 1, 1916, and remained married until Eisenhower's death. They had two sons, David Dwight and John Sheldon. David died early, at the age of four, while John followed in his father's footsteps, advancing to West Point and a military career.

Military trainer

By 1917, when the United States was about to enter World War I (1914–18), Eisenhower had risen to the rank of captain, mostly on his ability as an instructor. He knew how to discipline his men and gain their friendship. He was assigned during the war to Camp Colt near Gettysburg, Pennsylvania, a training camp for the infantry. After the war, he was promoted to major and sent back to school to learn about the new tank warfare. Two years later, still without a real career goal, he was assigned to Panama in Central America to serve under Brigadier General Fox Conner. It was one of the most fortunate turns of his military career.

Conner had played a central role in World War I and was also a student of military history. He taught Eisenhower the ways of the career officer and also renewed the younger man's keen interest in history. Eisenhower greatly respected the general and, for the first time, began to take a real interest in his career. In 1925, Conner secured an assignment for Eisenhower at the staff training school at Leavenworth, Kansas. Conner also pointed out a young colonel whom he guessed would be the next army leader and advised Eisenhower to seek the man out. The colonel was George C. Marshall (1880–1959), who would later become commander in chief of the army in World War II.

Eisenhower's change of attitude due to Conner's instructions showed in his record at staff training school. He finished first in a class of 215, yet attracted little attention among the army's ranking officers. From 1929 to 1933, he was just an aide in the office of the assistant secretary of war. Then, in 1933, he became an aide to **Douglas MacArthur** (1880–1964; see entry), then chief of staff of the army. Two years later, MacArthur accepted an assignment as field marshal of a new Philippine army. Major Eisenhower went along as his chief of staff, but tensions arose between him and MacArthur. In 1939, with World War II erupting in Europe, Eisenhower asked to return to the United States.

Outbreak of war

Eisenhower was serving as a colonel under General Walter Krueger with the Third Army when it joined in one of the army's most massive practice wars. Eisenhower devised the Third Army's plan of attack; it worked so well in the practice that he finally won recognition as a military planner. Army leaders found that Eisenhower could listen to others, then make sound judgments about what to do.

The day after these practice maneuvers, Japanese aircraft bombed Pearl Harbor in Hawaii, on December 7, 1941. Eisenhower became a brigadier general and was assigned to the War Plans Division in Washington, D.C. His first task was to plan the strategy for the Far East, but he was soon put in charge of the army's operations division. His task changed in 1942 to planning for a war to defeat Germany and Japan.

Planning the invasion of Europe

Eisenhower and his staff planned strategy to defeat the Axis powers, Germany, Italy, and Japan. Once its enemies were divided, the U.S. military reasoned, they would be easier to defeat. Eisenhower had been in the Far East and knew something about Japan. To attack Japan first, as MacArthur preferred, would require long lines of communication and, Eisenhower felt, consume too much in the way of U.S. energy and resources. Germany would meanwhile be left free to romp around Europe. The Operations Department decided to tackle Germany first.

Eisenhower liked to get the facts, make sense of them, and then take direct action. His plan to attack the Germans called for assembling some 3,500 ships to transport more than 150,000 troops, land these forces on beaches in France, and push the German army back until it submitted. At the same time, the Soviet Union would attack German holdings in Eastern Europe and move west toward Germany. Eisenhower presented the plan to Chief of Staff Marshall. Marshall then decided that Eisenhower was the man to get it started. Since it required gaining the cooperation of America's major allies (Britain and the Soviet Union) and Eisenhower's ability to get along with nearly everyone was well known, he was the logical choice. He headed for London to meet with the British leaders Winston Churchill and Field Marshall Alan Brooke, and a still unnamed Russian representative. With charm and modesty, the American general soon won both governments' cooperation. Eisenhower returned to Washington to prepare. President Franklin D. Roosevelt (1882–1945) and Marshall chose Eisenhower to direct the invasion.

The invasion of North Africa

Prior to other major invasions, the British wanted to drive out the German tank armies that were rapidly occupying Egypt and North Africa. Eisenhower felt that the allies needed all their resources for Europe, but President Roosevelt agreed with the British, so Eisenhower soon found himself directing attacks in Africa. Operation Torch began in November 1942. After an initial failure, the Allied forces finally captured the German supply port at Tunis, Tunisia. By May 1943, all of Africa was controlled by the Allied forces. Eisenhower, now a full general, could turn toward Italy.

Sicily and Italy

German soldiers had occupied northern Italy and established a strong line there. These would be the first targets for the Allied armies. From his headquarters on the island of Malta, southwest of Italy in the Mediterranean Sea, Eisenhower directed troops that drove toward the German lines. Sicily was taken in July and August 1943 and Italy was immediately invaded, but it was June 1944 before the Allies took Rome. The major assault on Germany was yet to come, although American and British bombers had already begun heavy bombing throughout Europe.

Normandy

In 1944, with Italy and Africa now under Allied control, there was another difference of opinion between Eisenhower and the British. They wanted to attack German forces through southern France. But Eisenhower again thought the long supply lines would be a problem, as would keeping Allied plans a secret. He preferred the shorter route from England across the channel to Normandy, on the northern French shore. This time Eisenhower persuaded the others to go along with his strategy. The invasion of France was planned for June 5, 1944. The week before, weather conditions had been very poor, and Eisenhower had begun watching them carefully. On the appointed day, the weather remained poor but was supposed to clear. Eisenhower believed the weather forecasters and set the invasion for the next day.

On June 6, 1944, hundreds of aircraft joined navy ships in bombarding the enemy as 156,000 Allied soldiers stormed the shores of Normandy. After heavy fighting, the Allies established themselves on European land. Eisenhower took an active interest in the soldiers, as he had in Sicily. Within forty hours after the invasion of Sicily, he had made a secret visit to the island and stopped to thank Canadian troops for their help there. After the Normandy landing, he made frequent trips over the battlegrounds to see for himself how the war was progressing. As the troops moved through France, he joined them often to talk with the leaders of the armies or just walk with the troops. His broad smile helped win people to his side even in battle conditions.

Impacted by horrors of war

By the end of the war, Eisenhower had commanded three million soldiers, airmen, and sailors and had succeeded in defeating the Germans. Along the way, he had witnessed the horrors of war. One grisly sight was a German concentration camp at Ohrdruf piled with the bones of victims. He called Washington to send reporters to the scene, then made German civilians aware of the sight by requiring a nearby town to clean up the mess. The town mayor and his wife were so overwhelmed that they committed suicide. Not every German was fully aware of the German war crimes, but Eisenhower set out to make them aware.

These experiences turned him against war. Eisenhower refused to talk with German officers except to remind the German general who signed the peace agreement that he would be held personally responsible for carrying out the conditions of surrender.

NATO

Eisenhower returned home a hero, not only in America but throughout the Allied nations. He became chief of staff of the army when Marshall left that office. In 1948, he retired from the active army to become president of Columbia University. Two years later, he returned to Europe as Supreme Commander of the forces of NATO, the North Atlantic Treaty Organization, set up to defend Europe from possible Soviet—communist—occupation. (Communism is a set of political beliefs that calls for the elimination of private property. It is a system in which goods are owned by the community as a whole rather than by specific individuals and are available to all as needed. The Soviet Union, made up of fifteen republics, including Russia, existed as a unified communist country from 1922 to 1991. The Soviet Union, for three decades after World War II, was seen as a threat to the United States, which practiced a capitalist economy, one in which individuals, rather than the state, own the property and businesses.)

President Eisenhower

In 1952, Eisenhower was nominated to be the Republican candidate for president. People throughout the nation campaigned wearing buttons reading "I Like Ike." While he was campaigning for the presidency, the United States was still locked in a stalemate in the war in Korea (1950–53). General **Mark W. Clark** (1896–1984) had recently taken over the

President-elect Dwight D. Eisenhower (left) has lunch with his old outfit, the Fifteenth Regiment of the Third Division, somewhere in Korea, December 1952. *Reproduced by permission of AP/Wide World Photos.*

supreme command of the United Nations (UN) forces in Korea. (The United Nations was founded by the Allies during World War II to maintain worldwide peace and to develop friendly relations among countries.) Clark almost immediately proposed a plan for an all-out assault on the enemy, including bombing mainland China and using Chang Kai-shek's Nationalist army troops, exiled in Taiwan (formerly Formosa), against the Communist Chinese forces. (**Chiang Kai-shek** [1887–1975] and and his forces were driven to the island of Taiwan after being defeated by **Mao Zedong** [Mao Tse-tung; 1893–1976; see entries] and the Communists in 1949 following the Chinese Civil War.) Clark also wanted to use nuclear weapons (atomic bombs), which devastatingly—but successfully—brought World War II to a close. The Joint Chiefs of Staff (the president's and secretary of defense's war advisors) held off making any decisions on Clark's proposals until they could see the outcome of the presidential election. Neither the Democratic nominee, Adlai Stevenson (1900–1965), nor Eisenhower had come out in favor of expanding the war, but for some the change to a Republican president suggested that such a change could take place.

"I shall go to Korea"

On October 24, 1952, Eisenhower made a speech in Detroit, Michigan, in which he promised to bring the war in Korea to "an early and honorable end," as quoted in Bevin Alexander's *Korea: The First War We Lost*. He did not specify how he would end the war other than a statement "I shall go to Korea." The speech was what the public wanted to hear. People feared that widening the war in Korea could bring about nuclear devastation throughout the world. They were tired of the war and sickened by the loss of America's young men. They were happy to have Eisenhower try to steer the United States out of it in whatever way he could.

Eisenhower declared that total war would be suicide for an American generation. As president, he directed the country through the stalemate and on to peace in Korea. Many Americans were not happy with the outcome of the Korean War, considering it the first war the United States had lost. But Eisenhower would always be very proud of his part in getting the United States out of that war without further disaster.

During his two-term administration, Eisenhower was responsible for several important changes at home, including tax reform. Although he suffered a mild heart attack during his first term in office, he was reelected in 1956.

In 1960, Eisenhower was once again a civilian. He continued to speak about public issues but finally found the time to return to his first love, sports, becoming an avid golfer. He died on March 28, 1969, in Washington, D.C., at the age of seventy-eight.

Where to Learn More

Alexander, Bevin. *Korea: The First War We Lost*. New York: Hippocrene Books, 1986, revised edition, 2000.

Ambrose, Stephen E. *Eisenhower, Soldier and President*. New York: Touchstone Books, 1991.

Brown, D. Clayton. *Dwight D. Eisenhower*. Berkeley Heights, NJ: Enslow, 1998.

Darby, Jean. *Dwight D. Eisenhower: A Man Called Ike*. Minneapolis, MN: Lerner, 1989.

Ellis, Rafaela. *Dwight D. Eisenhower. 34th President of the United States*. Ada, OK: Garrett Educational Corp., 1989.

Gunther, John. *Eisenhower: The Man and the Symbol*. New York: Harper and Brothers, 1952.

Lyon, Peter. *Eisenhower: Portrait of the Hero*. Boston: Little, Brown, 1974.

Miller, Frances Trevelyan. *Eisenhower: Man and Soldier*. Chicago: Winston Press, 1944.

Sandberg, Peter Lars. *Dwight D. Eisenhower*. New York: Chelsea House, 1986.

Marguerite Higgins

Born September 3, 1920
Hong Kong
Died January 3, 1966
Washington, D.C.

American journalist and war correspondent

It is difficult to find a history of the Korean War (1950–53) that does not feature Marguerite Higgins, the only female war correspondent reporting on combat in that war. Her presence at the battlefront caused a national sensation. In the 1950s, when many Americans were uncomfortable with women filling what were then considered strictly men's roles, Higgins was forced to prove herself at every step of the difficult path she had chosen. Young, attractive, and very determined, she made waves wherever she went. Her struggle against gender bias captured the American public's attention while she was bravely and skillfully carrying out her journalistic duties and winning a Pulitzer Prize for her coverage of Korea.

A childhood of glamor, adventure, and isolation

Marguerite Higgins was born on September 3, 1920, in Hong Kong, to Lawrence Daniel Higgins and Marguerite de Goddard. Her parents met in Paris during World War I (1914–18). Her father, a law student in California, was a natural adventurer and joined the French army as an ambulance driver when the war broke out. Higgins's mother was living in the French countryside and went to Paris looking for work. One day when the shelling in the city was intense, Lawrence and Marguerite both took cover in a metro (underground train) station. They fell in love and married. Lawrence took a job with the Pacific Mail Steamship Company, and the couple moved to Hong Kong, then a British colony in China. There Marguerite or "Maggie," their only child, was born. For five years the family lived a happy life in Hong Kong. They moved to California in 1925.

Settling down to a suburban life was not easy for the Higgins. Lawrence became a stockbroker, but hard times settled over the country during the Great Depression, and they were not well off. Higgins's mother got a job teaching French at a very exclusive girls' school in exchange for her daughter's scholarship. It is likely that both parents pressed their daughter to achieve the adventure and glamor in her life they had left behind. With her parents pushing her to excel, Higgins grew up to be an outstanding athlete and student, but she was poor and Catholic in a rich and Protestant school and never felt she fit in.

Higgins decided by the time she was sixteen that she wanted to be a journalist and never veered from this career choice. In 1937, she began her freshman year at the University of California at Berkeley and quickly joined the staff of the *Daily Californian,* a highly acclaimed school newspaper run entirely by students. Higgins was an extremely

Words to Know

cold war: the struggle for power, authority, and prestige between the communist Soviet Union and the capitalist Western powers of Europe and the United States from 1945 until 1991.

concentration camp: a camp where groups of people, such as prisoners of war, political prisoners, or refugees, are confined.

gender bias: sexual stereotyping; assuming someone will only perform certain functions because of his or her gender.

Great Depression: a decrease in economic activity and time of high unemployment that started with the stock market crash in 1929 and whose effects were felt throughout the 1930s.

leftists: people who advocate change and reform, usually in the interest of gaining greater freedoms and equality for average citizens and the poor; some leftist groups aspire to overthrow the government; others seek to change from within.

war correspondent: someone who provides news stories to a newspaper or television or radio news program from the battlefront or on location in a war.

dynamic young woman by this time. She liked to be the leader of anything she undertook and made things exciting for the people around her. Toward the end of her college days she took up leftist politics and began speaking at protest demonstrations. ("Leftists" generally hold radical political views seeking change and reform, usually including more freedom, more equality, and better conditions for common people.) Most of her colleagues of these days said she was very manipulative (scheming) and did not get close to other people. She was so competitive that she was often accused of stealing stories from other reporters on the paper.

A journalist in New York

Higgins graduated from the University of California with honors. She packed one suitcase and went to New York City with a reported $7 in her pocket. In New York, she tirelessly applied to every newspaper for work, but none were willing to hire her. Undaunted, she enrolled at the Columbia School of Journalism for the master's program. Her classmates there remember her as intelligent and beautiful, but unusually competitive and ambitious. While she was in school she landed a part-time job with the *New York Herald Tribune*. In June 1942, she managed to get an interview with the elusive Madame Chiang Kai-shek, the wife of the Nationalist leader of China. This accomplishment led to Higgins becoming the second woman ever to be hired as a news reporter at the *Tribune*.

World War II (1939–45) was in full swing when Higgins got her master's degree with honors. She married Stanley Moore, a handsome, intelligent, and politically radical philosophy student from an aristocratic background. Moore joined the air force and left for Europe soon after the marriage. Higgins continued to work for the *Tribune* as a member of its city staff. In 1944, she covered the story of a circus tent fire in Hartford, Connecticut, in which 186 people, most of them children, burned to death. The horror on the scene was felt deeply by the most hardened journalists and fire teams. One of Higgins's coworkers remembered with amazement how hard Higgins had worked to help out and to cover the story. It was good preparation for what was to come.

Overseas correspondent

Higgins had always wanted to be assigned to an overseas position. In 1944 she got her wish, when her paper sent her to London, England. By chance, her husband was stationed there as well, and the couple lived together for the first time in the midst of heavy bombing. Higgins reported on the bombings, on the British prime minister, Winston Churchill (1874–1965), the king, women in the war, and many other things. Her stories were very successful, but her marriage was not. She and her husband permanently separated by the end of the year and later divorced.

In February 1945, after recovering from a serious illness, Higgins was sent to Paris, France, as overseas correspondent for the *Tribune* because she spoke fluent French. There were few correspondents left in Paris and Higgins started out by handling all nonmilitary stories. She worked night and day, competing with the old hands, and churned out many key stories on war-torn France. Still, she longed to be at the battlefront, in the seat of the action.

War correspondent in Germany, 1945

In March 1945, Higgins joined the U.S. Seventh Army and went to Germany, where she witnessed, participated in, and reported on the last weeks of the war. Starting in Frankfurt, she reported on the recently released slave laborers from Poland, France, and Russia, freed from German labor camps by the Americans. She then hitched a ride on a cargo plane and made her way to Buchenwald, the concentration camp, only hours after it had been liberated by the American army. Her stories in the *Tribune* communicated the horrors she encountered at Buchenwald: the terrible suffering of the thousands of dead and dying prisoners she witnessed herself as well as the stories told to her by the survivors.

Higgins then met up with Peter First of the army newspaper *Stars and Stripes*. Prior to meeting First, Higgins had been excluded from the company of other journalists because of her gender. But First was an adventurer like herself. The two of them shared his jeep and traveled the towns of the German countryside at the same time as, and sometimes before, the Allies (the United States, the British Commonwealth, the

Soviet Union, and some other European nations) reached them. When they arrived at the Dachau concentration camp, Higgins's courage and spirit greatly impressed those around her. According to a *Time* reporter, "while some correspondents dodged SS [secret police] bullets," Higgins and First "jeeped blithely past and were the first reporters inside the central enclosure." According to her biographer, Antoinette May, Higgins entered the camp and demanded that the guards put down their arms and surrender. She then announced to the prisoners in three languages that they were free. The prisoners crowded around her in joy. For her courageous efforts at Dachau, the army awarded her a campaign ribbon "for outstanding and conspicuous service with the armed forces under difficult and hazardous conditions." She also won the New York Women's Club award for the best correspondence. In all, Higgins was only a World War II war correspondent for about six weeks, but it had been an impressive start.

From Berlin to Tokyo

In 1945, after the war, Higgins was made the *New York Herald Tribune*'s assistant bureau chief in Berlin, Germany. At the time, Berlin was occupied by four nations. The Soviet Union occupied East Berlin, and West Berlin was controlled by the British, French, and Americans. For Higgins, it was the perfect place to observe the beginnings of the cold war, the rising political tensions and military rivalry between the United States and the Soviet Union that persisted for decades after the war. She covered many central stories in the next couple of years, from the Nuremberg Trials for war crimes to an interview with Nazi (German) leader Adolf Hitler's (1889–1945) personal servant. She also witnessed the erupting political turmoil in Czechoslovakia and Poland. Despite her early allegiance to left-wing politics, Higgins strongly denounced the communist Soviet Union for its violent repression of democracy in Poland. (Some people who hold left-leaning beliefs also adhere to communism, a political theory and economic practice that advocates the elimination of private property. It is a system in which goods are owned by the community as a whole rather than by specific individuals and are available to all as needed. The Soviet Union existed as a communist country made up of fifteen republics from 1922 to 1991. Though its political ideology [set of beliefs] was attractive to many reform-minded people, its government practices were often brutal.)

In 1947, Higgins was promoted to bureau chief in Berlin, a highly unusual accomplishment for a twenty-seven year-old woman. She was happy there, living in a villa, working long, hard days, and enjoying an active social life as well. In 1948, the Russians set up a blockade around West Berlin (the city, as well as the country, was divided), stopping all supplies from entering by land and water in the hope that the Allies would abandon their section of the city. Instead, the American army began a huge airlift, bringing in food to feed more than two million people. The Berlin Airlift began on June 15, 1948, and did not end until May 12, 1949. Major General William Hall was in charge of the airlift, and although he was married, he and Higgins began a romantic involvement. They would later marry.

In April 1950, Higgins was transferred to Tokyo, Japan, as bureau chief there; she was not happy with the assignment. She shared an office there with Keyes Beech, a well-known Far East correspondent for the *Chicago Daily News*. Korea was part of her territory, but it was of little interest to her until June 25, 1950, when the North Koreans, backed by the Communist Chinese, invaded South Korea, backed by the United Nations forces, including the American military. Within two days Higgins was on her way to the front, where she would become as famous as she had always dreamed as the only woman war correspondent in the Korean War.

Early days at the front in Korea

After much difficulty, Higgins and three other correspondents from Tokyo arrived at Kimpo Airport at the Korean capital, Seoul. The advancing North Koreans were positioned only a few miles north of the city when Higgins arrived. Staying at the Military Government headquarters, she was awakened her first night as the North Koreans invaded Seoul. Fleeing the city, she marched along with thousands of refugees toward the city of Suwon. On the way, Higgins saw what was to become a very familiar sight: soldiers fleeing in disorderly retreats.

The next day, after filing her story in Japan and then returning to Korea, Higgins was typing a story at an airstrip in

Korea. General **Douglas MacArthur** (1880–1964; see entry), the commander of the United Nations (UN) Far East forces, saw her as he returned from the front. He invited her to fly back to Tokyo with him. MacArthur told Higgins that the South Korean Army just needed a little help from the United States. "Give me two American divisions and I can hold Korea," he told her, in one of his famous underestimations of the enemy, as quoted in Higgins's book, *War in Korea: The*

Report of a Woman Combat Correspondent. Higgins was accused of using her feminine appeal to gain access to the general.

Battle of sexes at battlefront

For days before the United States sent its troops to Korea, Higgins and her colleagues were caught up in the Republic of Korea (ROK) Army's rapid retreat to Taejon, constantly besieged by the advancing North Koreans and always in great danger. Along with covering the battles, Higgins was hit with another bomb. Her paper, the *New York Herald Tribune,* sent over its star war correspondent, the Pulitzer Prize-winning Homer Bigart, to cover the war. Bigart told Higgins to go home, saying she would be fired if she stayed in Korea. Higgins was dejected, but after thinking it over, simply stayed on, ignoring Bigart when she ran into him on the front.

Higgins was in the midst of intense combat as the city of Taejon fell to the enemy, when an officer delivered a message to her that she was under orders of the U.S. Army to leave the Korean theater of war at once. Lieutenant General **Walton H. "Johnnie" Walker** (1889–1950; see entry), commander of the Eighth Army, had issued the order because Higgins was a woman, and he believed Korea to be no place for women. With this second order to leave, Higgins felt she was being unfairly targeted, as she described in *War in Korea:*

> I had already been with the troops three weeks. . . . Realizing that as a female I was an obvious target for comment, I had taken great pains not to ask for anything that could possibly be construed as a special favor. Like the rest of the correspondents, when not sleeping on the ground at the front with an individual unit, I usually occupied a table top in the big, sprawling room at Taejon from which we telephoned. The custom was to come back from the front, bang out your story, and stretch out on the table top. You would try to sleep, despite the noise of other stories being shouted into the phone, till your turn came to read your story to Tokyo. Then, no matter what the hour, you would probably start out again because the front lines were changing so fast you would not risk staying away any longer than necessary.

After the fall of Taejon in July, Higgins made her way to Taegu in order to argue her point with General Walker at the new Eighth Army headquarters. Instead, she was unceremoniously put on a plane for Tokyo. Fortunately, when she arrived she learned that MacArthur had overturned Walker's order.

According to Antionette May's biography, MacArthur had written a message to the president of the *Herald Tribune* that read: "Ban on women in Korea being lifted. Marguerite Higgins held in highest professional esteem by everyone."

Pusan Perimeter

Higgins returned to Korea as Walker was bringing his forces into the concentrated defensive position in the Pusan Perimeter in the south and MacArthur was preparing the marines for the landing at the enemy-held Inchon to the north. Higgins was one of the few correspondents to cover the first fighting in the perimeter at Chindong-ni with the famous Twenty-seventh (Wolfhound) Regiment under Colonel John "Mike" Michaelis. After getting a story one day, she spent the night at the schoolhouse where the unit was temporarily stationed. The next morning as she ate breakfast with the officers and another correspondent, gunfire poured into the schoolhouse. Machine gun bursts ripped through the room, and grenades went off in several places. During the night the North Korean soldiers had snuck past the front lines and surrounded the unit. Diving out a window into the courtyard, Higgins learned that the enemy was massing all around them. In her memoirs, she described her brief, and rare, encounter with fear: "Then, suddenly, for the first time in the war, I experienced the cold, awful certainty that there was no escape. My reactions were trite. As with most people who suddenly accept death as inevitable and imminent, I was simply filled with surprise that this was finally going to happen to me. Then, as the conviction grew, I became hard inside and comparatively calm."

Michaelis regrouped his troops and Higgins helped out the busy medics, administering plasma to the many casualties that poured in while dodging enemy bullets. Michaelis later wrote a letter to the editors of the *Herald Tribune* praising Higgins for fearlessly volunteering to help in the desperate battle: "The Regimental Combat Team considers Miss Higgins' actions on that day as heroic, but even more important is the gratitude felt by members of this command towards the selfless devotion of Miss Higgins in saving the lives of many grievously wounded men."

Inchon, Chosin, and more

Higgins traveled by ship to the UN command's amphibious attack (involving land, sea, and air forces) on the port city of Inchon on September 15, 1950, landing on the shores with the first waves of troops. In early December, she was north of the 38th parallel (the dividing line between North and South Korea, at 38 degrees north latitude) at Hagaru, getting the stories from the surviving marines who were retreating from the unexpected assault by the Chinese in the Chosin (Changjin) Reservoir.

For many of her travels in Korea, Higgins teamed up with *Chicago Daily News* correspondent Keyes Beech, who had managed to find a jeep. They were in Seoul when it fell in June, then again in September, and when it fell the third time in January 1951. Although they fought with each other, Beech would later betray a reluctant admiration for her in his memoirs.

Out of Korea

Higgins returned to the United States in 1951. She married William Hall and the couple had two children. She was awarded the Pulitzer Prize for international reporting in 1951 (along with Keyes Beech and Homer Bigart). She also wrote her book, *War in Korea: The Report of a Woman Combat Correspondent,* which quickly became a bestseller. Higgins continued her journalism career. She went to Vietnam ten times between 1953 and 1965. In 1954, she reported on the defeat of the French army by communist forces at Dien Bien Phu in northwest Vietnam.

In 1955, Higgins traveled throughout the Soviet Union. On her return she wrote her book *Red Plush and Black Bread.* She next wrote a book about journalism, *News Is a Singular Thing,* in 1955. She then traveled to Africa to cover the civil war in the Congo.

In 1962, Higgins wrote about Cuban military activity, warning of the problems that were, in fact, about to surface between the United States and Cuba, which was an ally of the Soviet Union. In 1965, she reported on the American policy on Vietnam, and wrote the book *Our Vietnam Nightmare.* She took a last trip to Vietnam in 1965 to report on the combat. While there, she contracted leishmaniasis, a tropical disease. She died of the disease on January 3, 1966, at the age of forty-five. In honor of her war reporting, Higgins was buried at Arlington National Cemetery outside of Washington, D.C.

In the year 2001, Fox 2000 was at work on a romantic biographical movie called *Higgins and Beech,* about the relationship between the two correspondents in Korea.

Where to Learn More

Beech, Keyes. *Tokyo and Points North.* Garden City, NY: Doubleday, 1954.

Higgins, Marguerite. *War in Korea: The Report of a Woman Combat Correspondent.* Garden City, NY: Doubleday, 1951.

"Letter from Colonel John H. Michaelis." *New York Herald Tribune,* October 29, 1950, p. 67.

Life, October 2, 1950.

May, Antoinette. *Witness to War: A Biography of Marguerite Higgins.* New York: Beaufort Books, 1954.

Time, September 25, 1950.

Kim Il Sung

Born April 15, 1912
P'yongi, Korea
Died July 7, 1994
North Korea

Chief of state of the Democratic
People's Republic of Korea

Like many communist countries, political authority in the Democratic People's Republic of Korea (North Korea) is split between the government and a powerful communist party, the Korean Workers' Party. Kim Il Sung was premier and then president of the North Korean government and also the general secretary (leader) of the Korean Workers' Party from the foundation of the country in 1948. Holding the two most powerful positions in the country, he was the absolute ruler of North Korea for forty-six years, until his death in 1994. Developing a "cult of personality" around himself as a ruler of almost godlike stature, the "Great Leader" of the Democratic People's Republic of Korea governed his country with an iron grip.

Childhood of exile in China

Kim Il Sung was born Kim Sung-ju (Kim Sung-chu) on April 15, 1912, the son of a schoolmaster in Pyongyang in northeastern Korea. Korea was annexed by Japan (incorporated and forcibly ruled as part of Japan) two years before Kim's birth. Japan's colonial domination become progressively

"The juche idea is embodied, first of all, in the lines of independence in politics, self-sustenance in economy and self defense in national defense; the people themselves are the masters of the revolution and construction, they are the motive force to carry both to success."

Portrait reproduced by permission of AP/Wide World Photos.

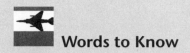

Words to Know

annex: to take over a nation that was independent, making it a dependent part of another nation.

colonial domination: a repressive rule imposed upon one nation by another, more powerful, nation.

Communism: a system of government in which one party (usually the Communist Party) controls all property and goods and the means to produce and distribute them.

dissent: disagreement or difference of opinion.

guerrilla: a warrior who performs an irregular form of combat; in Korea it usually involved hiding in mountains, enlisting the help of the local population, and setting ambushes and surprise attacks to harass or even destroy regular armies.

reunification: the process of bringing back together the separate parts of something that was once a single unit; in Korea, this usually refers to the dream of a single Korea ruled under one government, no longer divided into two nations at the demarcation line.

38th parallel: the 38th degree of north latitude as it bisects the Korean Peninsula, chosen by Americans as the dividing line between what was to be Soviet-occupied North Korea and U.S.-occupied South Korea in 1945.

harsher, and in about 1925 Kim fled with his parents to Manchuria, an area of northern China.

Kim spent the next fouteen years in Manchuria, attending middle school in Kirin. At the age of seventeen, he was arrested for belonging to a radical, communist youth organization. (Communism is a set of political beliefs that advocates the elimination of private property, a system in which goods are owned by the community as a whole rather than by specific individuals and are available to all as needed.) After his release from prison, he fought as a guerrilla (a warrior in a small band that fights the larger enemy with ambushes and surprise attacks) against the Japanese in the Yalu River region that marks the border between Korea and Manchuria. During this time he took the name Kim Il Sung, the name of a legendary anti-Japanese fighter from earlier in the century. Official North Korean biographies have exaggerated his role in the combat. According to one biography, Kim fought Japanese-Manchurian forces from 1932 to 1945 more than one hundred thousand times, never losing a single engagement. This means Kim fought more than twenty battles every single day in this period! Despite the doubtful numbers, Kim was an important member of the Korean movement that helped the Chinese Communists fight the Japanese in Manchuria in the 1930s.

Kim was forced to flee Manchuria for the Soviet Union around 1940, when Japanese imperial forces shattered the Chinese guerrillas with whom he was fighting. (The Soviet Union was the first communist country and was made up of fifteen republics, including Russia, and is sometimes simply called Russia. It existed as a unified country from 1922 to 1991.) In Russia, Kim received his military and political training at the Communist Party school in Khabarovsk in the Soviet Far East. He attained the rank of major in the Soviet army and, according to some accounts, fought with the Russians in Europe in World War II (1939–45).

Home to lead Korea

When the Japanese were defeated to end World War II in August 1945, the general order for the Japanese surrender included an arrangement for Korea in which the Americans were to accept the Japanese surrender south of the 38th parallel (the dividing line between northern and southern Korea, at 38 degrees north latitude), and the Soviets, who were already on the Korean border, would receive the surrender north of it. Kim accompanied the Soviet army to Pyongyang in the northern section of Korea in October, dressed in the uniform of the Soviet army.

Three distinct groupings of communists emerged in North Korea at this time: the Soviet-aligned group, including those Koreans who had returned from the Soviet Union; the Chinese-oriented, or the Yenan, faction, composed of those who had returned from China; and the domestic group, who had opposed the Japanese colonial rule within Korea. Meanwhile, in the southern section of the country, the United Nations (UN) was sponsoring elections in Korea, with the idea that Korea would become independent after a leader was elected. (The UN was founded in 1945 by the Allies to maintain worldwide peace and to develop friendly relations among countries.) The northern Koreans and the Soviets, claiming that the UN did not have the authority to determine the future of Korea, refused to take part in the elections. The vote was held in May 1948 nonetheless—without the northern Koreans —and a new government to rule over all of Korea, the Republic of Korea, was established.

Later in 1948, as the Soviets prepared to withdraw their troops from Korea, the northern authorities held an election that established a new government, the Democratic People's Republic of Korea. Kim Il Sung became its premier. Kim was picked by local Soviet commanders in Pyongyang to be northern Korea's leader in part because they knew few other Koreans. Kim's appeal to Koreans was that he had ties to both the Chinese and the Russians and would probably not answer solely to one or the other. Because Seoul, in the south, was the national capital, many of the Korean communist leaders, **Pak Hŏn-yŏng** (1900–1955; see entry) in particular, had remained there after liberation trying to work with the American Military Governmen. Thus they were not in the north when the leadership positions were being filled. It is not clear if Kim's rise to power was the result of a decision made by the Soviets or because of his effective organization of the People's Committees (units of local government the Korean people had established when the Japanese were defeated) or both. Nonetheless, the Soviets did support Kim as he took on increasing leadership.

Dreams of reunifying Korea

As premier of North Korea, Kim gave passionate speeches about the reunification of the country, and notably not about communism. From the beginning, Kim wished to sweep across the 38th parallel, conquer South Korea, and reunify the country. Soviet Premier **Joseph Stalin** (1879–1953; see entry), who was engaged in intense tensions with Western nations in European countries, had no wish to risk a war with the United States in Korea. By telegrams and in person, Kim convinced Stalin to at least give his approval to the venture, saying that he could finish the conflict and unify Korea in three weeks. Kim had been led to believe, probably through his vice premier Pak Hŏn-yŏng, that a force of about half a million members of the South Korean Labor Party were waiting in the south to join with North Korean forces in a war for reunification. He did not believe that the United States would intervene. Stalin at last gave his approval.

Kim invaded South Korea in June 1950, with arms purchased from, or left behind by, the Soviets. The invasion started out very successfully, and even when U.S. troops unexpectedly appeared, they were unable to hold a line against the well-trained North Korean People's Army (NKPA). By September, however, more and more United Nations troops were entering the battle, and the NKPA was driven north. Kim turned for help to the chairman of the People's Republic of China, **Mao Zedong** (Mao Tse-tung; 1893–1976; see entry). In October Mao, concerned about having U.S. troops so close to home, sent massive Chinese troops to North Korea's aid.

The cease-fire seven months later found the opposing forces near the war's starting point, the 38th parallel; Kim's reunification dreams were dashed. He would never give up hope of eliminating the South Korean (Republic of Korea) government, but there would never be another chance for reunification within his lifetime.

Democratic People's Republic of Korea after the war

After the Korean War ended in 1953, Kim established a rigid, militarized communist government that allowed no opposition. He ruled under the name "Great Leader," and placed himself in a position to be revered almost as a god by his people. Kim admired Stalin's methods and his bearing, and worked to develop his own status as an absolute ruler. As the "Great Leader" of the DPRK, he had a very energetic personal presence and was an impressive speaker who regularly made unexpected "tours" all over the country. The *New York Times* reported that citizens were encouraged to devote two to four hours daily to "Kim Study," during which they would reflect on their leaders' teachings. Throughout the streets of Pyongyang, there are thirty thousand statues of Kim. His birthday was celebrated as the most important of national holidays.

Kim developed and advanced a doctrine of nationalist self-sufficiency, known as "juche," which proclaims that the Korean people are masters of their own destiny. Juche was

The Cult of Personality

The three major communist heads of state in the Korean War, Soviet premier Joseph Stalin (1879–1953), Communist Chinese Chairman Mao Zedong (1893–1976), and Democratic People's republic of Korea (North Korea) premier Kim Il Sung, all purposely developed a "cult of personality" around themselves. Cult of personality is the elevation of a leader to the level of godlike infallibility, an object of adoration and veneration to the people of his nation. This is achieved through constantly bombarding the people with praise for the leader's virtues and achievements through every form of communication and art available. Some communist ideology (the philosophy behind the system) revolves around the concept of a personality cult. In order for people to work together for the communal good, the theory goes, they must be motivated by a deep adoration and unquestioning enthusiasm for their one absolute leader.

Stalin was a pioneer in developing the cult of personality. His predecessor, Vladimir Lenin (1870–1924), had utterly opposed the idea. Lenin believed that the masses should be elevated, not the leader.

But when Stalin was trying to stabilize his own power base after Lenin's death, he pursued the kind of religious adoration from the Russian people that had in the past been devoted to the Russian czar (or monarch). Stalin had his picture posted all over the Soviet Union. He rewrote history to take credit for Soviet achievements and to firmly associate himself with the beloved Lenin. Poems written at that time often sounded like hymns to Stalin, as the savior and father of the nation. The cult of personality allowed no dissent (disagreement). If artists or journalists did not worship him, they were often deported (sent out of the country), arrested, or even executed.

In his later years, Mao Zedong promoted himself as an almost religious figure in China. Some people began and ended their days praying to him. Every home had a picture or statue of Mao in it. His posters were all prepared to make him godlike, radiating light. Although Mao actively—and successfully—pursued the personality cult, the Chinese government functioned with input from many people. Mao's later periods of absolute rule alienated many people around him.

Kim's attempt to apply the ideas behind German philosopher Karl Marx's communism to the unique Korean society.

Kim repeatedly proved that he held the country in a tight control. For some time, his vision of the future worked.

In the Soviet Union and China, the idea of the cult of personality was rejected after Stalin's deadly purges (elimination, often by murder) of enemies and Mao's brutal Cultural Revolution (1966–76). In 1956, Soviet premier Nikita Khrushchev (1894–1971) delivered a scathing speech against the cult of personality and Stalin's use of it, saying that "Stalin had so elevated himself above the party and above the nation that he ceased to consider either the central committee [government] or the [Communist] party." He also said that Stalin believed "he could decide all things alone and all he needed were statisticians; he treated all others in such a way that they could only listen to and praise him." Khrushchev later visited Mao and made a similar pronouncement about his use of the personality cult.

As has been noted by many historians and journalists, in many ways Kim Il Sung surpassed both Stalin and Mao with his own cult of personality campaign. This is particularly notable since the cult lasted after his death and well into the twenty-first century. In North Korea at the turn of the twenty-first century, every home had a picture of both Kim Il Sung and his son, Kim Jong Il, the new leader of North Korea. People bowed to these images morning and night. There were markers to Kim Il Sung, the "Dear Leader," everywhere throughout the country. His books—twenty-seven volumes of his teachings—provided the center of education in the nation. He was often called the "eternal" leader of North Korea, in effect, still ruling along with his son, the "Great Leader." Whether Kim Il Sung was so successful in his cult of personality because he was so thorough in establishing it—spending millions of dollars annually, instilling great fear of punishment for expressing contradicting opinions, touring the country personally and checking up on the people—or because the North Koreans believed in him as a great leader, will require the passage of time to understand.

Source: Modern History Sourcebook. "Nikita S. Khrushchev: The Secret Speech—On the Cult of Personality, 1956, Secret Speech Delivered by First Party Secretary at the Twentieth Party Congress of the Communist Party of the Soviet Union, February 25, 1956." [Online] http://www.fordham.edu/ halsall/mod/1956khrushchev-secret1.html (accessed on August 14, 2001).

From 1953 until the 1970s, Kim emphasized heavy industry and collective farming, and he was able to push people to work long hours. During this period, North Korea was a model of state-controlled development, and was economically better off

than South Korea. Yet North Korea under Kim was a true dictatorship that did not permit disagreement with the government of any kind. Each of the country's twenty-two million people was classified according to their degree of loyalty to Kim. The "core class" (25 percent) lived in the big cities and received the best jobs, education, and food. The "wavering class" (50 percent) had second-rate jobs and homes, and their loyalty was monitored by internal security forces. The people in the "hostile class" were assigned to hard labor and most lived in remote villages. Dissent did not exist in North Korea, at least not out loud; according to *Amnesty International,* there were tens of thousands of dissidents and political enemies in concentration camps during Kim's reign, and untold numbers had been executed.

As an economic program juche began to decline in the 1970s. Kim's military spending reached 25 percent of the entire national budget (in South Korea, it was 4 percent); harvests declined; the Soviets no longer wanted to import North Korea's tractors and trucks; and public works spending increased greatly, most of it on monuments to Kim. For his sixtieth birthday in 1972, Kim erected a huge bronze statue, among other things; for his seventieth, it was an Arch of Triumph taller than the original in Paris, France, and the Tower of the Juche Idea, which consisted of 25,500 white granite blocks, one for each day of Kim's first seventy years.

Conflicts with Western powers

North Korea remained isolated from capitalism and the West longer than any other communist nation. (Capitalism, the economic system of the United States and most Western powers, is based on the idea that individuals, rather than the state, own property and businesses, and the cost and distribution of goods are determined by the free market. Capitalism is fundamentally at odds with communism, in which goods are owned by the community as a whole rather than by specific individuals and are available to all as needed.) The country has been involved in several terrorist attacks, including one against South Korea's president in 1968. A blown-up South Korean airliner has also been credited to North Korean terrorists. When, in 1968, the American ship the U.S.S. *Pueblo* was intercepted on a spying mission in North Korean waters, Kim managed to embarrass the United States by imprisoning the crew for eleven months. In 1993, with nuclear materiel in his country, possibly a bomb or even two, Kim announced that North Korea would withdraw from the longstanding international Nuclear Nonproliferation Treaty. On a visit to North Korea, former U.S. President Jimmy Carter managed to ease tensions, and new United Nations talks had begun when Kim died on July 8, 1994, in North Korea, of an apparent heart attack.

The depth and character of North Korea's mourning for Kim was difficult for Westerners to comprehend. A 273-member committee, chaired by his son, Kim Jong Il, organized the funeral in Pyongyang. An estimated two million North Koreans attended the three-and-a-half hour procession. After the mourning period, Kim was succeeded by his son Kim Jong Il, who had been placed in many key positions in the government as far back as 1980 and was already groomed for the public as the "Dear Leader."

Where to Learn More

Baik Bong. *Kim Il Sung: Biography.* 3 vols. Tokyo: Miraisha, 1969–70.

New York Times, July 10, 1994; July 11, 1994.

Newsweek, June 27, 1994.

Suh Dae-sook. *Kim Il Sung: The North Korean Leader.* New York: Columbia University Press, 1995.

Suh Dae-sook. *The Korean Communist Movement, 1918–1948.* Honolulu: University of Hawaii Press, 1967.

Time, June 13, 1994; June 27, 1994.

U.S. News & World Report, June 27, 1994.

Web sites

"Kim Il Sung, 15 April 1912–8 July 1994." [Online] http://www.geocities.com/CapitolHill/Lobby/1461/kimilsung.htm (accessed on August 14, 2001).

Douglas MacArthur

Born January 26, 1880
Little Rock, Arkansas
Died April 5, 1964
Washington, D.C.

American military leader

Most people who came into contact with General Douglas MacArthur during his long career as a military commander were taken aback by the power of his personality. He was described as "larger than life" by many, with a remarkable gift for making compelling speeches and bringing drama and high passion to battlefields and military command offices worldwide. His military accomplishments from World War I (1914–18) and II (1939–45) and on through the Korean War (1950–53) were numerous and significant, and his courage in the face of grave danger became a matter of legend. With his corncob pipe and sunglasses and his well-kept uniforms, he cut a very impressive figure, and the press kept busy photographing him walking fearlessly in the face of flying bullets. Yet, despite his near perfect American hero image, MacArthur became the most controversial military figure of the Korean War and was relieved of his command. Some of his admirers remember him as a strong and appealing military hero, while others remember him for his arrogance and disdain for the chain of command.

"In war there can be no substitute for victory."

A general's son

Douglas MacArthur was born on January 26, 1880, in Little Rock, Arkansas. He was the son of a very distinguished military leader, Arthur MacArthur, who had won the Congressional Medal of Honor during the Civil War (1860–65). In 1898, as a brigadier general, Arthur MacArthur led troops as they shattered Filipino resistance to the American takeover of the Philippines. He then became military governor of the Philippines. By the time he retired in 1909, Lieutenant General Arthur MacArthur had become commander of the U.S. forces in the Pacific.

Military background

Douglas MacArthur was the third son in his family. His brother, Arthur II, was a navy captain whose career was marked by outstanding service in the Spanish-American War (1898) and World War I. His paternal grandfather was a lieutenant governor (and briefly governor) of Wisconsin and a federal judge. MacArthur often attributed his inspiration and success to his family heritage.

Douglas took an early liking to the military. He was born at a military station, and for much of his early life his family moved from post to post. He spent three early years, from age four to six, at Fort Selden near the Mexican border, watching the drills and parades of the fifty soldiers stationed there. He remembered learning to ride and shoot at Fort Selden even before he could read or write.

Probably the strongest influence on the young MacArthur was his mother, Mary Pinkney ("Pinkie") Hardy, the ambitious, strong-willed daughter of an aristocratic family from Norfolk, Virginia. Pinkie MacArthur spent much of her time persuading her son Douglas that he was special and destined for greatness. A very dominating parent, she nagged and pushed him to do great things, and also pushed the people around him to appreciate him. As a result, Douglas was, from an early age, a leader and an achiever. He earned high grades and found time to be active in sports but never participated much in the social activities at school. An acquaintance later said he was arrogant, or overly proud, from the age of eight.

The illustrious military career begins

In 1899, at the age of nineteen, MacArthur entered the military academy at West Point. His mother rented a room at a hotel overlooking her son's room at the academy. She is said to have watched over him very closely, making sure that he worked hard. He did. He earned top grades while playing baseball and managing the football team. In his senior year, he also served as president of the student body of West Point. MacArthur graduated in 1903 with a grade average of 98.14 percent, first in his class. He held the third best academic record in the history of the academy. On top of this, he clearly had an active social life, for he is said to have been engaged to eight women at the same time while still in school.

MacArthur rose rapidly in the service. His first assignment was in Leyte in the Philippines as an aide to his father. In 1906 and 1907, he attended the Engineer School of Application in Washington, D.C., receiving a degree in 1908, and he worked in the Office of the Chief of Engineers. By 1911, he had risen to the rank of captain. In 1913, after serving as an aide to President Theodore Roosevelt (1858–1919), MacArthur found himself in Vera Cruz, Mexico, with the Corps of Engineers. The next year, he was promoted to the rank of major, at first supervising the State Department Building in Washington and then joining the general staff of the army. He was on the general staff in 1917 when the United States entered World War I.

World War I

Still only a major, MacArthur was lower in rank than most of the army staff. Yet he now began to show the arrogance and determination that would mark his military career. The wartime army needed more men to fight in Europe. To remedy this, MacArthur was strongly in favor of enlisting the National Guard into the regular army, but most generals on the staff were against it, believing that the part-time volunteer guard was not properly prepared. MacArthur argued so violently on the issue that one superior officer threatened to block any more promotions for him. Eventually, though, President Woodrow Wilson (1856–1924) came to hear of the young officer's proposal of forming a single battalion from National Guard volunteers of every state, a Rainbow Battalion. Wilson liked the idea, and soon MacArthur found himself a colonel helping to form the Rainbow Battalion and then a brigadier general leading the battalion into battle.

Even as a general, MacArthur was defiant of army ways, particularly in regard to his dress. Once he climbed out of the trenches in France to lead his men into combat wearing a West Point letter sweater with no helmet or gas-mask, armed only with a riding crop. He continually exposed himself to enemy fire. Winning many medals for his bravery and leadership, MacArthur was wounded twice and disabled by a gas attack once during World War I.

Postwar duty

After the war, MacArthur was appointed superintendent of West Point. He was the youngest commandant of the academy ever to serve. He stayed in that position for three years until, in 1923, he followed in his father's footsteps on assignment to the Philippines. Back in the United States a year later, he took command posts of several army corps before returning to the island nation in 1928. He had married Henrietta Louise Cromwell Brooks, a wealthy divorcee, on February 14, 1922; they had no children. Seven years later they were divorced.

President Herbert Hoover (1874–1964) appointed MacArthur army chief of staff in November 1930, with the temporary rank of general. Because of the worsening Great Depression (a worldwide economic downturn prompted by the U.S. stock market crash of 1929 that lasted throughout the 1930s), much of his time and energy went toward preserving the army's already meager manpower and equipment. MacArthur served the army well as its directing officer. His work was so impressive that President Franklin D. Roosevelt (1882–1945) asked him to stay in the position until 1935—one year beyond the normal tour for a chief of staff. From 1935 to 1937, MacArthur headed the U.S. military mission to the Philippine Commonwealth, given the task of developing Philippine self-defense in preparation for independence in 1946.

Field marshall

In 1935, MacArthur suffered a very difficult loss when his mother died. Two years later, in 1937, he wed Jean Marie Faircloth. This second marriage endured and the couple had one son, Arthur MacArthur III. Also in 1937, MacArthur retired from the U.S. Army. His old friend Manuel Quezon (1878–1944), then president of the Philippines, had asked him to serve as a military adviser. He became a field marshall in the Philippine army, with an assistant appointed by the U.S. Army, a young major named **Dwight D. Eisenhower** (1890–1969; see entry). (The United States at this point in Philippine history was in charge of the island nation's defense and so could make such appointments.)

Pacific commander

When it appeared that the United States would soon be involved in World War II, MacArthur was recalled to serve in the U.S. Army. In 1941, President Roosevelt appointed him a major general, and one day later promoted him to lieutenant general in charge of the U.S. forces in the Pacific.

For some reason, MacArthur felt that the Philippines were not threatened by the war. He told John Hersey of *Time* magazine in May 1941 that "if Japan entered the war, the Americans, the British and the Dutch could handle her with about half the forces they now have deployed in the Far East." He held to this idea even after, on December 7, 1941, Japanese airplanes struck Pearl Harbor in Hawaii. Ten hours later, the Japanese struck Clark Field in the Philippines, destroying most of MacArthur's planes.

A Japanese invasion and takeover of the Philippines followed, with forces far beyond the numbers the U.S. leaders thought possible. Once the fighting on the island began, MacArthur spread his poorly equipped forces far too thin and greatly exaggerated Japanese strength. MacArthur and his troops were penned up in the jungles with little possibility of escape or reinforcement. Still, MacArthur took personal command of his army's defenses, and to his credit he saved the city of Luzon from immediate destruction. He concentrated his forces on the Bataan peninsula and established his headquarters on the island of Corregidor. By moving food supplies away from the troops at Bataan and over to Corregidor, he created hardships for the soldiers. At this time, too, he accepted a personal gift of $500,000 from Philippines president Quezon, which violated army rules. Although MacArthur was known throughout his career for exposing himself, sometimes recklessly, to enemy fire, he did not visit the exhausted troops at Bataan even once.

It became clear that the U.S. forces in Bataan faced defeat, but MacArthur refused to leave the desperate situation until he was commanded to do so by President Roosevelt. In March 1942, he left the Philippines for Australia, taking with him a few of his men who could not become Japanese prisoners because they knew key military secrets. Typically, MacArthur revised his last message to the Japanese and Filipinos. In the message, he used the words "I shall return" instead of the army's recommendation, "We shall return."

In early April, the Filipino and American troops on Bataan surrendered; a month later Corregidor fell to the Japanese. Meanwhile, MacArthur was awarded the Medal of Honor, and to most of the public in the United States he emerged as the first American hero of the war.

A hero again in the Southwest Pacific

In mid-April 1942, MacArthur took command of the Southwest Pacific Area, a newly formed theater in which the principal forces for many months would be Australian. In the Papuan (New Guinea) campaign of July 1942 through January 1943, MacArthur's forces stopped a Japanese thrust and then counterattacked, annihilating the enemy army in several battles. The Papuan victory, though, was very costly, with nearly nine thousand combat casualties (and even more felled by diseases) out of thirty-three thousand troops engaged.

After Papua, MacArthur was determined to avoid frontal assaults and to bypass enemy strongholds. From this victory, he went on to a series of brilliant amphibious (land, water, and air) assaults throughout the Southwest Pacific, securing important harbors and air and land bases. His ground actions spanned fourteen hundred miles: his forces suffered some sixteen hundred combat casualties while killing more than twenty-six thousand enemy troops. A master of publicity, MacArthur obtained great press coverage. His popularity was rapidly increasing in the United States, and in 1944 he threw in his name as a presidential candidate in the primaries. The bid was unsuccessful and was quickly dropped.

Return to Bataan

On September 20, 1944, the chiefs of staff of the branches of the U.S. military (who advise the president and the secretary of defense on matters of war) ordered MacArthur back to the Philippines to attack Leyte, and on October 3 to invade the northern island of Luzon. MacArthur's orders limited him to Luzon, but he wanted to conquer the entire Philippines. Acting contrary to instructions from Washington, he foolishly divided his forces by sending the equivalent of five divisions to conquer one island after another in head-on strikes. The Japanese then engaged his troops in guerilla action, with ambushes and surprise attacks from mountain hideaways, and the campaign became one of the bloodiest operations of the Pacific. But MacArthur won back Bataan.

Adviser to Japan

The dropping of the atom bombs on Hiroshima and Nagasaki in Japan ended the war, calling for major decisions by the Allies (the United States, the British Commonwealth, the Soviet Union, and other European nations) as to what should be done about the government of Japan. As commander of the U.S. forces and of the Allied forces in the Pacific, MacArthur accepted the Japanese surrender. He was then charged with building a new government in Japan.

The Japanese government had been based on a belief in an emperor chosen by heaven and a government dominated by the military. MacArthur, as usual, was prepared. He had planned to turn Japan into a democracy. His arrogant ways in this instance proving useful, he marched into the Japanese capital of Tokyo with a handful of aides, all without weapons, and established his office there. The emperor was allowed to continue as the symbol of unity for the Japanese but without any power to govern. MacArthur directed the emperor and his officials in a change toward elected government.

For five years, MacArthur held several positions: commander of the U.S. forces in the Pacific, commander of the Allied and then the United Nations forces, and military commander of Japan. He worked seven days a week long into the night to form a Japanese constitution and a form of govern-

And the Oscar Goes to . . . Douglas MacArthur

Nearly everyone who came into contact with U.S. Army general Douglas MacArthur commented on his extraordinary presence. Everything from newspaper reports to official documents from the Korean War note the general's corncob pipe and sunglasses, his voice, his gestures, his range of expression, and the charismatic power of his speech. Here are a few out of many quotes describing the commander's remarkable acting skills:

- General Matthew B. Ridgway (1895–1993), who replaced MacArthur as the supreme commander of the UN Far East forces, described a meeting between MacArthur and him in December 1950: "I was again deeply impressed by the force of his personality. To confer with him was an experience that could happen with few others. He was a great actor too, with an actor's instinct for the dramatic—in tone and gesture. Yet so lucid [clear] and so penetrating were his explanations and his analyses that it was his mind rather than his manner or his bodily presence that dominated his listeners." (Source: Matthew B. Ridgway. *The Korean War*. Garden City, NY: Doubleday, 1967.)

- When Dwight D. Eisenhower (1890–1969), army commander, president of the United States, and one-time assistant to MacArthur, was asked if he had ever met MacArthur. He replied: "Not only have I met him, ma'm; I studied dramatics under him for five years in Washington and four years in the Philippines." (Source: William Manchester. *American Caesar: Douglas MacArthur, 1880–1964*. Boston: Little, Brown, 1978.)

- At a meeting in Tokyo with the Joint Chiefs of Staff and others, MacArthur defended his plans for an amphibious attack at Inchon. Army chief of staff J. Lawton Collins (1896–1987) described him as follows: "MacArthur was cool and poised as always. He spoke with confidence and élan as he paced back and forth in his customary fashion. He always gave the impression of addressing not just his immediate listeners but a large audience unseen." (Source: J. Lawton Collins. *War in Peacetime: The History and Lessons of Korea*. Boston: Houghton Mifflin, 1969.)

ment much like that of the United States. Although MacArthur was one of the most conservative figures in American public life, during his administration of Japan many reforms were put into place, in such diverse areas as women's rights, trade unions, education and police systems, and land

- Frank Pace (1912–1988), the secretary of the army who was chosen to deliver the news to MacArthur that he had been relieved of command, formed his own opinion about the purpose of some of the general's theatrics in the Korean War. His idea was not held by others: "I believe that General MacArthur really created the basis for his firing. I felt that the crowds around the Dai-Ichi Building [MacArthur's headquarters in Tokyo, Japan] were getting to be very small; I felt that his period of glory there had passed; he was a great student of history; I felt he felt Mr. Truman would be easily defeated [in the next election for president] and that if he could be fired under dramatic circumstances he could return and get the Republican nomination for President and run for President against Mr. Truman. I felt he engineered his own dismissal. The kind of letters that he wrote, a man steeped in military and national tradition knew very well was out of order. I can't believe that he would undertake such an action without realizing what the consequences would have to be. (Source: "An Oral Interview with Frank Pace Jr., New York, N. Y., February 17, 1972, by Jerry N. Hess." Truman Presidential Museum and Library. [Online] http://www.trumanlibrary.org/oralhist/pacefj3.htm [accessed on August 14, 2001]).

- John J. Muccio (1900–1989), ambassador to the Republic of Korea during the first years of the Korean War, visited MacArthur in the fall of 1950 and described him thus: "I can still picture him 'posturing' with his corncob pipe. The two of us were alone at the time. MacArthur was a very theatrical personality. . . . I don't think MacArthur even blinked his eyes without considering whether it was to his advantage to have his eye blink or not. Everything was thought through, but it became so [much] a part of his nature, and his personality, that it seemed to be automatic. (Source: John J. Muccio. "Oral History Interview Transcripts." Harry S. Truman Library, Independence, Missouri. [Online] http://www.trumanlibrary.org/oralhist/muccio.htm [accessed on August 14, 2001]).

redistribution. MacArthur was particularly proud of his hand in the drafting of the Japanese constitution of 1947. Provisions included universal adult suffrage (the right to vote), a bill of rights, a clause outlawing discrimination, and the renunciation of war.

In fact, MacArthur's job in Japan was to carry out the policies dictated by the heads of the branches of the U.S. military, who served as advisors to the president and secretary of defense in matters of war, and a council of the Allied powers. But by most accounts, he ruled as if he were a prince. MacArthur's personality and distinctive style of leadership so dominated his headquarters that the Japanese people generally came to view the occupation as personified in his image. To some, he seemed to provide strong, inspiring leadership at a time when they had despaired of their old leaders, who had brought the country to ruin. His imperious and dignified manner, dramatic flair, dedication to his mission, and empathy for the war-ravaged nation were esteemed by many Japanese, particularly during the early phase of the occupation (1945–47).

The Korean War

After 1946, MacArthur was also head of the Far East Command, which consisted of all American ground, air, and sea forces in Japan, the Ryukyus, Korea (to 1948), the Philippines, the Marianas, and the Bonins. Trouble had been brewing in Korea—the country had come to be divided between the communist North (supported by the Soviet Union) and the nationalist South (allied with the United States) after World War II, and both sides sought to reunify the country with its own government ruling—but MacArthur was not prepared for what was to come. By 1950, the new nation of North Korea had built an army of 135,000 soldiers, trained by Soviet advisers. The force was well armed, with 120 tanks supplied by the Soviets along with 40 fighter aircraft and 70 bombers. Battles had been going on at the border for over a year, some of them resulting in hundreds of casualties, and many started by the South Koreans. But on June 25, neither the South Koreans nor the Americans were aware that the North Koreans were gathering their forces along the border. North Korea had 90,000 soldiers prepared to attack across the border. They faced 10,000 unprepared South Korean troops. The attack was so sudden and so unsuspected that within a few days the capital city of Seoul collapsed.

At first, from his headquarters in Japan MacArthur believed that the South Koreans were strong enough to repel

the invasion. When Seoul fell, however, he called the media and told them to prepare for a very dangerous trip to Korea. He was photographed at the battlefront, undaunted by the bullets flying everywhere. On the flight back to Hawaii, he told a reporter that with two U.S. divisions, he could stop the communist forces. Within a couple of days, President **Harry S. Truman** (1884–1972; see entry) authorized two U.S. divisions to go to Korea at once. Soon after, the United Nations agreed to enter the conflict. But stopping the North Koreans proved much more difficult than anyone imagined. As the U.S. troops went in and took up positions with the South Korean army in an attempt to delay the North Koreans' southward advances, they were shattered over and over again, incurring heavy losses. By late August 1950, they had taken up a defensive position at the southern end of the Korean peninsula, called the Pusan Perimeter. By September even this line was being threatened.

Brigadier General Courtney Whitney, Douglas MacArthur (seated), and Edward M. Almond observe the shelling of Inchon from the deck of the U.S.S. McKinley, September 15, 1950.
Reproduced by permission of Double Delta Industries, Inc.

MacArthur defends South Korea

MacArthur had been caught unprepared, but he now planned a counterattack. Inchon was a port city near Seoul in the area captured by the communists. Rather than fight back from the base at Pusan, MacArthur led a landing at Inchon, cutting off the North Korean army from its supplies in the north. So effective was MacArthur's plan that the North Korean forces were soon in retreat. Supported by a United Nations General Assembly resolution calling for the reunification of Korea, MacArthur sent the UN forces in an advance toward the Yalu River at the northern border of North Korea. On October 15, he and Truman conferred at Wake Island, mainly about plans for the postwar rehabilitation of Korea, so near did victory seem.

Two weeks later, however, UN troops near the Yalu were severely attacked by Communist Chinese forces. Then, mysteriously, the Chinese withdrew and disappeared after ten days of combat. MacArthur chose to ignore their warning and launched his "end-the-war" offensive at the end of November. Much to the concern of many military leaders, MacArthur divided his army in two, weakening it. Although his orders were to send only South Korean troops to fight near the border with China (to avoid an American conflict with China, which would certainly lead to expanded warfare), MacArthur ordered U.S. troops to advance to the Yalu. Within two days, a massive Chinese offensive routed his forces in the worst defeat ever suffered by an American army.

By January 1951, General **Matthew B. Ridgway** (1895–1993), had halted the communist advance. MacArthur was soon complaining that the U.S. government had tied his hands. On March 7, he accused the Truman administration of preventing him from directly bombing China's war-making potential. A week later, he called for the unification of Korea, a goal abandoned by the Truman administration. On March 24, knowing that Truman was in the process of trying to start peace talks with the communists, MacArthur called upon the Chinese commander in chief to negotiate directly with him or face U.S. strikes on mainland China. On April 5, House Minority leader Joseph E. Martin released a letter MacArthur had written about the usefulness of enlisting Nationalist Chinese troops supplied by **Chiang Kai-shek** (1887–1975) against the

Chinese Communists. (Communist Chinese leader **Mao Zedong** [Mao Tse-tung; 1893–1976; see entries] had driven the American-backed Chinese Nationalist forces, led by Chiang, to the island of Taiwan [formerly Formosa] in October 1949 following a bloody civil war.) Engaging the Chinese Nationalists had long since been considered and vetoed by the Truman administration; MacArthur's letter could only be read as a weapon against the U.S. president and his administration.

Douglas MacArthur waves to the crowd during a tickertape parade in his honor in New York in April 1951, after he was relieved of command. *Reproduced by permission of AP/Wide World Photos.*

Fired

MacArthur had more than once taken action without the approval of his superiors or of the president. Now he was publicly speaking out against the president's actions. The Joint Chiefs of Staff (the president's military advisors) and the Departments of State and Defense met to consider whether he could be trusted to carry out the orders he received. The majority felt that he could not. Truman listened to all of his advisers and then stated his decision. On April 11, 1951, the president fired his most famous and popular general, replacing him with General Ridgway.

MacArthur had served in the military for fifty-two years. He had won nearly every medal for valor and courage awarded by the United States. He had been the highest-ranking officer in the military forces of another nation and had earned great respect for the defense of the Philippines and the peace in Japan. He served his nation so continuously that he had been out of the United States for sixteen years. When the news was brought to him, his only response was to his wife, "Jeanie, we're going home at last," as quoted in Joseph C. Goulden's *Korea: The Untold Story of the War.*

A career change

MacArthur returned to Washington, D.C. Though he arrived after midnight, twenty thousand admirers were on hand to welcome him. He was invited to speak to Congress, where he denied that he had acted in opposition to the president's directives. He became a popular speaker throughout the country. Public clamor against Truman's action subsided during the Senate hearings in May and June on the general's dismissal, especially after the Joint Chiefs testified that MacArthur's proposals for winning the war had been strategically unsound and might have resulted in a greatly expanded conflict.

In 1944, 1948, and 1952, conservative Republican factions tried to have MacArthur chosen as the party's presidential candidate, but these plans never went very far. After failing to get the nomination in 1952, MacArthur became the chairman of the board of Remington Rand (later Sperry-Rand). One of his final visitors was President Lyndon B. Johnson. MacArthur advised Johnson, as he had John F. Kennedy, not to send ground forces to Vietnam or anywhere else in mainland Asia.

MacArthur died in Washington, D.C., on April 5, 1964, at the age of eighty-four. For his funeral, in keeping with his own request, his body was dressed in one of his old tropical uniforms decorated with only the U.S. and five-star general insignias. He once said that if history a hundred years in the future remembered him only briefly for contributing to the advance of peace, he would gladly yield every honor which has been accorded by war.

Where to Learn More

Darby, Jean. *Douglas MacArthur.* Minneapolis, MN: Lerner, 1989.

Finkelstein, Norman H. *The Emperor General: A Biography of Douglas MacArthur.* Minneapolis, MN: Dillon Press, 1989.

Goulden, Joseph C. *Korea: The Untold Story of the War.* New York: Times Books, 1982.

James, D. Clayton. *The Years of MacArthur.* Vol. 3. Boston: Houghton Mifflin, 1985.

Kawai, K. *Japan's American Interlude.* Chicago: University of Chicago Press, 1960.

Long, Gavin. *MacArthur as Military Commander.* New York: D. Van Nostrand Company, 1969.

MacArthur, Douglas. *A Soldier Speaks.* Westport, CT: Praeger, 1965.

Perret, Geoffrey. *Old Soldiers Never Die: The Life of Douglas MacArthur.* New York: Random House, 1996.

Petillo, Carol Morris. *Douglas MacArthur: The Philippine Years.* Bloomington: Indiana University Press, 1981.

Scott, Robert A. *Douglas MacArthur and the Century of War.* New York: Facts on File, 1997.

Jacob A. Malik

Born February 11, 1906
Kharkow, Ukraine
Died February 11, 1980
Moscow, Russia, USSR

Soviet diplomat

For years, many American historians accepted almost without question that the Soviet Union was the power behind the Korean War (1950–53) from the start. It was believed that North Korea was merely a satellite of the Soviets, a country completely ruled by a larger and more powerful country, and that the North Korean army was in fact carrying out a Soviet plan when it attacked South Korea to begin the war. Indeed, the cold war belief that the Soviets were attempting to take over as much of the planet as possible was not without basis. Soviet premier **Joseph Stalin** (1879–1953; see entry) and the Soviet military were heavily engaged, mainly in Europe, in creating Soviet satellite nations. By the early 1990s, however, the release of formerly top secret government and military documents in the United States and in Russia convinced a significant number of historians that the Soviet Union's role in the Korean War was not as clear cut as had been thought. Like the United States, the Soviet Union had left behind a military government when it withdrew its troops from Korea in 1948 and it had armed the North Koreans, continuing throughout the war to supply them with weapons. But the prospect of war in

Korea seems to have had little appeal for the Soviets. Their involvement in the war was based on a complicated foreign policy in which strained relations with China—an ally in communism—played a large part

Jacob A. Malik, a top Soviet diplomat, became the permanent Soviet representative to the United Nations in 1948. He was a skilled ambassador, solidly holding his nation's line in highly charged and difficult circumstances in the cold war years while managing to maintain friendly personal relations with diplomats from hostile nations. Malik made a tremendous effort, before and during the Korean War, to win Communist China membership in the United Nations; the new People's Republic of China, under its leader **Mao Zedong** (Mao Tse-tung; 1893–1976; see entry), was eager to receive international recognition as a powerful nation. As the Korean War heated up, Malik made it clear that the West needed to communicate with China in order to avoid a wide-scale war. He persistently tried to make arrangements for such discussion at the United Nations (UN), but was voted down by other member nations. Finally, the Chinese intervened in the war and—with the largest military in the world—quickly proved themselves to be a formidable world power. When the Western powers decided to negotiate a truce in the war with China and North Korea, they sought out Malik. Although the gist of his response was that the UN powers should engage in conversation with its real opponents, China and North Korea, rather than the Soviet Union, his conversations with American diplomat George F. Kennan (1904–) and his subsequent UN radio broadcast provided the course for the UN command to begin the truce process.

Early years

Jakob (or Yakov) A. Malik was born and grew up in Kharkov, Ukraine, in 1906. He attended university in Kharkov at the Institute of People's Education with a major in economics. Later, he moved to Moscow, the capital of the Soviet Union, where he graduated from the Soviet Institute for Foreign Affairs at the University of Moscow in 1937. (The Soviet Union existed as a unified country from 1922 to 1991. It was the first communist country and was made up of fifteen republics, including Ukraine and Russia. Sometimes Soviets are called simply Russians.)

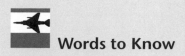

Words to Know

biological warfare: the act of spreading disease germs or other living organisms through enemy territory, using the germs as a weapon with which to kill or disable the enemy.

boycott: a refusal to participate in something (purchasing from a store, working, attending an organization) until stated conditions are met.

cold war: the struggle for power, authority, and prestige between the communist Soviet Union and the capitalist Western powers of Europe and the United States from 1945 until 1991.

communism: an economic system that does not include the concept of private property. Instead, the public (usually represented by the government) owns the goods and the means to produce them in common.

diplomat: a professional representative of a nation who helps handle affairs and conduct negotiations between nations.

resolution: the formal statement of an organization's intentions or opinions on an issue, usually reached by vote or general agreement.

satellite: a state or nation that is controlled by a stronger nation.

Soviet bloc: The Soviet Union and all the nations within the Soviet empire during the second half of the twentieth century.

Western nations: the noncommunist nations of Europe and America.

Malik served as a Soviet diplomat in a variety of positions, becoming the ambassador to Japan in 1942. When Japan surrendered at the end of World War II (1939–45), Malik returned to Moscow, where he worked in the foreign ministry. In December 1945, with the Soviets occupying North Korea and the United States occupying South Korea as part of the peace agreement (Japan had occupied that country for forty years), Malik wrote a report on the five-month long divided occupation of Korea, "On the Question of a Single Government for Korea." He concluded that the Soviet Union should not try to oppose the establishment of a single government in Korea. He believed that the Koreans should establish an independent nation with an elected government and a constitution. He recommended preparing the Korean population for democracy (a government based on election of its leaders) through education and suggested a joint commission of Soviet and U.S. representatives to help to prepare the newly liberated nation for elections.

Ambassador to the United Nations

Malik became the deputy foreign minister of the Soviet Union in 1946. In May 1948, he assumed his position as the permanent Soviet representative to the United Nations. The United Nations had been formed at the end of World War II as a body dedicated to preserving peace and friendly relations among countries. With the cold war taking hold of international politics, his role within the UN became increasing isolated as the West grew suspicious of the Soviets and communism. The cold war was a time of political anxiety and military rivalry—that stopped short of full-scale war—between the United States and the Soviet Union. It began at the end of World War II (when the two countries were allies) until the Soviet Union dissolved in 1991. The Soviets had a communist government, which worked to eliminate private property. Communism is a system in which, in theory, goods are owned by the community as a whole rather than by specific individuals and are available to all as needed. The United States, on the other hand, has a capitalist economy, in which individuals, rather than the state, own the property and businesses.

In 1949, the Chinese Communists under Mao Zedong forced the American-backed Chinese Nationalists under **Chiang Kai-shek** (1887–1975; see entry) out of mainland China and into exile on the island of Taiwan (formerly Formosa). Mao proclaimed the new People's Republic of China in October. Still, the United Nations continued to recognize the government of Nationalist China. Malik strongly protested the presence of a representative from Chiang's government in the UN. On January 10, 1950, he stormed out of the UN Security Council, beginning a Soviet boycott of the institution that would still be in effect when the war in Korea broke out six months later.

War in Korea

Both North and South Korea wanted to reunify Korea. When North Korea invaded South Korea on June 25, 1950, the Security Council of the United Nations met immediately to determine what was to be done. After some heated debate, it passed a resolution that condemned North Korean aggression, demanded the withdrawal of North Korean troops from South Korea, and called on member nations to aid South Korea against the invaders. Because of Malik's boycott, the Soviet Union lost its chance to veto the resolution.

Malik had returned to the Security Council by August 4, when he proclaimed to the Security Council that the Korean War was a civil war among the people of a nation and that foreign troops should leave the nation at once. In September 1950, he lodged a complaint that civilian targets, including hospitals and villages, were being bombed in Korea by U.S. forces. The Security Council voted against the complaint. Malik called the vote illegal, bitterly adding that great evils were being done in Korea under the direct orders of General **Douglas MacArthur** (1880–1964; see entry), commander of the UN forces in Korea.

That same August, Malik became president of the UN Security Council. On August 22, he delivered a warning that, unless something were done, the Korean War would widen into a large-scale war, pointing to the possibility that Communist China would intervene. At that time he pushed relentlessly to gain UN membership for the People's Republic of China. He also attempted to provide a forum in the United Nations for discussion of the Korean War that included representatives from North Korea and China. Things were becoming more intense in China and, on August 25, China accused the United States of firing heavy weapons on its mainland. Malik proposed that the United Nations invite the Chinese to come in and present their case. On September 6, the Security Council voted against Malik's proposal for Communist China's membership in the United Nations. They also declined on providing a forum for Chinese and North Koreans to discuss the war. Malik was frustrated and angry at the losses, but maintained social relations with key Western diplomats.

In January 1951, after several powerful Chinese offensives in Korea had severely smashed the UN forces, the UN General Assembly Truce Commission proposed a plan to urge the People's Republic of China to agree to a truce. The United States was all for the plan. Malik and the Soviet bloc voted against it because it was created without any consultation with China or North Korea.

The Malik-Kennan Conversations

The UN forces recovered their position at the 38th parallel (the original dividing line between North and South Korea) after the Chinese spring offensives of 1951. By that time, MacArthur had been relieved of command for insubordination. MacArthur had been the most staunch advocate of fighting the Korean War with no holds barred. Many, but certainly not all, of the other top military officials believed that the military could be used to support peace negotiations in limited warfare. The United States was in position to negotiate for peace and **Dean Acheson** (1893–1971), secretary of state under President **Harry S. Truman** (1884–1972; see entries), sought a way to begin the process.

The United States still would not deal with China as a nation, and therefore the State Department started contacting Soviet officials around the world. For several weeks, none of the contacts could help. Then Acheson decided to ask the renowned Soviet expert George Kennan, who was temporarily

Jacob A. Malik casts the only dissenting vote in the United Nations Security Council to the resolution calling on the People's Republic of China to withdraw its troops from Korea. *Reproduced by permission of Double Delta Industries, Inc.*

George Kennan and the Cold War Containment Policies

In 1933, when President Franklin D. Roosevelt opened diplomatic relations with the Soviet Union by recognizing it as a nation, George F. Kennan (1904–), a foreign relations diplomat with a background in Russia, joined the staff at the embassy in Moscow. Soviet premier Joseph Stalin (1879–1953) was reaching his height of power at that time. Kennan knew as much as any outsider could of the purges, executions, terror, and concentration camps in the Soviet Union. He left Moscow in 1937 with a new understanding of—and a deep distrust for the Russians.

Kennan returned to Moscow during World War II in 1944 as an aide to U.S. ambassador W. Averell Harriman (1891–1986). He witnessed the Soviets' harsh treatment of Poland, the wartime repression in the Soviet Union under Stalin, and the ease with which the Soviets acquired control of much of Eastern Europe and the eastern sector of Germany following the postwar conferences. Kennan despaired at U.S. willingness to allow Stalin so much leeway simply because he had been a U.S. ally during the war. Realizing that the Soviets were playing by a different set of rules than the Americans, he urged U.S. officials to treat the Soviets with far more suspicion and caution. No one paid much attention to him.

In February 1946, the Soviets refused to participate in the new World Bank and International Monetary Fund, taking U.S. policy-makers by surprise. Kennan, in charge of affairs in Moscow in the absence of the ambassador there, could answer the stream of questions that arose. He sat down to write what would become known as the "Long Telegram," an eight-thousand-word report on the Soviet threat.

The Soviets, Kennan argued, simply dismissed the idea that international agreements must be respected or treated as law. Stalin and his negotiators would certainly seek to turn all negotiation and treaties to their advantage: they were unlikely even to consider conforming to a previous agreement if it conflicted with their interests. U.S. diplomacy, Kennan concluded, must adjust itself to two compelling realities: first, America would have to assume a "Great Power" role, an active position in international politics. The Western world, Kennan believed, depended upon America's overcoming its isolationist tradition, its tendency not to get involved in conflicts elsewhere in the world. Second, the Soviet Union had learned from the European experience only to be more cynical (disbelieving) and duplicitous (deceitful) than its opponents. Such a state of affairs, Kennan emphasized, would

George F. Kennan. *Reproduced courtesy of the Library of Congress.*

require a complete revision of U.S. diplomacy. Kennan did not believe that the Soviet Union would instigate another great war in pursuit of world domination. What was needed was a United States plan to *contain* communism. This could be done, advised Kennan, by strongly upholding American positions and by supporting noncommunist countries wherever help was needed.

Americans were ready to hear Kennan's message when the Long Telegram arrived. The U.S. government reacted by providing huge sums of economic aid to European countries that were in danger of communist overthrow, through the Truman Doctrine and the Marshall Plan. Fears inspired by Kennan's telegram as well as the later National Security Memorandum No. 68 (NSC 68), which recommended massive military buildup to counter the threat of Soviet worldwide expansion, loomed when, on June 25, 1950, the North Koreans invaded South Korea. What might have passed as an isolated civil war was quickly regarded as Soviet expansionism and an immediate threat to the West.

Kennan believed that the United States overreacted to his message. What had begun as a caution to the United States to better understand its rival and potential enemy was quickly developed into a rigid and very expensive foreign policy. As a political realist, Kennan believed that as circumstances change, policies should change with them. But at that point his concept of containment of Soviet expansion had taken hold so firmly it would rule U.S. foreign policy for decades to come.

on leave from the State Department, to contact Malik. Malik agreed to a meeting.

Malik and Kennan met twice in the Soviet compound at Glen Cove in Long Island, New York. At the first meeting on May 31, 1951, Kennan told Malik, although not with any official authority, that he believed a cease-fire could be arranged in Korea with both sides holding their existing battle lines. He asserted that the United States wished to come to an agreement with the Soviet Union in order to carry out this armistice. Malik responded that the United States had a conflict with China, not with the Soviet Union. He urged that Communist China, rather than Taiwan, receive recognition in the United Nations, and that discussions about a cease-fire take place between the United States and China and North Korea. Kennan told Malik that the United States did not trust the Chinese and did not feel it could count on them to keep any promises made during negotiations. Malik told Kennan that his government would like to hear more about the cease-fire proposal, and the meeting ending with little resolved, but another meeting planned.

At the second meeting, on June 5, 1951, Malik was much more clear about the Soviet position, probably having received thorough instructions on what to say. He told Kennan that the Soviet Union wished the Korean War to be resolved as soon as possible. Once again, he said that the United States would have to speak directly with the Chinese and North Koreans about a cease-fire, because the Soviets had nothing to do with it. But the Soviets felt an armistice was possible. For the Americans, this was the first sign their enemies would negotiate.

The radio broadcast

On June 23, 1951, Malik announced the Soviet position again on a taped fifteen-minute broadcast of the UN radio program "The Price of Peace." Although much of the speech focused on the United States's responsibility for the war, he ended by saying that the Soviet Union believed that the Korean conflict should be brought into a cease-fire, adding again that the opposing parties—the United States on one side, and the Chinese and North Koreans on the other—would have to sit down and talk among themselves. After his speech, the American ambassador to the Soviet Union spoke to the Soviet first deputy for foreign affairs, Andrei A. Gromyko (1909–1989), who confirmed that the Soviet Union supported the position expressed by Malik on the radio. Gromyko made it clear that the Americans and the Chinese/North Koreans should agree at first only to a cease-fire and the withdrawal of troops from the 38th parallel; the nonmilitary negotiations could begin after the fighting had stopped.

For a couple of weeks after the radio broadcast, Malik never commented on it to anyone. The United States did send a message to North Korea and China through the UN commander General **Matthew B. Ridgway** (1895–1993; see entry) on June 30. The beginning of the two-year truce negotiations began on July 10, 1951, in the village of Kaesong, just over the 38th parallel in North Korean control. Sadly, the United States decided that because it did not trust the Chinese to stop fighting, there was to be no cease-fire during the long peace process. Tens of thousands were killed in those years.

Malik remained in his position as permanent representative to the United Nations until October 1952. In his last year in that position, he brought the complaint to the UN that the United States was using biological, or germ, warfare against the Chinese in their own country. The United Nations voted him down once again.

In 1952, Malik became the first deputy foreign minister of the Soviet Union. In 1953, he began a seven-year stint as ambassador to the United Kingdom. He served another eight-year term as permanent representative to the United Nations from 1968 to 1976. He died in Moscow in 1980.

Where to Learn More

Goulden, Joseph C. *Korea: The Untold Story of the War.* New York: Times Books, 1982.

Matray, James I. *Historical Dictionary of the Korean War.* New York: Greenwood Press, 1995.

Varhola, Michael J. *Fire and Ice: The Korean War, 1950–1953.* Mason City, IA: Savas Publishing, 2000.

Web sites

Matray, James I. "Korea's Partition: Soviet-American Pursuit of Reunification, 1945–1948." [Online] http://www.mtholyoke.edu/acad/intrel/korpart.htm (accessed on August 14, 2001).

Weathersby, Kathryn. "Soviet Aims in Korea and the Origins of the Korean War, 1945–50: New Evidence from Russian Archives." Cold War International History Project, Woodrow Wilson International Center for Scholars. [Online] http://cwihp.si.edu (accessed on August 14, 2001).

Mao Zedong

Born December 26, 1893
Shoashan, China
Died September 9, 1976
Beijing, China

Chinese revolutionary and political leader

Few twentieth-century leaders have left such a profound imprint on modern times as did the Chinese revolutionary Mao Zedong. Born among China's peasants, Mao grew up in a country weakened by overpopulation and by a failing government. He spent decades fighting against all odds to empower the peasants and to restore the strength of China, and he succeeded in his purpose. He was one of the central forces to reshape the social and political structures of the ancient and populous country of China. Highly literate and sensitive, he dedicated himself to a relentless struggle against inequality and injustice. Placing ideals above all else, he could be utterly ruthless in his efforts to achieve them. His revolutionary idealism would take a heavy toll on China in the years to come.

The good student in rocky times

Mao Zedong (Mao Tse-tung) was born on December 26, 1893, in the small village of Shaoshan in Hunan, a province in central China that had remained isolated from the modern world. Although his parents, Mao Jenshen and Wen Qimei,

"In a very short time, in China's central, southern and northern provinces, several hundred million peasants will rise like a mighty storm, like a hurricane, a force so swift and violent that no power, however great, will be able to hold it back."

Portrait reproduced by permission of AP/Wide World Photos.

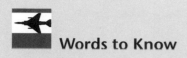

Words to Know

collective farm: a farm under government control, in which the government dictates what will be grown, how much of it, and what the farmworkers will be paid for their work.

Communism: a system of government in which one party (usually the Communist Party) controls all property and goods and the means to produce and distribute them.

cooperative farm: a farm owned and run by the farmworkers who use its goods or sell them for profit.

dynasties: periods in China's history in which one particular family ruled, sometimes for centuries.

guerrilla warfare: an irregular form of combat; in Korea it usually involved small groups of warriors who hid in mountains, enlisted the help of the local population, and used ambushes and surprise attacks to harass or even destroy much larger armies.

Marxism: the belief, originating with German political philosopher Karl Marx, that a revolution by the working class would eventually lead to a classless society.

Nationalists (Chinese): the ruling party led by Chiang Kai-shek in China from the 1920s until 1949, when the Nationalists were defeated by the Communists in the Chinese Civil War and forced to withdraw to the island of Taiwan (formerly Formosa).

rightist: a person who advocates maintaining tradition and the status quo and generally supports a strong and authoritarian government by the elite.

socialism: a system in which there is no private property, and business and industry are owned by the workers.

warlord: a leader with his own military whose powers are usually limited to a small area that, in most cases, he took by force.

were peasants, his family never lacked food or clothing. Mao began working in the fields around his home when he was five and did not begin school until he was seven. The part of China that was his childhood home was beautiful, with rolling hills and abundant rice paddies. But Mao's early years were shadowed by the angry temperament of his father, who was quite cruel to the whole family. Mao and his mother became very close because of this.

In 1910, Mao was sent to a modern school in a nearby town. There, he studied traditional works of Chinese history and literature, but also modern works. He was an excellent student and did so well that the next year he went to a teacher's training college in Changsha, the capital of Hunan.

At this time, China was collapsing. For thousands of years, the country had been controlled by emperors (kings) in a series of dynasties, periods in which one particular family rules, sometimes for centuries. Under the Manchus or the Qing (Ch'ing) dynasty in the nineteenth century, foreigners had invaded China, sparking civil wars. The Chinese peasants had suffered gravely. In 1912, a revolution led by Sun Yat-sen (1866–1925) overthrew the Manchus and a new government was formed. However, Sun could not unify the country and by 1916 power had fallen into the hands of military generals, or warlords, who controlled the numerous provinces in the country.

Learns from the Russian Revolution

While chaos reigned over China, Mao completed his education in Changsha. Hoping to find a solution to China's crisis, he and other young intellectuals began to look to the communist government recently formed in Russia by Vladimir Lenin (1870–1924). (The Soviet Union was the first communist country and was made up of fifteen republics, including Russia, which it is often simply called. It existed as a unified country from 1922 to 1991.) The Russian Revolution of 1917 had shown that workers could carry out a revolution and gain control of the government. Mao believed Chinese peasants could do the same. He became very active in the world of political discussion, forming student groups, editing magazines, and leading in student protest demonstrations. Along with other intellectuals around him, he became interested in the works of Karl Marx (1818–1883), a German political philosopher who developed a theory of socialism, a system in which there is no private property, and business and industry are owned by the workers. (Communism is a political ideology based on socialism.) In 1921, he met with others who shared his interest, and helped found the Chinese Communist Party, which grew rapidly over the next few years.

From 1924 until 1927, Mao and the communists put their forces behind Sun Yat-sen, who had gotten the support of the Soviets for his mission to unite China under one ruler. Mao spent most of this period working among peasants in the countryside. At this time he came to the conclusion that socialism in China would take a different form than in Russia: in China, the poor farmers from the country would carry out the revolution rather than the workers in the cities of Russia.

By 1927, when Sun died, there was a great deal of conflict among the communist groups in China, and the country came under the control of the Nationalist government party (the Kuomintang; pronounced KWOE-min-TANG) led by the anticommunist **Chiang Kai-shek** (1887–1975; see entry). The Nationalists wanted to keep control of China in the hands of landowners and businessmen, but the communists wanted the country turned over to the peasantry. Although at first the Kuomintang worked with the communists in order to establish bases of power, in April 1927, Chiang turned his army against the communists, slaughtering thousands.

The Long March

During the next seven years, Mao and other communists hid in remote mountainous regions in southern China. There they built a strong rebel government, attracting more and more people to their cause. After repeated attacks by Nationalist forces, the communists were forced to flee their base, and began a six-thousand-mile journey called the Long March in 1934. During the Long March, the communists fought constant battles and suffered incredible hardships. By the time they reached their destination the following year, more than half of the original marchers had died. For his courage and leadership during this journey, Mao was elected chairman of the Chinese Communist Party.

Creates a communist nation

A truce between the communists and the Nationalist government was declared when Japan invaded China in 1937. During World War II (1939–45), the two sides fought against this common enemy. But right after the war they resumed their battle against each other. By 1949, the Nationalist government had lost popular support because of corrupt practices that had impoverished parts of China. Although the communists had less money and were poorly armed, they had received the support of China's large peasant class. With the

people's support they were able to drive the Nationalists out of mainland China and onto the island of Taiwan (formerly Formosa). On October 1, 1949, Mao proclaimed the founding of the People's Republic of China, saying "Today the Chinese people stood up!"

There was much to be done as the new republic took shape. China's economy was in shambles. Mao immediately ordered the peasants to seize property from the landlords who controlled almost all the farmland. Over the next few years, life improved for the peasants as they grew more than enough food to eat. Mao also faced the rebuilding of China to the status of a world power, to which he felt it was entitled. But because of the years of war and extreme need, China had become backward in terms of technology and education. The Chinese were isolated in relation to other world powers. The Chinese Communist Party had conflicts with the Soviets, and the United States had supported Chiang Kai-shek against them. The United Nations (UN) would not recognize the Peo-

Reviewing the Chinese troops at Yenan airfield while on a peace mission in 1946; (left to right) Zhou Enlai, future premier and foreign minister of the People's Republic of China; George C. Marshall, U.S. Secretary of State; General Chu Teh, commander in chief of the Communist Chinese forces at Yenan; General Chang Chi-chung; and Mao Zedong.
Reproduced by permission of AP/Wide World Photos.

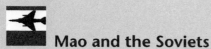

Mao and the Soviets

In 1917 and 1918, Chinese revolutionaries watched as the masses took power and overthrew the government in the Russian Revolution. The Russian revolutionaries were equally interested in China. It was obvious to them that China was on the verge of a major upheaval which, with proper assistance, might become a second communist revolution. The Russians sent political advisors to the radical (extremist) Chinese groups.

But as the Russians looked about China, they found their interests drawn not to the newly emerging Chinese Communist Party, but to a far larger and better organized group, the Nationalist party (Kuomintang), begun by revolutionary leader Sun Yat-sen (1866–1925). A frustrated Chinese Nationalist seeking money from abroad, Sun Yat-sen had welcomed help from the Soviets. With their assistance, he had built the Kuomintang military organization and modern party along Soviet lines.

In 1921, the Chinese Communist Party was founded in Shanghai, and Mao Zedong was one of its founding members. The Soviets immediately requested that the new Chinese Communist Party cooperate with the Kuomintang. The young communists threw their energies into helping prepare the Nationalist army for the march north, in the hope of unifying China and freeing it from the warlords and foreign interests that had long fragmented it. Mao worked willingly for the Kuomintang for several years. But in 1925, as the combined forces of the Kuomintang and Communists drove north, Mao was sent back to Hunan, shunned by the Soviet-influenced Chinese Communist because he did not have first-hand Soviet training or a top-notch education.

In Hunan, Mao worked with peasants and developed his theory that in China it was the peasant farmers—not the proletariat, or workers in the cities—who would drive the revolution. After the Kuomintang army turned on the Communists in 1927, killing them in huge numbers, Mao made his way into the countryside, where he was able to rally the peasants to join him. The leaders of the Communist Chinese Party as well as the Soviets ordered him to move into the cities to organize the workers there. But Mao

ple's Republic of China, and in fact still recognized Chiang's fallen Nationalist government as the legitimate government of China. (The UN was founded right after World War II to maintain worldwide peace and to develop friendly relations among countries.)

knew that the Communist Party's real support was to come from the peasants.

By the early 1930s, the new Communist leaders, called the 28 Bolsheviks for their schooling in the Soviet Union and adherence to Russian-style principles of revolution, rejected Mao's theories on building a peasant base for revolt and initiating guerrilla warfare. Although Mao was made leader of the communist government in name, he was not allowed to act as a policymaker. He did not regain any real control of the Chinese Communist Party until 1935. Once in power, he worked to break with the Russian model of communism and called for a "Sinification" of Marxism, that is, making it apply to Chinese life and culture. By the late 1930s, Mao was trying to eliminate the Soviet orientation held by a faction of his party. He initiated a campaign that prohibited imitation of Soviet communism or obedience to the Soviet's directives. In the early 1940s, the Soviets accused Mao of waging a purge: getting rid of the Soviet-influenced leaders of the Communist Chinese Party, sometimes through violence or murder.

Later, as the war between the Chinese Communists and the Nationalists came to a head, it is said that Soviet premier Joseph Stalin (1879–1953) was not eager for the Chinese Communists to win, fearing that Mao and his brand of communism would mean trouble for the Soviets.

As the Communists came into power in China in 1949, the new government faced an unfriendly world. Mao understood that China would need support from the Soviet Union and also that China could benefit from the lessons already learned by the Russians. Mao's dealings with Stalin were strained, but in December 1949, he traveled to Moscow. It took Mao two months to convince Stalin to join in a treaty of mutual assistance accompanied by economic aid, but the treaty was signed. There was a bond between two communist nations through the Korean War, but the ties were fragile and the suspicions were ever-present.

During the Korean War, many U.S. policy-makers believed that China was a satellite of—or indirectly ruled by—the Soviet Union. They did not understand Mao Zedong.

China enters the Korean War

Initially Mao and his party threw China's huge military forces to the regaining of Taiwan from Chiang's Nationalists and to reestablishing their footing in Tibet, which had recently been resisting the "special relationship" China claimed with it.

But Mao watched the situation in Korea carefully. In August 1945, when the Japanese, who were occupying Korea, were defeated to end World War II, the general order for the Japanese surrender included an arrangement for Korea in which the Americans were to accept the Japanese surrender south of the 38th parallel (the dividing line between northern and southern Korea) and the Soviets, who were already on the Korean border, would receive the surrender north of it. Soon the UN was sponsoring elections in Korea, with the idea that Korea would become independent after a leader was elected. The Soviet Union and the northern Koreans did not believe that the UN had authority to decide the future of Korea, so they refused to take part in the elections. The vote was held in southern Korea, nonetheless, and a new government was formed to rule a united Republic of Korea. Not accepting that government, the Koreans in the north held their own elections and established the Democratic People's Republic of Korea (DPRK).

In the summer of 1950, as North Korea invaded South Korea, the United States entered the war. (The governments of both communist North Korea and nationalist South Korea hoped to reunify Korea under their leadership.) Mao prepared for the emergency in Korea by sending large forces of troops to towns along the Chinese-North Korean border. Then, only one year after he proclaimed a Chinese republic, Mao felt it necessary to stop the American and UN troops that were advancing up to China's borders as they overwhelmed the North Koreans. After repeated warnings and attempts to negotiate through the United Nations, Mao sent his long-time comrade, General **Peng Dehaui** (P'eng Teh-huai;1898–1974; see entry), to command the Chinese forces being sent into Korea to assist the shattered North Koreans.

China was already weakened by its prolonged civil war and many of Mao's top generals argued strongly against getting involved. But Mao believed that if the United States succeeded in toppling the North Korean nation on China's border, there could never be peace in Asia. He sent in massive numbers of well-trained, though poorly equipped, troops. None of the Western powers (the United States and Western Europe) had taken China very seriously as a nation up to that point. But China's powerful offensives in November and December 1950 threw the UN troops into a retreat, and after two more years of battle, all the forces of the United Nations were unable to overcome the Chinese. China lost hundreds of thousands of soldiers in the Korean War, but it made the world stand up and pay attention to its power as a new nation.

Putting ideals to practice at home

In 1953, with the Korean War over, Mao turned his attention back to reforms at home. He directed that all farms be pooled into cooperatives, where numerous peasant families would work together on a large tract of land. Within two years, almost two-thirds of all peasants had joined cooperatives. Farm output increased dramatically. Peasants sold the extra food they grew and many of them became prosperous.

Mao had a vision of an industrial China. To raise the money needed to build industries, Mao turned to the peasants. In 1956, he decreed that all farms, animals, and tools be placed under government control. Peasants were forced to work on what were called "collective" farms. The government dictated what would be grown, how much of it, and what the peasants would be paid for their work. Within months, all of China's six million peasants were working in collectives. They lost what little wealth they had.

That same year Mao encouraged people to offer helpful criticism of the Communist Party, a policy he called Let One Hundred Flowers Bloom. Party leaders, quickly attacked for being corrupt, convinced Mao to reject this policy. In 1957, Mao called those people who spoke out enemies or rightists (reform-seeking individuals, often communist, are referred to as leftists). Nearly one million people were condemned as rightists and sent to jail or prison camps during the next year.

The Great Leap Forward and the Cultural Revolution

To make China equal with industrial nations, Mao launched his Great Leap Forward program in 1958. With the promise of a better future, the government encouraged people to work day and night to increase production. In a drive to make steel, people melted all the tools they had, but their primitive methods produced useless steel. To win the favor of high government leaders, local party officials inflated farm output figures. The government took grain from the peasants based on these high, false amounts. As a result, the peasants were left with nothing. A time of horrifying famine followed: the farmers were forced to eat tree bark, grass roots, and earth in their attempts to survive. Between 1959 and 1961, about twenty-five million peasants starved to death.

In the early 1960s, Mao stepped down as leader of the government, but still controlled the Chinese Communist Party. The new leaders, more moderate, worked to rebuild the country. They relaxed government controls and China prospered over the next few years. In 1966, however, Mao attacked these leaders, saying they were betraying the radical ideas of the original revolution. He then called on young Chinese to rebel against party officials, starting the Cultural Revolution. Bands of young Chinese, called Red Guards, ransacked museums, libraries, temples, and people's homes. They captured and publicly beat millions of officials, intellectuals, and former landowners. At least four hundred thousand of these people were beaten to death.

Establishes contact with United States

In 1967, the Red Guards began to fight among themselves. By summer, with millions of workers and soldiers joining the battle, China was in turmoil. The following year Mao ordered the Red Guards to disband and peace was restored. Mao then regained authority in the government and worked to improve relations with other countries. A visit by United States President Richard Nixon in 1972 eventually led to diplomatic contact with the United States after decades of hostile relations. Mao's health declined in the next few years, and moderates and radicals in the government fought for control. When Mao died in Beijing (Peking) on September 9, 1976, the new leaders began to steer China away from his strict policies.

Where to Learn More

Chou, Eric. *Mao Tse-Tung: The Man and the Myth*. New York: Cassell, 1982.

Garza, Hedda. *Mao Zedong*. New York: Chelsea House, 1988.

Hoyt, Edwin P. *The Day the Chinese Attacked Korea, 1950: The Story of the Failure of America's China Policy*. New York: McGraw-Hill, 1990.

Kolpas, Norman. *Mao*. New York: McGraw-Hill, 1981.

Marrin, Albert. *Mao Tse-Tung and His China*. New York: Puffin, 1993.

Stefoff, Rebecca. *Mao Zedong: Founder of the People's Republic of China*. Brookfield, CT: Millbrook Press, 1996.

Roe, Patrick C. *The Dragon Strikes, China and the Korean War: June-December, 1950*. Novato, CA: Presidio, 2000.

Terrill, Ross. *Mao: A Biography*. New York: Simon & Schuster, 1993.

Whiting, Allen S. *China Crosses the Yalu: The Decision to Enter the Korean War*. Stanford, CA: Stanford University Press, 1960.

Joseph McCarthy

Born November 14, 1908
Grand Chute, Wisconsin
Died May 2, 1957
Washington, D.C.

American politician

"In my opinion the State Department . . . is thoroughly infested with Communists. I have in my hand fifty-seven cases of individuals who would appear to be either card-carrying members or certainly loyal to the Communist Party, but who nevertheless are still helping to shape our foreign policy."

Joseph McCarthy rose to fame in 1950 when he shocked the nation with his claims that communists had infiltrated every segment of American society, including the government. His timing for making these accusations was impeccable, with the cold war heating up in post-World War II Europe and in the battlegrounds of Korea. McCarthy was a master of drumming up emotions and making powerful implications. From the winter of 1950 to the summer of 1954, he made outrageous charges and prompted numerous unnecessary investigations, always accompanied by tremendous publicity and minimal evidence. A little-known senator from Wisconsin, he had somehow stumbled onto a means to manipulate America's anxieties over communism, a set of political beliefs that advocates the elimination of private property and that is at odds with the American economic system of capitalism, in which individuals, rather than the state, own property and businesses. McCarthy's slanders caused untold hundreds to suffer. Journalists, professors, senators, generals, cabinet members, presidents—no one was safe from his attacks. He was able to disrupt the Truman and Eisenhower administrations, lower morale throughout the entire federal government, and impede serious congressional business for months at a time.

Early years

Joseph Raymond McCarthy was born on November 14, 1908, in Grand Chute, Wisconsin, the son of Timothy Thomas McCarthy, a farmer, and Bridget McCarthy. The McCarthy family was a happy one: hardworking, devoutly Catholic, and proud of its Irish ancestry. One of seven children, Joe grew up on farms outside Appleton and Manawa and was educated in the one-room Underhill country school. He completed the eighth grade at age fourteen and then quit to work on the family farm, run his own chicken farm, and manage a Cash-Way grocery store. In the fall of 1929, at age twenty, he decided to go back to school. He entered Manawa's Little Wolf High School, where he completed the whole four-year program in nine months with honors. Enrolling in Marquette University in 1930, he graduated with a law degree five years later. Throughout his school years, McCarthy supported himself by part-time jobs as a grocery worker, flypaper salesman, theater usher, construction worker, dishwasher, and manager of a filling station.

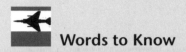

Words to Know

censure: an official scolding.

intelligence (military): information about the enemy.

isolationism: the view that a country should take care of its problems at home and not interfere in conflicts in other countries.

ostracize: to exclude from the rest of the group.

resolution: the formal statement of an organization's intentions or opinions on an issue, usually reached by vote or general agreement.

subversion: the destruction or overthrow of an institution or government by people within it.

witch-hunt: an extreme form of seeking out and harassing people whose views are for some reason against the standard.

Admitted to the Wisconsin bar, McCarthy first practiced law in Waupaga, then in Shawano. In 1936, he ran unsuccessfully as a Democrat for district attorney. A strong admirer of President Franklin D. Roosevelt (1882–1945), he adamantly supported New Deal relief programs, programs Roosevelt developed in the 1930s during the Great Depression to help the needy and unemployed and stimulate the economy. McCarthy voted for Roosevelt three times.

Three years later, McCarthy was elected circuit judge. At age thirty, he was the youngest circuit judge in Wisconsin history and he was known for being loose with the law, but many local attorneys liked working with him.

In 1941, World War II was raging in Europe and the Pacific. Though too old to be drafted into the military, McCarthy enlisted in the Marine Corps. He was commissioned a lieutenant and assigned to intelligence. His job was to gather data about enemy forces in the Pacific area from fighter and bomber pilots returning from raids over enemy territory. He returned to the United States with awards for his devotion to duty, a Distinguished Flying Medal and an Air Medal. He would later use his war effort in political campaigns, inaccurately claiming a leg injury from a shipboard fall as a war wound.

In July 1944, while still on active duty, McCarthy returned to Wisconsin. Campaigning that year on his war record as "Tail Gunner Joe," he entered the Republican senatorial primary against Alexander Wiley, the incumbent (someone already holding the office). He was easily beaten.

Elected to the Senate

In 1946, McCarthy again sought the Republican Senate nomination. This time he made his bid against another Republican incumbent, Robert M. La Follette, Jr. Backed by the conservative Republican Voluntary Committee, McCarthy received the nomination. In his campaign against Democratic nominee Howard J. McMurray, McCarthy branded McMurray as "communistically inclined." In part of a general Republican sweep that encompassed both houses of Congress, he won seventy of the state's seventy-one counties. (Political conservatives, also known as the right-wing, generally seek to maintain traditions and establish strong, authoritative governments. They tend to favor big business and power in the hands of an elite and are always anticommunist, since communists tend to be concerned with the plight of the common people.)

At thirty-eight years old, McCarthy was the Senate's youngest member. He rapidly developed a reputation for his brash, arrogant, and unpredictable behavior. He often questioned the integrity (truthfulness) of witnesses and fellow senators. He made many enemies even among conservative Republicans, but there were some within his closest circles who found him kind and amusing. Disliking formality, he asked everyone to call him "Joe."

The crusade against communists

When faced with reelection, McCarthy could see that he had little to recommend him. The State of Wisconsin was preparing to investigate him for tax evasion and ethics violations. His record in the Senate was fairly weak. He needed an issue. At a dinner party in January 1950, McCarthy and his friends determined a strategy that would grab public favor: he would take up a crusade against communists in the government.

On February 9, 1950, McCarthy made his famous speech at Wheeling, West Virginia. What attracted everyone's attention was one claim: "And ladies and gentlemen, while I cannot take time to name all the men in the State Department who have been named as active members of the Communist Party and members of a spy ring, I have here in my hand a list of 205—a list of names that were made known to the Secretary of State as being members of the Communist Party and who nevertheless are still working and shaping policy in the State Department" (as quoted from *Congressional Record of the Senate, 81st Congress 2nd Session, February 20, 1950*). Most of the text for the Wheeling speech had been prepared by a newspaper man from the ultraconservative *Washington Times-Herald*.

McCarthy's source for the number 205 was a letter written almost four years earlier by Secretary of State James F. Byrnes to Congressman Adolph Sabath, an Illinois Democrat, in which Byrnes spoke in general of State Department personnel policies. The letter did not mention Communist Party membership, any list of names, or the current secretary of state, **Dean Acheson** (1893–1971; see entry). Nevertheless, with this speech, McCarthy ushered in an era of anticommunist hysteria.

McCarthy's timing was perfect, because fears about communism in the United States were on the rise. Three weeks earlier, evidence in a trial had shown that a former State Department official, Alger Hiss (1904–1996), had been part of a spy ring while serving in the Roosevelt administration. And the world was still adapting to two major communist feats of 1949: the Communist Chinese victory over the Nationalists in the Chinese Civil War, and the Soviet Union's successful testing of an atom bomb. Unfortunately, the people in the government who were experts on the Chinese and the Soviets—and therefore the most crucial to understanding the demands of the communist North Koreans—were the ones in most danger of being accused of being communists. Driven out of the State Department, they were unable to advise on American foreign policy during the Korean War (1950–53), when their expertise was most needed.

How to stop McCarthy?

For anyone seriously trying, it was easy to refute McCarthy's accusations. His figures varied: first there were 205 communists in the State Department and then it was 57. When it was clear that McCarthy was basing his accusations on the four-year-old list of employees, the matter would no doubt have been dropped if the public wasn't already in a state of panic.

The Democrats made an early move to stop McCarthy's irresponsible accusations. Senator Millard Tydings, a Democrat from Maryland, headed a congressional investigation into McCarthy's accusations and found them unsubstantiated. But somehow McCarthy was able to skillfully use the hearings as a personal forum. At one point in the investigation, lacking any evidence, McCarthy accused left-wing Asian expert Owen Lattimore of being a top Russian spy and Philip C. Jessup, State Department ambassador-at-large, of having too much sympathy for communist causes.

McCarthy faced another investigation, this one held in the fall of 1951, to examine his financial dealings. It failed to turn up any irregularities. In the meantime, McCarthy's language became increasingly reckless. In June 1951, in the wake of President **Harry S. Truman**'s (1884–1972) dismissal of General **Douglas MacArthur** (1880–1964), commander of the U.S. forces in the Far East, for insubordination, McCarthy claimed that Truman was a drunkard. Furthermore, McCarthy claimed, Secretary of Defense George C. Marshall (1880–1959) was involved in some vast conspiracy. Marshall soon resigned from his position. Perhaps the most savage attack of all came against Secretary of State Dean Acheson, whom McCarthy implied was a tool of Soviet premier **Joseph Stalin** (1879–1953; see entries). "It has not been," McCarthy said in his Wheeling speech, "the less fortunate or members of minority groups who have been selling this Nation out, but rather those who have had all the benefits the wealthiest nation had to offer—the finest homes, the finest college education, and the finest jobs in Government we can give." McCarthy's accusations were so specific, they sounded as if they must have been the result of an investigation. He professed to have documents and names, but they never appeared. If one of his charges proved to be untrue, he was already on to another.

In 1953, with the Republican President **Dwight D. Eisenhower** (1890–1969; see entry) in office and a Republican majority in Congress (Republicans are conservative and tend to be fiercely anticommunist), McCarthy got himself appointed chairman of the Senate Committee on Government Operations and its investigative arm, the Permanent Subcommittee on Investigations. Chief counsel was Roy Cohn, a twenty-five-year-old lawyer whose arrogance made him detested by everyone on the senator's staff, but his intelligence and breadth of knowledge made McCarthy increasingly dependent upon him. The Republicans had hoped to rein McCarthy in with the new administration, but this was not to be. Within a month he was accusing the Eisenhower administration of communist subversion as well. His Senate investigations were often irresponsible witch-hunts.

Senate holds Army-McCarthy hearings

In the fall of 1953, McCarthy claimed that a communist spy ring operated at the Army Signal Corps Center at Fort Monmouth, New Jersey. From April to June 1954, the Senate's "Army-McCarthy hearings" were held. Its aim: to investigate all the recent charges and countercharges. At Eisenhower's request, they were conducted before a television audience. In fact, twenty million viewers—two-thirds of American televisions—caught this show. At last McCarthy's bad temper and irrational behavior were fully exposed to a disgusted nation. Yet fear of communism was so great that not a single subcommittee member questioned the validity of the Fort Monmouth investigation, nor did a senator challenge any of McCarthy's claims concerning an America permeated with subversion (disloyalty to a society and its institutions). In many ways, the climax of the hearings took place on June 9. McCarthy had just attacked the secretary of the army, saying he had once belonged to a procommunist organization, when finally, the army's chief attorney, Joseph Welch, challenged the senator, as quoted in Thomas Reeves' biography: "Until this moment, senator, I think I never really gauged your cruelty or your reck-

Joseph McCarthy points to a map as chief attorney to the army Joseph Welch, head in hand, looks on. *Reproduced by permission of the Corbis Corporation.*

lessness. Let us not assassinate this lad further, senator. You have done enough. Have you no sense of decency, sir, at long last? Have you no sense of decency?"

In the end, the American public was turned against McCarthy because, as Welch pointed out, he seemed to have no sense of decency. McCarthy spent the hearings bullying and badgering witnesses, interrupting loudly, making vicious personal attacks, and making very long speeches.

Censure

On June 11, 1954, Senator Ralph Flanders, a Vermont Republican, introduced a resolution calling for McCarthy's censure (formal criticism). Senate Majority Leader Lyndon B. Johnson (a Democrat) formed a special committee to investigate the accusation, carefully handpicking conservatives in an effort to maximize the credibility of the committee. Arthur V. Watkins of Utah, a Republican who was an isolationist and moderate on domestic policy, chaired the group. Charges included contempt of the Senate and its committee and abuse of fellow senators and of an army general. Particularly appalling to the committee were McCarthy's attacks on Senate colleagues, which were vicious and demeaning, and unsupported.

McCarthy left the spotlight far more rapidly than he entered, spending his last years in relative obscurity, totally ostracized by former colleagues and by the Eisenhower administration. Full of despair and self-pity, he would arise late in the morning and watch television soap operas all day. He increasingly skipped Senate sessions. In 1957, he and his wife, former staff member Jean Fraser Kerr, adopted a child but little else interested him. McCarthy had always been a big drinker. On May 9, 1957, at the age of forty-eight, he drank himself to death.

Where to Learn More

Bayley, Edwin R. *Joe McCarthy and the Press*. Madison: University of Wisconsin Press, 1981.

Cohn, Roy. *McCarthy*. New York: New American Library, 1968.

Cook, Fred J. *The Nightmare Decade: The Life and Times of McCarthy*. New York: Random House, 1971.

Crosby, Donald F. *God, Church, and Flag: Senator Joseph R. McCarthy and the Catholic Church, 1950–1957*. Chapel Hill: University of North Carolina Press, 1978.

Ewald, William Bragg, Jr. *Who Killed Joe McCarthy?* New York: Simon & Schuster, 1984.

Fried, Richard M. *Men Against McCarthy*. New York: Columbia University Press, 1976.

Griffith, Robert. *The Politics of Fear: Joseph R. McCarthy and the Senate*. Lexington: University of Kentucky Press, 1970.

Matusow, Allen J. *Senator Joe McCarthy*. New York: Prentice-Hall, 1970.

McCarthy, Joseph R. *America's Retreat from Victory: The Story of George Catlett Marshall*. Greenwich, CT: Devin-Adair, 1951.

McCarthy, Joseph R. *McCarthyism: The Fight for America*. Greenwich, CT: Devin-Adair, 1951.

Oshinsky, David M. *A Conspiracy So Immense: The World of Joe McCarthy*. New York: Macmillan, 1983.

Reeves, Thomas C. *The Life and Times of Joe McCarthy: A Biography*. New York: Stein & Day, 1982.

Rovere, Richard. *Senator Joe McCarthy*. New York: Harcourt, 1959.

John J. Muccio

Born March 1900
Naples, Italy
Died 1989
United States

American diplomat

American ambassador to South Korea throughout most of the Korean War, John J. Muccio had the difficult job of persuading Syngman Rhee to enter his country into peace talks to bring an end to the bloodshed.

Portrait reproduced by permission of AP/Wide World Photos.

John J. Muccio was the U.S. ambassador to the Republic of Korea (ROK) from 1949 until 1952, just before and during the crucial years of the Korean War, from 1950 to 1953. When he took office, he inherited powerful problems left behind by the American Military Government's occupation of the southern section of the country and more problems ahead in his dealings with the repressive regime of ROK President **Syngman Rhee** (1875–1965; see entry). When war broke out in Korea, it was Muccio who informed the U.S. government and oversaw the evacuation of Americans and the Rhee regime from the capital, Seoul. Over time, he developed an acute diplomat's understanding of Korea and its president. He found ways to coax the elderly man to cooperate with the Americans, sometimes by tricking him to do so. While he may have had some reservations about the Korean president, Muccio deeply respected the Korean cause and used his skills effectively to persuade the United States to aid Korea, and, when appropriate, to allow the fledgling nation to stand on its own. The ambassador was invaluable to the United Nations' side of the war for his insight into the ROK Army and the Korean people, and perhaps even more so for his ability to elevate Rhee's morale and to restrain him from rash decisions.

Background of a diplomat

John Joseph Muccio was born near Naples, Italy, in 1900, but came to the United States when he was five months old. His family settled in Providence, Rhode Island, where he went to school and attended Brown University. In 1918, he took out one year to serve in the U.S. Army in World War I (1914–18). He graduated from Brown in 1921 and then pursued a master's degree from George Washington University.

After leaving school, Muccio spent the rest of his career life working in diplomatic service in a variety of places, notably eight years in China and nine years in Latin America, in Bolivia, Panama, Nicaragua, and Cuba. In 1945, at the conclusion of World War II (1939–45), he was sent to Germany as the assistant of the U.S. political advisor on German affairs. In this capacity he attended the Potsdam Conference, a meeting between the heads of state of the United States, Britain, and the Soviet Union, where he met **Harry S. Truman** (1884–1972; see entry), who had just become U.S. president upon the death of Franklin D. Roosevelt (1882–1945).

When the United States recognized the Republic of Korea as a nation in 1948, Truman sent Muccio there as his special representative. Muccio was particularly fit for this position because of his experience in Asia and with U.S. military occupations abroad. In Korea, his first job would be the transfer of responsibilities from the American Military Government to the new Korean government under its president, Syngman

Words to Know

armistice. talks between opposing forces in which they agree to a truce or suspension of hostilities.

diplomat: a professional representative of a nation who helps handle affairs and conduct negotiations between nations.

evacuate: to remove people from a dangerous area or a military zone.

intelligence (military): information about the enemy.

mop up: the clearing of an area of all enemy troops or resistance.

morale: the way that a person or a group of people feels about the job they are doing or the mission they are working on.

reunification: the process of bringing back together the separate parts of something that was once a single unit; in Korea, this usually refers to the dream of a single Korea ruled under one government, no longer divided into two nations at the demarcation line.

Rhee. Establishing a relationship with the seventy-year-old ruler was a difficult job. The temperamental Rhee exhibited mixed feelings toward the American presence in his country. Although he desperately needed the U.S. troops' strength in conflicts with North Korea, he resented American influence in Korean politics. He was not sure he liked Muccio, either: he may have viewed the diplomat's light-hearted style as a lack of manners.

Muccio was a bachelor known for his taste for wine, women, and song. His first secretary, Harold Noble, wrote in his memoirs about the Korean War, *Embassy at War,* that Muccio was the best man for the job in Korea: "The Republic of Korea was so new, it had so much to learn, it was bound to make so many mistakes, and its officials were so thin-skinned in their personal and national pride, that Muccio's relaxed calmness and sympathy were ideal. He genuinely liked Koreans and most Koreans genuinely liked and respected him."

The first U.S. Ambassador to Korea

At the end of World War II, in August 1945, the general order for the Japanese surrender included an arrangement in which the Americans were to accept the Japanese surrender in Korea south of the 38th parallel (the dividing line between northern and southern Korea) and the Soviets, who were already on the Korean border, would receive the surrender north of it. The United States and the Soviet Union had originally agreed to occupy Korea after the war because, after forty years of being occupied by Japan, it was feared that the Koreans would not have enough experience to govern themselves right away. The Koreans, naturally, wanted to rule themselves.

In early 1948, at the urging of the United States, the United Nations (UN) sponsored elections in Korea, after which Korea would become an independent nation. (The UN was founded in 1945 by the Allies to maintain worldwide peace and to develop friendly relations among countries.) The northern Koreans and the Soviets, claiming that the future of Korea should not be determined by the UN, refused to take part in the elections. The vote was held in May anyway, without the northern Koreans, and a new government to rule over all of Korea, the Republic of Korea (ROK), was established, with Rhee installed as its president. Rejecting the ROK and Rhee's authority, the northern Koreans soon held their own elections and established their own new government, the Democratic People's Republic of Korea.

In 1949, the United States named Muccio ambassador to the Republic of Korea. Muccio immediately had some tough problems to handle. The United States was ready to withdraw its troops, and Rhee firmly opposed the withdrawal. Muccio's job was to change that attitude, as he explained to Jerry N. Hess in a 1971 interview, the transcript of which is housed at the Harry S. Truman Library:

> My first aim was to make clear to President Rhee and his whole hierarchy that they were responsible for what was being done in Korea, and it was no longer the United States running the show. And the Koreans were very slow in really seriously taking on the task of developing a defense force, a defense capability. The whole aim, until the final unit of American armed forces left on June 29, 1949, was to keep us there militarily. But once that final unit left, the Koreans did more for themselves in the one year from June 1949 until 1950, than they had done for themselves in all the four previous years.

Muccio had to do some backpedaling as well: before he became ambassador he had criticized Rhee and his government for serious political repression (stifling of any opposition to government policies). Now he had to convince the ruler that he and the United States had Korea's best interests in mind. With remarkable persistence, Muccio managed to arrange an agreement with the United States to provide strong economic aid to the Republic of Korea. He also convinced Rhee to take steps to correct the inflation that was rocking Korea's economy.

Many other things in Korea disturbed the ambassador. Although the United States did not want to be involved in a war, the withdrawal of U.S. troops from Korea brought about new violence at the border, as the South Koreans closely faced the North Koreans across the 38th parallel. Muccio frequently heard of skirmishes, as he recalled in his 1971 interview:

> While we were in the Blue House, the presidential residence, Lee Bum Suk, who at that time was Prime Minister and Minister of Defense and head of the National Youth Corps, came in joyfully exalting that his boys had just taken over Haeju, which is just beyond the 38th parallel opposite Kaesong. That was his news, that his boys had entered Haeju, he didn't go on to say that practically every one of them were killed on the spot. But that's the sort of thing that was going on from both sides.

John J. Muccio (left) leaving the Third Division command post after a brief visit, March 1951. *Reproduced by permission of AP/Wide World Photos.*

War breaks out

At 8:00 A.M. on the morning of Sunday, June 25, 1950, Muccio got word that the North Korean People's Army (NKPA) had attacked the ROKs at various points along the border. By 9:00 he had sent word to Washington, and his message ended, as quoted in John Toland's history *In Mortal Combat: Korea, 1950–1953:* "It would appear from the nature of the attack and the manner it was launched, that it constitutes an all-out offensive against the Republic of Korea." In Korea, President Rhee was in a panic. The news from the battlefront was not good, and air strikes were rapidly approaching Seoul.

By Monday it was clear the NKPA would soon be in Seoul. Muccio remained calm, delivering hourly radio announcements stating that the ROK army was holding its own. At the same time, he was organizing the evacuation of the wives and children of Americans stationed in Korea. Later that day, he arranged for air evacuation of all American embassy workers. When he went to tell Rhee about the evacuation, he found that the president had already fled Seoul. Muccio himself planned to stay in Seoul with a few volunteers, but Secretary of State **Dean Acheson** (1893–1971; see entry) ordered him to leave before the enemy got him. He made his first move, setting up a temporary headquarters in Suwon. From there, the embassy and the Rhee government were forced to flee again, first to Taejon and then to Taegu in the Pusan Perimeter.

Rhee, utterly confounded by the steady defeat of the ROK army and the arriving U.S. troops, frequently threatened to go back across the new defensive lines into enemy territory. Repeatedly, Muccio convinced him that the war was not lost and that the president must save himself in order to lead his people. He described to Hess in the 1971 interview how he found a little help in dealing with the unpredictable Rhee from the president's Austrian-born wife:

> Mrs. Rhee and I developed, more or less unconsciously, a little procedural understanding. She would get on the phone and call (and she didn't have to say anything on the phone), the call itself was just a tip-off to me that he was about to do something that she thought was not advisable. I would then find some excuse for dropping in on the old man. And if I sat there long enough he'd come out with what he had in mind. She did this repeatedly during those very crucial days.

Diplomacy in the hot seat

Muccio came to know all the significant players in the Korean War. In his interview, he described his observations of General **Douglas MacArthur** (1880–1964; see entry), commander of the U.S. Far East forces and later the commander of the UN forces in Korea: "I think MacArthur is one of the biggest brains I've ever come in contact with, but he had gotten to the age where he was no longer in touch with the situation. And I think that was very, very evident in the developments in November and December, in northern Korea. There was a failure of intelligence more than anything else for the mess that we got into." In his dealings with the commander, Muccio's efforts were often stymied by his staff. "I found that the occasions when I had direct access to MacArthur to have gotten the greatest backing and support. When we—I personally—or the American Mission in Korea—tried to deal through the hierarchy, it was quite different."

While MacArthur and the X Corps (the First Marine Division, the Third and Seventh Infantry divisions, and ROK I Corps) split off from the Eighth Army in the Pusan Perimeter to launch their successful invasion at Inchon, Muccio was with the Eighth Army, penned in by the enemy and in very desperate circumstances. Muccio in his interview recalled with admiration the leadership of the American military he observed during the war:

> The thing that impressed me most about the whole U.S. operation, the U.S.-UN operation in Korea, was that the U.S. military leadership, that is General [Matthew B.] Ridgway, General [James] Van Fleet and General MacArthur, General [Walton H. "Johnnie"] Walker, General [John H.] Church, and General [William F.] Dean, were men who were still in their physical and mental prime, who had come to the fore during World War II. And it was really a tremendous satisfaction to have dealings, direct dealings, with men of that caliber. I think that we should be very proud of the leadership that we had available at that time, right in the prime of their physical and mental vigor, it was a tremendous experience.

Muccio was also highly impressed with the Republic of Korea Army. Having only started training as a military force after the U.S. troops left Korea in 1949, the ROKs were certainly not prepared for war, as Muccio noted in the interview:

> This was enough time, of course, to train squads and companies, but they did not have time to get the leadership personnel organized and trained for large-scale operations. But in spite of that, there wasn't a *single* Korean unit that gave up as a unit. . . . They held on desperately, they gave us time, and for awhile, several months, the U.S. and other UN forces were so desperately pressed that we didn't have the time to train and refurbish and reorganize the Korean forces. . . . And once we had the time and the resources to start reorganizing, and retraining, the Koreans fitted in beautifully and did an excellent job.

Wake Island

On the night of October 14, 1950, Muccio was mysteriously summoned to an airport and the next day he was on his way, with General MacArthur, to Wake Island to meet with President Truman. MacArthur, a soldier at heart, told Muccio that he was angry to have to deal with "politics" at such a time. He put on a good face, however, for the conference.

At Wake Island, MacArthur claimed he was certain that the Chinese were not going to intervene in the Korean War. (In fact, since August China had said that it would enter the war if American troops crossed the 38th parallel into North Korea, China's ally.) Soon after he and Muccio returned to their positions, the first Chinese attacks were made on ROK units, but MacArthur still dismissed them as random help from Chinese volunteers.

Retreat and a change of command

When the Communist Chinese Forces attacked again in late November 1950, this time pushing the UN forces back down below the 38th parallel, Muccio was forced to flee Seoul for a second time. He visited MacArthur soon after, and recalled that MacArthur was still thinking that the rest of the war would be a "mop-up" operation: one in which they would simply eliminate the random North Korean soldiers that remained in the fight. By this point in the war, however, there was worldwide concern that the United States might provoke World War III in Korea; most of Washington agreed that it was time to pursue peace. But when the Joint Chiefs of Staff (the president's and the secretary of defense's war advisors) informed MacArthur of their plan to try to work out a cease-fire with the Chinese, MacArthur sent his own communique to the Chinese, threatening them with bombs in their homeland and contradicting the intention of the Truman administration. This was one in a series of acts that Truman felt compromised the security of the country. After the commander was relieved of duty by the president, the pursuit of an armistice (truce) began for real. Muccio went to work on the very unhappy Syngman Rhee, who wanted to continue the war for reunification of Korea. Muccio continued this difficult work until he was called back to the United States in September 1952.

After the Korean War, Muccio was made envoy extraordinaire to Iceland and then ambassador to Guatemala. After forty-two years in diplomatic service, he retired in 1962 at the highest rank available to career ministers. He lived in retirement for another twenty-seven years, dying in 1989.

Where to Learn More

Matray, James I. "John J. Muccio." In *The Korean War: An Encyclopedia,* edited by Stanley Sandler. New York: Garland, 1995.

Noble, H. J. *Embassy at War.* Seattle: Univeristy of Washington Press, 1975.

Toland, John. *In Mortal Combat: Korea, 1950–1953.* New York: William Morrow, 1991.

Websites

Muccio, John J. "Oral History Interview Transcripts." Harry S. Truman Library, Independence, Missouri. [Online] http://www.trumanlibrary.org/oralhist/muccio.htm (accessed on August 14, 2001).

Paik Sun Yup

Born November 23, 1920
Pyongyang, Korea

South Korean military leader and chairman of the Joint Chiefs of Staff, diplomat, and business executive

When the North Koreans invaded the Republic of Korea (ROK, or South Korea) at the start of the Korean War in 1950, the ROK Army was unprepared. Its soldiers fought without training or good leadership, and, most of all, without adequate weapons and ammunition. In the initial two weeks of attack, thousands of ROK soldiers died or suffered severe wounds and the rest were sent off in disorganized retreat by an onslaught of well-trained, well-armed North Korean soldiers. Yet the army reorganized and came back whenever it suffered a setback, at times demonstrating selfless heroism and determination. One of the key players in bringing the stricken ROK Army to combat efficiency was Paik Sun Yup. Only twenty-nine years old when the war began, he led his ROK First Division so skillfully that it was quickly recognized as a reliable combat unit by all the United Nations (UN) forces. In their introduction to Paik's book, *From Pusan to Panmunjom: Wartime Memoirs of the Republic of Korea's First Four-Star General,* the American general **Matthew B. Ridgway** (1895–1993), commander of the UN forces, and **James A. Van Fleet** (1892–1992), the American commander of the Eighth Army, said of Paik that "he was, without question, the

"The war managed to exchange the '38th parallel' for the 'DMZ' and drench mountains of Korean soil with oceans of blood; it had not done a hell of a lot more."

Portrait reproduced by permission of AP/Wide World Photos.

135

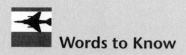

Words to Know

armistice: talks between opposing forces in which they agree to a truce or suspension of hostilities.

constabulary: a police force, separate from the regular army, but organized in the same manner as the army.

grenade: a small explosive weapon that can be thrown, usually with a pin that is pulled to activate it and a spring-loaded safety lever that is held down until the user wants to throw the grenade; once the safety lever is released, the grenade will explode in seconds.

guerrilla: a warrior who performs an irregular form of combat; in Korea the warriors generally hid in mountains,

enlisted the help of the local population, and used ambushes and surprise attacks to harass or even destroy much larger armies.

infiltrate: to enter into enemy lines by passing through gaps in its defense.

morale: the way that a person or a group of people feels about the job they are doing or the mission they are working on.

suicide mission: an activity taken on with the knowledge that carrying it out will mean one's own death.

unification: the process of bringing together the separate parts of something to form a single unit; in Korea, the hoped-for act of bringing North and South Korea together under a single government.

finest operational commander in the Republic of Korea." Paik was a hands-on general who saw most of the combat in the Korean War firsthand. He was an active participant in the rebuilding and reshaping of the ROK army throughout the war. Paik was staunchly anticommunist and devoted to the cause of a unified, independent Korea. As a general, he was utterly loyal to the Republic of Korea and its often difficult leader, **Syngman Rhee** (1875–1965; see entries). The young general's courage and commitment were well known and in the twenty-first century he is still considered a legend in his homeland.

Background

Paik Sun Yup was born in 1920 in the small town of Tokhung in Kangso County, seventeen miles southeast of Pyongyang (later the capital of the Democratic People's Republic of Korea, or North Korea). When Paik was five, he moved with his mother, brother, and sister to Pyongyang. There, severe poverty ruled their lives. They lived in a small room, frequently going hungry. His mother and sister eventually found jobs at a rubber factory, enabling Paik to attend primary school and later a five-year training course for teachers at the Pyongyang Normal School.

As a senior at the normal school, Paik realized he wanted to be a soldier, so upon graduation he went to Manchuria, China, to the Mukden Military Academy. In 1942, he became a second lieutenant in the Manchurian Army. At the end of World War II in 1945, Paik returned to Pyongyang. He hoped that Korea, recently liberated from decades-long Japanese rule, would achieve independence. Instead he found the Soviet Army occupying his homeland (the Soviets and the United States had agreed to both occupy Korea after World War II until the country could successfully rule itself; the Soviets were in the area north of the 38th parallel, the dividing line, while the Americans were in the south) and the young communist leader **Kim Il Sung** (1912–1994; see entry) was rapidly rising to power in the north. For a time, Paik worked for a rigidly anti-Japanese nationalist (one who wanted to see a united, independent Korea) who served as a provincial ruler in Pyongyang. When the Soviets imprisoned his boss in December 1945, Paik fled south across the 38th parallel.

Invasion from the north

In the south, Paik was commissioned a first lieutenant in the South Korean Constabulary, which would later become the ROK Army. During the next four years, he moved up the ranks to the position of colonel. On June 25, 1950, when the North Korean People's Army (NKPA) invaded, he had just taken over the command of the ROK First Division, which was positioned to defend Seoul, the capital city.

On the day of the invasion, however, Paik had been away from the ROK First for ten days, attending infantry school in Seoul. When he learned of the attack, he hurried to ROK headquarters. He soon learned that a good portion of his division had been given leave while he was away. When he got to the battlefront he found his Thirteenth Regiment fighting well, although just beginning an orderly withdrawal. The

Eleventh Regiment, which had been on reserve, was beginning to muster its soldiers and appear on the scene. But the Twelfth Regiment had been almost entirely wiped out near the border town of Kaesong.

"T-34 Disease"

On that first afternoon, what was left of the First Division entered into a fierce battle with the NKPA, which had crossed the Imjin River with a tank column composed of Russian T-34 tanks. Paik's men had no training with tanks and no ammunition that could penetrate the armor. In his memoirs, Paik recalled the "T-34 disease": panic at the mention of the word "tank." Despite the general panic, a number of courageous soldiers formed suicide squads to stop the tanks. These men climbed onto the tanks and detonated grenades and explosives, dying in the explosions that successfully destroyed the tanks. Paik remarked: "Although such desperate acts brought tears to my eyes, the bravery of these men prevented NKPA armored units from getting past the Thirteenth all that first day, earning precious time for division troops on leave and pass to return to the Eleventh."

The North Koreans pushed through the ROK First the next evening. Under heavy attack, Paik realized what a powerful, massive, and well-prepared enemy he faced. On the third day of the war, Paik's troops were fighting better than ever but there was no way to continue to hold their position, and Paik asked for permission to withdraw. Orders came back from headquarters to stay there and fight to the death. Paik understood that his division would be mauled, but he obeyed.

Things went from very bad to worse. On the afternoon of the June 28, the ROK First sent an ambulance to Seoul only to find that the capital had fallen to the enemy and they were completely isolated from support. The Han River Bridge, which the First Division needed to cross in retreat, had been destroyed. Soon the enemy was completely surrounding the ROK First. Paik's officers reported that ammunition was nearly gone. When things seemed as if they could not get any worse, the U.S. Air Force began to bomb the ROK First units, mistaking them for the enemy. Although his men were angry at the grisly mistake, Paik took heart at the sight of the American aircraft, realizing that it meant the United States was going to support the Republic of Korea in this war. After holding out against the enemy longer than anyone could have expected, the First Division began a very difficult withdrawal to the Han River south of Seoul. Paik had held his position against overwhelming odds for four days, but the survivors of his division were badly scattered in retreat.

The two-hundred-mile retreat to the Pusan Perimeter

By the beginning of July, Paik was able to assemble only two to three thousand men of his formerly ten-thousand-man division. With them he began the long retreat south to the city of Taejon. The United States had decided to send ground troops into Korea and the first units of the U.S. Army were starting to arrive under the resolution of the United Nations, which had agreed to supply forces to help the Republic of Korea. The U.S. Army was taking responsibility for the Seoul to Pusan Highway area; the ROK Army would handle the central and eastern fronts. They were all beginning a strategy of delaying the enemy in its relentless drive south. In vicious warfare with very few victories and terrible losses, the First Division fell back a grueling two hundred miles over the next month.

On July 27, much to his own surprise, Paik was promoted to the position of brigadier general. Still there was no rest for him or his troops in the bloody retreat. On August 1, thoroughly exhausted and spent, the First took a position on the Naktong River in the Pusan Perimeter, where the U.S. and South Korean forces had concentrated at the southern tip of Korea. There, the ROK Army was responsible for the fifty-five-mile front on the northern boundary of the perimeter and the United States for the seventy-five-mile western boundary. Stretched too thin, the First could barely defend itself against the North Koreans during the day when the U.S. air support was there to help. On August 8, during the night, the North Koreans completed an underground bridge across the river—made up of sandbags, rocks, logs, and barrels built up from the river bottom to about a foot below the river's surface—and crossed it with their tanks. The ROKs had obtained an antitank weapon that worked against the T-34 tanks and ten enemy tanks were destroyed that night, but the enemy had still infiltrated their position.

"If I turn back, shoot me"

After further withdrawal and heavy fighting in the Pusan Perimeter, Paik teamed up with U.S. Colonel John "Mike" Michaelis, commander of the famous Wolfhounds, the U.S. Twenty-seventh Regiment, in the defense of the city of Taegu. The First Division held the hills around the town of Tabu-dong and fought the North Korean soldiers while the Twenty-seventh held the road and fought the NKPA tanks. For Paik's troops, the battles consisted mainly of intense, exhausting hand-to-hand combat. On August 18, the enemy had penetrated into the foothills outside of Taegu. The fighting was furious. Night after night, the North Korean tanks rode down a 2.5-mile road called the "Bowling Alley" toward the ROKs. Colonel Michaelis's Twenty-seventh Regiment repelled them with its own tanks.

On August 20, the North Koreans launched a fierce attack, and Paik learned that his Eleventh Regiment had been thrown into a retreat. Michaelis's Twenty-seventh Regiment was made vulnerable by the Eleventh's withdrawal, and the colonel told Paik he had no choice but to withdraw his own forces. Paik urged him to hold off and jumped into a jeep heading for the front. He found the soldiers of the Eleventh in a full retreat. The commander of the Eleventh told him the men were totally exhausted; supplies had been cut off, and the men had not even had any water for two days. Paik recalled in his memoirs summoning the troops to him and delivering a speech:

> I want to thank you for fighting like you have. But we just don't have room to retreat any more. The only place left for us to go is into the ocean. If we run now, Korea is done for. Look at those American troops over there. They're fighting because they trust the ROK Army, and if we retreat, we bring shame down on the entire ROK Army. We are men of Korea; let us fight for this land. We're going to turn around and kick the enemy off our ridge, and I shall be at the front. If I turn back, shoot me.

With Paik at the front, the regiment retook the hill it had just lost and held its position. After the battle, Paik recounted in his book, Michaelis said: "When I saw the division commander himself leading that attack, I knew the ROK Army was God's own force." Paik had instigated a crucial reversal in the battle, but he had lost many soldiers in the campaign: "ROK First Division losses were so great that I just wanted to fall down and bawl," he recalled.

Return to his home

While the ROK First Division continued to fight in the Pusan Perimeter, General **Douglas MacArthur** (1880–1964; see entry), the commander of the UN forces in Korea, carried out his plan for an amphibious assault (using land, sea, and air forces) at the port city of Inchon. The attack at Inchon, carried out by the new X Corps MacArthur had put together (consisting of the First Marine Division, the Third and Seventh Infantry divisions, and ROK I Corps), was a complete success. UN forces had invaded Korea well behind the enemy and gained access to Seoul. The North Koreans fighting at Pusan fled when they learned of Inchon, allowing the Eighth Army troops that had been penned in there to advance north. Paik then led the UN forces in the capture of his home town, Pyongyang. The assault was successful and one of Paik's great memories: "I shall remember our final assault on Pyongyang to my dying day. My two regiments attacked in line abreast across the vast plain, supported by fifty tanks and no fewer than four battalions of artillery—more than one hundred howitzers and mortars. This was my moment in the sun."

On to the Yalu River

After Pyongyang, Paik's First Division pushed up to the northern city of Unsan. Then, on October 25, 1950, an unknown enemy surrounded the entire division. The ROK First had stepped into a huge trap set by the recently arriving Communist Chinese Forces and a furious battle began. Paik, who spoke fluent Chinese, interviewed a prisoner of war (POW) and learned that tens of thousands of Chinese troops were in position in the valley around them. This was reported to MacArthur and his staff. MacArthur, despite this and other statements made by officials of the Chinese government, chose not to believe that the Chinese were intervening in the war. Six days into the battle, Paik's men were exhausted and the losses were terrible. He received permission to withdraw, and during the night his division made a six-mile retreat.

On November 6, the Chinese mysteriously withdrew from battle. For the first time since the war began four months before, the First Division was allowed to rest. When they returned, they joined in the Eighth Army's advance up to the Yalu River at China's border with North Korea. On the second morning of this offensive, November 25, 1950, the Chinese counterattacked the Eighth Army with incredible force. That day, the ROK Seventh and Eighth divisions were totally destroyed. By November 28, the entire army was in retreat. The First Division along with several other UN divisions tried to hold a line at Pyongyang, but on December 3 they were given orders from MacArthur to withdraw down to the 38th parallel. Paik recalled in his memoirs: "For us in the ROK Army, December 3, 1950, lives as the day when our dream of national unification by force was dashed forever." His soldiers were badly demoralized. "This reversal was so total and so swift that soldiers couldn't deal with it. . . . When morale sinks to such depths, units simply ignore orders and directives."

The third Chinese offensive

On December 31, 1950, the ROK First Division returned to defensive positions along the 38th parallel. In a surprise attack, the Chinese penetrated into the right wing of Paik's Twelfth Regiment. As night fell, the Chinese attacked the Fifteenth Regiment with fury. Both regiments were in an impossible situation and there was nothing left for Paik to do but issue the order for the whole division to withdraw. In fact, all of the ROK divisions were forced to withdraw. On January 2, 1951, Seoul was once again abandoned to the North Koreans, and the retreats continued into the south, far enough from enemy fire to allow rehabilitation for the demoralized and exhausted UN forces.

As Chinese offensives continued in the months to come, Paik observed that Chinese POWs were increasingly exhausted, starving, and often infected with disease. The enemy that had once seemed unstoppable was wearing down visibly. General Ridgway had taken command of the Eighth Army in December and began to launch counterattacks, chasing the Chinese back up to the north. When the ROK First joined with the other divisions in advancing northward, they moved slowly and with the support of adjoining units in standard, tight military formation. Although fiercely resisted in further Chinese offensives, the UN command worked its way north again, recapturing Seoul in March 1951 and positioning itself near the 38th parallel by the end of that month.

A new command

In April, Paik was promoted to major general and given command of the ROK I Corps. Leaving what he called the "magnificent ROK First Division" was emotional, as he described in his memoirs: "I had shared the joys and sorrows and the life and death pressures of combat with these men for ten long months, and we had grown as close as brothers." In Pusan, for the first time since the war had erupted, Paik was reunited with his family. He found his mother, wife, and three-year-old daughter living in one small room in Pusan, without money or food. His wife was critically ill with typhoid fever.

As a corps commander, Paik oversaw the operations and training of the divisions in his corps. He traveled to the front to inspect the troops and confer with the commanders. He served as a liaison between the commanders and headquarters and coordinated their efforts with those of the U.S. Navy and air forces. Throughout the spring of 1951, the Chinese offensives took a tremendous toll on the South Korean forces. The Chinese were singling out the ROK units for attack, knowing that they were poorly armed. Some of the ROK performances were not good; the ROK III Corps, for example, disintegrated under intense enemy attack, leaving surrounding divisions vulnerable. Paik's leadership of the ROK I Corps, though, was credited for repelling a brutal attack at Taegwall-yong and inflicting tremendous damage to the Chinese.

Retraining the ROK

The ROK had failed in many of its missions in the spring attacks and all agreed that something needed to be done. Korean President Syngman Rhee wanted to increase his army from ten divisions to twenty and he wanted the United States to provide the equipment. The U.S. military leaders believed that it was useless to create more divisions when the existing ones were not living up to expectation. Paik, usually loyal to Rhee, sided with the Americans.

In July 1951, General Van Fleet decided to take all the ROK divisions out of the line and retrain them, one at a time. His training program was intensive. Paik recalled in his book: "Training lasted nine weeks and consisted of basic individual, squad, platoon, and company training. The center started

South Korean soldiers rest during a lull in a retreat and rearguard fighting. *Reproduced by permission of the Corbis Corporation.*

from scratch, assuming nobody knew anything. Every man in a division, with the exception of its commander, was required to undergo the training, and when the training was over, a unit had to pass a test before being assigned to the front." After training, the ROKs were finally provided with a more reasonable supply of arms and ammunition. When they went back to the line, the ROK Army was strong and skilled and had no more disorganized retreats. By December 1952, three out of four Eighth Army soldiers at the battlefront were ROKs.

Peace talks, hostile action

Armistice talks between the United Nations and the North Koreans and Chinese began in July 1951. Paik was selected as the South Korean representative at the meetings. Paik was opposed to the peace negotiations, fearing that the dream of Korean unification would be lost. He spoke up whenever it seemed that someone might listen, but he felt that his country's views were not being considered.

By August, Paik was told to report back to the ROK I Corps where he oversaw the heavy fighting around the 38th parallel at the Punchbowl, a large crater surrounded by hills, and Heartbreak Ridge. His troops were now fighting a war that barely moved, with both sides well entrenched and facing each other. The casualties were heavy and there was little to show for it on either side.

Operation Rat Killer

By November, with the front stable, Paik was called on to head Operation Rat Killer, which was formed to seek out and destroy communist guerrilla fighters in the southern part of South Korea. (Guerrilla warfare usually involves small groups of warriors who hide in mountains, enlist the help of the population, and use ambushes and surprise attacks to harass or even destroy much larger armies.) Two divisions were taken from the front for his use. Although Rat Killer did not eliminate all guerrillas, it dealt them a harsh blow. During this operation, Paik was again promoted, to lieutenant general.

When Operation Rat Killer was done, Paik was instructed to build a new ROK corps, the II Corps. It was complete with three divisions and ready for action by April 5, 1952. The United States was actively promoting the increase in the ROK Army, pushing it to take over as much of the combat as possible.

Honors

On July 22, 1952, Paik became chief of staff of the ROK Army. On January 31, 1953, he was promoted to four-star general. He was the first Korean officer to reach that rank. "If we lived in former times, you would be king of a new dynasty today," Syngman Rhee addressed the general during the ceremony for this honor, quoted in Paik's book. "Generals as powerful and successful as you in the dynastic years weren't satisfied to serve as mere subjects to the old king. But we are now a republic, not a kingdom, so you must be content with the stars of a full general."

End of battle

In May 1952, Paik took his first trip to the United States to learn more about how military training and organization were done there. He managed to meet with President **Dwight**

D. Eisenhower (1890–1969; see entry), who himself had been supreme commander of the NATO forces in Europe during World War II, and relayed to him the strong opposition of the Korean people to an armistice that left Korea divided. Paik then visited West Point Academy; the Army's Infantry School in Fort Benning, Georgia; and the Army Command and General Staff School at Fort Leavenworth, Kansas, where he enrolled in a two-week course. He never finished it, because President Rhee called him home. Rhee was trying to throw a monkey wrench in the truce negotiations. Soon after Paik's return, Rhee secretly directed the ROK prison camp guards to release about twenty-five thousand North Korean POWs into the population of the Republic of Korea. The United States then bargained with Rhee, promising great amounts of economic and military aid so he would not obstruct the armistice. At the same time the Chinese viciously attacked the ROK units at the front, making it clear that they could still exercise their might against the small nation. Rhee agreed to the armistice and the final prisoner exchange began. The war in Korea was basically over, although for the Koreans it remained unresolved.

After the war

For Paik, the postwar years were extremely busy, with overseeing the prisoner exchange, and, as the U.S. troops withdrew, strengthening the ROK Army and its position at the demarcation line that separated North and South Korea. He remained the chief of staff until 1954, and was chairman for the ROK Joint Chiefs of Staff from 1957 to 1959. By 1959, Rhee had lost the support of the Korean people as a result of his strong-arm tactics and corruption. Angry student protesters forced him to flee to the United States. In the years after Rhee's presidency, Paik served his country as ambassador to France, Taiwan, and Canada, as well as other postings in Europe and Africa. In 1969, he retired from diplomatic service, and in 1971 he served as the Minister of Transportation. He has also held high positions in corporations. He lived with his wife in Seoul at the turn of the twenty-first century.

Where to Learn More

Paik Sun Yup. *From Pusan to Panmujom: Wartime Memoirs of the Republic of Korea's First Four-Star General.* Dulles, VA: Brassey's, 1992.

Ra, J. Y. "Paik Sun Yup." In *Historical Dictionary of the Korean War,* edited by James I. Matray. New York: Greenwood Press, 1991.

Toland, John. *In Mortal Combat: Korea, 1950–1953.* New York: William Morrow, 1991.

Web sites

Franklin, Mark R. "Paik Sun Yup." State of New Jersey, U.S. Military Biographies: Korea. [Online] http://www.state.nj.us/military/korea/biographies/yup.html (accessed on August 14, 2001).

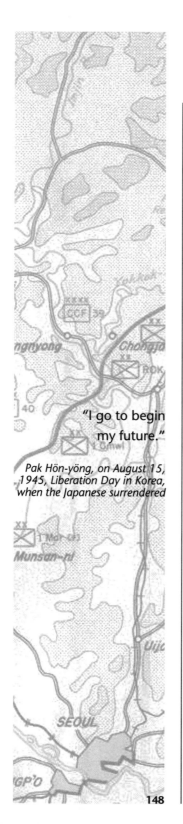

Pak Hön-yöng

Born 1900
Yesan, South Ch'ungch'öng Province, Korea
Died December 1955
North Korea

Korean political leader

"I go to begin
my future."

*Pak Hön-yöng, on August 15,
1945, Liberation Day in Korea,
when the Japanese surrendered*

W hen the American and Soviet troops liberated Korea from Japan in 1945 at the end of World War II, several factions of Korean communists had developed, most in exile and arising from the strong anti-Japanese activism of Koreans abroad. One faction of Korean communists had trained in the Soviet Union, another in China, and another had arisen from the guerrilla armies that had fought the Japanese (**Kim Il Sung** [1912–1994], the future leader of North Korea, among them). The "home" faction had carried on secretly within Korea during the Japanese occupation. Pak Hön-yöng was the popular and respected home leader of the Korean communists at the time of liberation. His base of operations was in the southern part of Korea that the Americans occupied after the Japanese left. Pak had a strong following and worked in concert with the more moderate leftist (reform-oriented) groups following the lead of **Yö Un-yöng** (Lyuh Woon Hyung; 1885–1947; see entries). He was one of the top candidates to head the new government in southern Korea, but the American Military Government opposed him vigorously because he was a communist.

Rising to leadership in secret

Pak Hön-yöng was born in 1900 in the village of Yesan, in the province of South Ch'ungch'öng in southern Korea. He grew up during the hated Japanese occupation of Korea: in 1910, Japan had annexed Korea, incorporating it as a part of Japan with the help of a very weak Korean monarch whom they had helped to the throne, and ruled it with an iron fist. As a young man Pak traveled to Shanghai, China. Soon after the Russian Revolution of 1917, which saw the Russian people rise up and overthrow the monarchy, he was drawn to communist ideology. (Communism is a political belief system that advocates the elimination of private property. It is a system in which goods are owned by the community as a whole rather than by specific individuals and are available to all as needed.) Pak joined a communist youth league in Shanghai in 1919, and became a leader of the Korean Communist Party of Shanghai by 1921. During the 1920s, he returned to Korea as a guerrilla—fighting the enemy with ambushes and surprise attacks—and organized anti-Japanese and communist activists there. He was arrested by the Japanese several times, but never stopped his political efforts.

Most of the Korean communist movement at the time was taking place outside of Korea, particularly in Shanghai and Manchuria, China, and in Siberia and other parts of Russia. By 1928, there were four different Korean communist parties. Pak decided to combine them all and in 1939 formed the Communist Group. He led the group for its two years of existence and became well known as a revolutionary leader.

Liberation from the Japanese

On August 15, 1945, the Japanese surrendered to end World War II and were ordered to withdraw their forces from Korea. In Korea, the top leaders, including Pak, were busy trying to form a transition government that could maintain order until a constitution could be created and a new government elected into office. A group of Korean leaders from all political sectors formed the Committee for the Preparation of Korean Independence (CPKI), organized to function as a temporary governing body. This group of leaders was selected primarily by Pak and the more moderate leftist Yö Un-hyöng. On August 16, the Korean public learned that the CPKI was effectively rul-

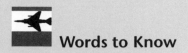

Words to Know

annex: to take over a nation that was independent, making it a dependent part of another nation.

Communism: a system of government in which one party (usually the Communist Party) controls all property and goods and the means to produce and distribute them.

exile: forced or voluntary absence from one's home country.

guerrilla warfare: an irregular form of combat; in Korea it usually involved small groups of warriors who hid in mountains, enlisted the help of the local population, and used ambushes and surprise attacks to harass or even destroy much larger armies.

interim government: a government formed after the ruling government in a nation is eliminated; when necessary, an interim government fills in until a permanent one can be established.

leftists: people who advocate change and reform, usually in the interest of gaining greater freedoms and equality for average citizens and the poor; some leftist groups aspire to overthrow the government; others seek to change from within.

moderate: of neither one extreme nor the other; having political beliefs that are not extreme.

occupation: taking over a state or nation and ruling it by a foreign military force.

socialism: a system in which there is no private property, and business and industry are owned by the workers.

ing Korea. By radio and other media, the committee instructed the people of Korea to form local committees to govern locally until a new government could be put in place. Within two weeks, there were 145 branches of this government. The branches were called People's Committees and they ruled in the cities and villages throughout the country, assuming the function of government on the local level.

In the capital city of Seoul, the CPKI leaders separated into two factions: the communists, who followed Pak, and a more moderate leftist group led by Yö Un-hyöng. (In politics, leftist refers to people who seek change and reform, usually including more freedom, more equality, and better conditions for common people. Leftism may include communism, but many leftists are not communists. They seek reform either within the existing government or through revolution.) But it was no time for any divisions among factions. By September 6, the Americans were on their way to Korea, in theory to accept the surrender of the Japanese. (By agreement, the Americans were to receive the Japanese surrender south of the 38th parallel, while the Soviets were to receive it north of the 38th parallel.)

Most Koreans understood that it was essential that they have a functioning government in place if they wished to remain independent when the large powers arrived. The CPKI hurriedly announced the formation of the Korean People's Republic (KPR). Fifty-five Korean leaders were selected to serve in an interim (temporary) government until elections could put a democratic administration in place. The leaders of the KPR included people from all of the political factions. In fact, the future president of South Korea, **Syngman Rhee** (1875–1965; see entry), in exile at the time, was named president of the interim group, since his name was associated with the independence movement of earlier days.

None of these preparations mattered to the Americans, who thought the transitional government leaned too far to the left. The KPR was never recognized by the new American Military Government, nor would they even speak to its leaders when they arrived.

Communism in southern Korea, 1945–1947

Despite the American Military Government's rejection, the Korean People's Republic had the popular support of the Korean people. Although Pak and Yö had very different political values, they tried at first to maintain unity. In 1946, they formed the Korean National Democratic Front, an alliance among many of the communist and moderate left-leaning groups that replaced the Seoul Central People's Committee. For a time the two leaders fought a vigorous battle for leadership of the Front. The Americans, seeing how much popular support the Front was able to draw from, and fearing that it would soon be in the communist hands of Pak, convinced Yö to break off altogether from the Front and the communists. With Yö gone, Pak organized the South Korean Workers' Party and again found strong support. In spite of American efforts, he was emerging as one of a few top leaders of southern Korea.

The American Military Government decided to move against him. A warrant for his arrest on charges of organizing disruptive activities was issued at the end of 1946. Early the next year, Pak and other southern communists were forced to flee to the Soviet-occupied north.

In the Democratic People's Republic of Korea

Pak and some of his followers settled at Haeju, in Hwanghae Province. There they established the Kangdon Political Institute, a school for training guerrillas to fight for independence and communism in the south. Through these activities, Pak began to gather support in the north. Kim Il Sung, the premier of the newly formed Democratic People's Republic of Korea (North Korea), did not like the competition for power. He closed Pak's institute, but because Pak was popular and respected, and because his following in the south would be very important in an invasion, Kim brought him into the new government as vice-premier and minister of foreign affairs.

Pak's main interest in these years was to unify his country. In 1948, he initiated a meeting of North and South Korean leaders in Pyongyang, the capital of North Korea. Although some powerful South Korean leaders attended, the meeting did not accomplish very much. The next year, in 1949, Pak tried once again with the formation of the Democratic Front for the Unification of the Fatherland. The group's goal was to eliminate the Americans and the Japanese influences from South Korea. It opposed Syngman Rhee's government and fully supported Kim Il Sung's leadership and communism.

The plan to invade

During 1949 and 1950, border skirmishes between North and South Korea were fairly common. Both sides initiated battles. North Korea's army was becoming increasingly fit, with more men, superior training, and better arms than South Korea could muster. Kim Il Sung was ready to invade. Many of the histories of the war say that Pak convinced Kim that there were hundreds of thousands of his supporters in the south who would join with the North Korean army and rise up against Syngman Rhee and his army if the North invaded.

There had indeed been many guerrillas in the south. Severe guerrilla warfare had raged in the southern part of the Republic of Korea (ROK; South Korea) in the years from 1946 until 1949. With the help of the American Military Government, however, Rhee had devoted the ROK army, the military police, youth groups, and paramilitary groups to the brutal elimination of the guerrillas, as well as many other opponents to his rule. By the time the North Koreans invaded on June 25, 1950, there was very little support for their efforts from within South Korea. Kim Il Sung had boasted to Soviet Premier **Joseph Stalin** (1879–1953) and Communist Chinese leader **Mao Zedong** (Mao Tse-tung; 1893–1976; see entries) that he would win back South Korea in three weeks. In the three-year war that followed, he never did win back the south.

At the end of the Korean War, Kim Il Sung was bent on eliminating any threats to his own power. Setting himself up as the almost godlike leader of North Korea, he jealously guarded against rivals to his command. It has been suggested that he had Pak arrested because he feared Pak's natural ability to lead the communist North. It has been traditionally held, however, that Pak's overestimation of communist support in the South angered the leader. Pak was charged with espionage (spying) and executed in 1955.

Where to Learn More

Cumings, Bruce. *The Origins of the Korean War.* 2 vols. Princeton, NJ: Princeton University Press, 1981.

Deane, Hugh. *The Korean War, 1945–1953.* San Francisco: China Books, 1999.

Kim, Joungwon Alexander Kim. *Divided Korea: The Politics of Development, 1945–1972.* Cambridge, MA: East Asian Research Center, Harvard University, 1975.

Matray, James I. *Historical Dictionary of the Korean War.* New York: Greenwood Press, 1991.

Varhola, Michael J. *Fire and Ice: The Korean War, 1950–1953.* Mason City, IA: Savas Publishing, 2000.

Peng Dehuai

Born October 24, 1898
Shixiang, Hunan, China
Died November 29, 1974

Chinese military leader and minister of defense

Although he was in charge of the Chinese forces in Korea, Peng Dehuai was barely known to Westerners, who for years assumed another general led China in the Korean War (1950–53). Peng had been with Communist Chinese Chairman **Mao Zedong** (Mao Tsu-tung; 1893–1976; see entry) as a commander in the Red Army since the early days in the 1920s. His skill and integrity as the commander of the Chinese forces in Korea led to tremendous successes in the first Chinese offensives, and his troops were responsible for some of the worst U.S. defeats in combat yet known.

An impoverished childhood

Peng Dehuai (P'eng Teh-huai) was born in the village of Shixiang in the southern province of Hunan. His home was not far from the birthplace of Mao Zedong. Peng's early years were marked by poverty. After the death of his mother in 1904 and the failure of the family's business, Peng and one of his brothers were forced to beg for food in their neighborhood. The times were difficult in China, after years of the unsteady leadership of the ruling family of China, the Manchu–Qing

(Ch'ing) dynasty. In 1911, the Manchus were overthrown by the revolutionary Sun Yat-sen (1866–1925) and his Kuomintang party (pronounced KWOE-min-TANG). Sun briefly established a republic, but it did not hold together, and soon the country was under military rule. Several provinces declared their independence, and separate rulers, or warlords, took over. The country was falling apart in many ways.

In 1913, there was a large demonstration in Shixiang, the result of hardships due to a bad drought. Peng took part in breaking into a grain storehouse and giving the grain to the demonstrators. After the demonstration, he was forced to flee in order to avoid arrest for his part. After working at a number of jobs, in 1915 he joined the Hunan warlord army, one of several regional military forces controlling sections of China. Peng distinguished himself as an excellent soldier and chose to further his military career by entering the Hunan Military Academy in September 1922. After his graduation, Peng served in several armies fighting to unify China. Sun Yat-sen died in 1925 and was succeeded by **Chiang Kai-shek** (1887–1975; see entry), in whose Nationalist army Peng rose to the rank of major. During all the years of his military service, Peng's interest in politics and political philosophy grew stronger and he found himself deeply drawn to the ideals of communism. Communism is a set of political beliefs that advocates the elimination of private property; it is a system in which goods, owned by the community as a whole rather than by specific individuals, are available to all as needed. Impressed especially with the communists' sympathy for the common man, Peng began to align himself with the communist faction within the Nationalist forces.

Joining the communists

In 1927, Chiang accepted the help of the communists to take over the city of Shanghai in an offensive. When the mission was accomplished, Chiang set his army against the communists who had just helped him, slaughtering them in the streets and having them arrested and executed. The few communists who survived the incident had to flee to the countryside. A small group formed in remote mountains on the border of Hunan. One of the leaders that emerged in the mountains was the revolutionary Mao Zedong.

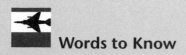

Words to Know

armistice: talks between opposing forces in which they agree to a truce or suspension of hostilities.

bayonet: a steel blade attached to the end of a rifle or other firearm, used as a sword or knife in hand-to-hand combat.

bunker: a reinforced underground room dug into a battle area for protection against enemy gunfire and bombs.

Communism: a system of government in which one party (usually the Communist Party) controls all property and goods and the means to produce and distribute them.

grenade: a small explosive weapon that can be thrown, usually with a pin that is pulled to activate it and a spring-loaded safety lever that is held down until the user wants to throw the grenade; once the safety lever is released, the grenade will explode in seconds.

guerrilla tactics: an irregular form of combat, in which warriors generally rely on ambushes and surprise attacks to harass or even destroy much larger armies.

intervention: the act of a third party who steps into an ongoing conflict in the attempt to interfere in its outcome or stop it altogether.

Nationalists (Chinese): the ruling party led by Chiang Kai-shek in China from the 1920s until 1949, when the Nationalists were defeated by the Communists in the Chinese Civil War and forced to withdraw to the island of Taiwan (formerly Formosa).

stalemate: deadlock; the state in which the efforts of each party in a conflict cancels out the efforts of the other party so that no one makes any headway.

warlord: a leader with his own military whose powers are usually limited to a small area that, in most cases, he took by force.

Peng joined the Chinese Communist Party in February 1928, although he remained in Chiang's Nationalist army. That summer, his regiment was sent to hunt down communists in Hunan. Under his leadership, his troops revolted. Rather than going after the communists as they were ordered, they arrested and executed the Hunan landowners, establishing the Hunan Provincial Soviet Government. Peng's unit became the Fifth Corps of the Chinese Workers' and Peasants' Army. When the Nationalist army came after them, they fled to join Mao in the mountains.

The Long March

The group of communists in the mountains grew steadily and by 1930 had become such a threat to Chiang that he continually sent his troops on missions to annihilate them. Peng had become a leader in the Red Army, commanding a unit of eighteen thousand men, when Chiang's troops totally surrounded the communist base, forcing the whole group to embark on what became known as the Long March. The march began with eighty thousand communist troops heading westward in October 1934. One year later only ten thousand men were left, and they had traveled eight thousand miles, fighting in fierce combat all the while. Only three thousand of Peng's men survived the one-year trek, but Peng, a burly man with a flair for the dramatic, emerged from the Long March a hero of the Red Army. At this time, Mao Zedong took his place as leader of the Communists, with Peng serving as commander of the First Front Army.

From this time, the Communist Party and army grew and took over more and more of China. By 1938, the Red Army had 156,000 men and at the close of World War II (1939–45) it was estimated at 800,000. The Communists had fourteen bases and controlled about one-fifth of the population of China. Peng, as commander of the army, wished to bring his troops up to date in military procedures and technology. Mao, on the other hand, wanted to promote political idealism in his soldiers and preferred to use guerrilla tactics such as ambushes and surprise attacks.

A united front

In 1937, with the Chinese Communists and the Chinese Nationalists involved in utter conflict with each other, they barely noticed that their country was being invaded by Japan. Chiang was in the middle of preparing his army for the final extermination of the Communists when Japan invaded China in July. Although Chiang would have preferred to go after the Communists, the public demanded that he create a united front of Communists and Nationalists against the invading Japanese. Chiang and Mao agreed to form a united front army comprised of both Nationalists and Communists to the common enemy. They called a very reluctant truce to their own hostilities as World War II ignited worldwide and they began to receive help from the Allies against Japan.

As desperate as the situation was, with Japan occupying large parts of China, Mao wanted to save the Red Army for the fight against Chiang's Nationalist army after the war. But he deployed three divisions in the war against the Japanese and Peng became a general in one of them. Peng also occasionally led guerrilla forces on surprise attacks on the Japanese. Peng disagreed with Mao on the overall use of the armed forces. Peng believed that the Japanese were such a potent enemy that all the forces of the Communist troops should be used against them. In the end, it was the atomic bombs dropped on mainland Japan by the United States that forced the Japanese to surrender and end World War II.

Chinese Civil War

As soon as the Japanese surrendered, the Communists and the Nationalists rushed in to accept the Japanese surrender in various parts of China, both wanting to claim as much of the formerly occupied territory as possible. This led to resumed fighting between the two groups, which became a civil war. During the Chinese Civil War (1946–49), Peng commanded the 175,000-man Northwest Field Army. He was given the difficult task of protecting the Communist capital of Yenan. The opposing general, Hu Tsungnan, was one of Chiang Kai-shek's best strategists. In March 1947, Hu launched a 260,000-man offensive that pushed Peng's forces back toward the Inner Mongolian border in northwest China. Peng's troops were able to save Mao from being captured in one of the battles, and Mao honored his general's courage and skill by dedicating a poem to him. Peng's troops recaptured Yenan in April 1948. Hu evacuated his troops to the island of Taiwan (formerly Formosa) in the fall of 1949, signaling a Communist victory. On October 1, 1949, the People's Republic of China (PRC) was proclaimed by the Chinese Communist Party, of which Mao Zedong was chairman.

Korean War

After winning the civil war, the new Chinese Communist government faced a ruined economy and an urgent need to get control over the fragmented country. They were also fighting nationalist guerrillas in the south and trying to reunite Taiwan with the rest of China and eliminate Chiang Kai-shek's hold there. After years of war, China was in need of a period of restoration, not involvement in the Korean War. But for a variety of reasons, when United Nations (UN) troops crushed the North Korean Army and drove up to China's border in October 1950, Mao argued fiercely that China must help out their neighbor. (The UN was founded right after World War II by the Allied Powers—the United States, the British Commonwealth, the Soviet Union, and other European nations—as an international body devoted to maintaining worldwide peace.) Most of the generals and top officials argued against intervention. Peng Dehuai was almost alone in his support of Mao in this. When Mao coaxed the skeptical PRC leadership to agree to enter the war, it was Peng who was named commander in chief of the Chinese forces assigned to save North Korea. Peng commanded the 380,000-man Chinese People's Volunteers (CPV), who were actually taken from the regular army.

At the time of this appointment, Peng Dehaui was fifty-three years old and had been with Mao and the Red Army for twenty-two years. On October 8, he flew to Shenyang to take command of the CPV. Then he went on to the town of Andong, where he brought together five field armies near the border of North Korea. On October 14, he started sending trainloads of advance units across the Yalu River to various strategic destinations in North Korea. On October 19, the rest of the troops began their journey, but the going was slow. Supplies had been transported across the border beginning October 11.

On October 21, Peng met with the North Korean premier **Kim Il Sung** (1912–1994) to form a joint plan of action. He determined that his best course was to stop the UN forces' advances by surrounding the widely scattered units with hidden troops, and then to kill as many of them as possible. That same morning, Peng's advance units first met with the Republic of Korea (ROK, or South Korean) troops advancing toward the border. "On the morning of October 21, a division of our 40th Army encountered Syngman Rhee's puppet troops," he wrote in his memoirs of meeting the South Korean troops, whose government was headed by **Syngman Rhee** (1875–1965; see entries). "Our troops displayed characteristic flexibility and mobility and wiped out some Syngman Rhee units, forcing the pursuing U.S. and puppet troops to retreat." This initial offensive was brief and scattered, mostly hitting the ROKs but also some Eighth Army troops, and lasted until November 6. On that day, although the Chinese were winning the battles, Peng ordered all units to cease combat and withdraw. The Chinese troops did not reappear to the UN forces for three weeks, giving the United Nations plenty of time to reconsider the invasion of North Korea. In the meantime, Mao was sending more armies and Peng's troops had a chance to resupply.

The attack at the Chosin Reservoir

On November 8, 1950, Peng and his generals began planning their next offensive. They were more optimistic about the outcome than when they decided to enter the war one month previously. There were by November about 380,000 men available in the area, and they had found the UN forces weak and unprepared in combat. Still, Peng was realistic about the ends that could be achieved, hoping only to push the enemy back to the 39th parallel. They planned to wait for the UN to attack northward into the mountainous areas in the Chosin (Changjin) Reservoir, and then attack. The greatest effort would be against the First U.S. Marine Division, which the Chinese understood to be the most challenging opponent they would face. Mao sent Peng extra divisions for this encounter. Surprise would be a great asset. The United States still believed that the Chinese force in Korea was small, about 60,000 men.

Peng's military strategy was to lure unsuspecting UN forces into a huge and well-laid trap. He was very skillful in moving hundreds of thousands of troops into North Korea without alarming the UN command. His troops marched at night to avoid being seen by air or on land. They marched in the mountains, brushing the snow over their tracks as they went. With great discipline, they hid while UN units marched past them, waiting for the trap to be laid. To form a trap, they often formed a giant V shape in front of the enemy troops. When the enemy was inside the V, the Chinese would close up the back opening, and attack at very close range. The trapped UN units were cut off from help and outnumbered. Their military training was for organized combat rather than hand-to-

American soldiers examine the bodies of dead Chinese soldiers killed in a central front attack on UN forces near Chunchon. *Reproduced by permission of AP/Wide World Photos.*

hand fighting. Peng's attacks were usually short and fierce, with many deaths on both sides.

From November 25 until December 6, the Chinese struck full force against the UN forces, which were divided in half and separated by mountains. Peng described the attack in his memoirs: "Our main force swept into the enemy ranks with the strength of an avalanche and engaged the enemy at close quarters with grenades and bayonets. The superior firepower of the enemy became useless." The Eighth Army was forced into retreat on November 28. The X Corps in Chosin were trapped, surrounded by massive Chinese forces in the bitterly cold reservoir: there were twelve Chinese divisions facing three U.S. and two ROK divisions. Casualties on both sides were heavy. Although the Chinese did not annihilate the First Marines, Chosin was the worst marine defeat in history. In the first days of December, the surviving marines fought their way to the fortified town of Hagaru; from there they would begin their journey to the coast, where they were evacuated by ship from North Korea. On December 2, Peng ordered a halt to the combat for a few days. China had suffered grave losses, with whole divisions so battered they could no longer operate. Reserves were moving in, but the freezing weather and UN air attacks were killing many soldiers before they ever saw combat. Several days later, the Chinese forces advanced to the south.

The Eighth Army was quickly retreating south, not realizing that the Chinese forces had been so badly damaged. They stopped at a line roughly along the 38th parallel, the original dividing line between North and South Korea. Slowly, over the next few weeks, the Chinese built up their troops on the other side of the line, with a concentration just north of Seoul. The Chinese struck again on New Year's Eve, sending the Eighth Army into a disorderly retreat. They quickly recaptured the city of Seoul.

Reaching a stalemate

The recapture of Seoul was a great victory for Peng, but he was deeply concerned, as he wrote in his memoirs of the winter of 1951: "By now the Chinese People's Volunteers had fought three major campaigns. . . . They had neither an air force nor sufficient antiaircraft guns to protect them from enemy bombers. Bombed by aircraft and shelled by long-range guns day and night, our troops could not move about in daytime. And they had not had a single day's good rest in three months." Mao and Kim Il Sung both urged that the Chinese offensives continue until the UN troops could be driven from Korea altogether. The next offensive failed, and Seoul was lost to the UN forces a second time, on March 14. A large offensive in April was successful in killing many of the enemy, but failed to gain much ground. Another massive attack in May began favorably for the Chinese and North Koreans, but this time the UN forces, now under the command of General **Matthew B. Ridgway** (1895–1993; see entry), held their ground firmly. Peng reported the heaviest losses yet in the war. After that the Chinese forces dug into a defensive position, creating tunnels and bunkers that were nearly impenetrable. In the next two years of warfare, neither the U.S. nor the Chinese forces made great advances. They fell to positions near the 38th parallel and held their own in a stalemate that cost of hundreds of thousands of lives.

By the summer of 1953, Peng had amassed a huge and powerful army in North Korea. But after two years of negotiating, the UN and the communists finally arranged a truce. Peng personally signed the armistice agreement at Panmunjom on July 27, 1953. "This is a happy day for our people," read Peng's public statement upon the signing, as quoted in his memoirs. "Through three years of fighting together, the Volunteers had forged a comradeship in blood with the North Korean people and their army—a friendship which further deepened and strengthened our international feelings." North Korean premier Kim Il Sung hailed him as a Korean national hero.

Although Peng exhibited deep concern about his troops consistently throughout the war, he was also known to throw them into short, fierce battles in which huge numbers would be killed. Peng's strategy during the Korean War was to use the CPV's advantage—numerical superiority—to overwhelm UN forces. Swarms of soldiers using bayonets advanced, with little to no artillery, tank, or air support, into the teeth of concentrated UN fire. Chinese losses during the war were appallingly high. Western estimates place the losses at a minimum of 450,000, although the exact figure is not known.

Minister of Defense

In the spring of 1954, Peng was named China's minister of defense, becoming, in effect, the supreme commander of China's army, the People's Liberation Army (PLA). On January 18, 1955, Peng used his new position to lead twelve thousand soldiers on an attack of the Dachen Islands. Chiang Kai-shek, the Chinese Nationalist leader who escaped to Taiwan in December 1949, was in possession of the islands and had been using them as a base from which he could launch commando raids into mainland China. The United States persuaded Chiang to evacuate his ten thousand soldiers from the Dachens by promising U.S. congressional approval of the Taiwan Straits Resolution, which gave the U.S. president authority to use force to protect Taiwan. In addition to the Dachens assault, the Communist Chinese were shelling two other strategic islands, Quemoy and Matsu, just off the mainland. Quemoy received the brunt of the assault. Hostilities mounted between China and the United States and at one point U.S. Secretary of State John Foster Dulles (1888–1959) made a nuclear threat against China. In the summer of 1955, the PLA stopped its shelling.

Peng's forces shelled Quemoy again in August 1958, using as many as sixty thousand artillery shells a day. Peng's navy blockaded the island, hoping to "starve" Quemoy into a surrender. The United States intervened, protecting Chiang's supply lines from Taiwan to Quemoy with its Seventh Fleet. Peng's air force sustained heavy losses while engaging Taiwan's fighter planes. Thirty-seven of Peng's planes were shot down. The Chinese eventually ended the blockade and shelling in October 1958 after more threats from the United States. Peng's mission was a failure.

A warning to Mao

In the late 1950s, Peng tried to use his influence to upgrade the PLA. His objective was to rebuild the military with modern weapons and disciplined training. This effort did not get far. Mao was more interested in his new economic program, the Great Leap Forward, in which he wanted to promote rapid agricultural and industrial growth by developing "people's communes" that combined farming and industry. Many Chinese leaders believed Mao's plan was dangerous to the economy, but few dared to say anything. In 1959, at Communist Party meetings at Lushan, a mountain resort in Jiangxi (Kiangsi) province, Peng Dehuai spoke out bluntly against the plan, warning Mao that a terrible famine loomed in China and that his idea could cause disaster. Mao did not listen to the warning, and his program collapsed by 1960. Mao was by this time becoming paranoid (thinking people wanted to do him harm) and relentless in his revolutionary idealism. He launched an even more radical plan; more than twenty-five million people died in the Great Leap famines of 1959 to 1961.

In the meantime, for voicing disagreement with Mao, Peng Dehuai lost his position, was banished from the Communist Party, and was soon arrested and imprisoned in 1959. He remained in prison for fifteen years. In 1974, Peng became ill but was denied medical treatment. He died in prison on November 29. After Mao's death, Peng's memory was openly honored again in China. He is now regarded as a hero in China.

Where to Learn More

Deane, Hugh. *The Korean War: 1945–1953*. San Francisco: China Books, 1999.

Domes, Jurgen. *Peng Te-huai: The Man and the Image*. Stanford, CA: Stanford University Press, 1987.

Peng Dehuai. *Memoirs of a Chinese Marshal: The Autobiographical Notes of Peng Dehuai (1898–1924)*. Translated by Zheng Longpu and edited by Sara Grimes. Beijing: Foreign Languages Press, 1984.

Roe, Patrick C. *The Dragon Strikes, China and the Korean War: June-December 1950*. Novato, CA: Presidio Press, 2000.

Spurr, Russell. *Enter the Dragon*. New York: Newmarket, 1988.

Whiting, Allen. *China Crosses the Yalu*. Stanford, CA: Stanford University Press, 1960.

Syngman Rhee

Born April 26, 1875
Pyong-san, Korea
Died July 19, 1965
Honolulu, Hawaii

President of the Republic of Korea

"I will never accept the armistice terms as they stand. The Republic of Korea will fight on, even if it means a suicide, and I will lead them."

Portrait reproduced courtesy of the Library of Congress.

Syngman Rhee had been in exile from his native country for most of thirty-three years when he returned in 1945 at the age of seventy. He became the first president of the Republic of Korea in 1948. After spending most of his life in the United States petitioning for help in the cause of Korean independence from Japan, Rhee was single-mindedly devoted to his country. Rhee was called a puppet of the United States by the communists, but the United States in fact had far less control over his actions than they wished. Rhee was tough, cunning, and manipulative, and one of the more skilled politicians in the country. He did not represent the majority of South Koreans, but, backed by wealthy bureaucrats and the national police force, he managed to build a power base in the U.S.-occupied country. For some who lived through the tumultuous times of his rule, Rhee seemed to be the glue that held the war-torn Republic of Korea together. To others, he was an autocrat and zealot who oppressed his country and extinguished chances of reconciliation between North and South Korea.

Yangban youth

Yi Sung-man, who later Westernized his name to Syngman Rhee, was born on April 26, 1875, the only son of Yi Kyong-sun, a member of the local gentry in the village of Pyong-san in Hwanghae Province. When he was very young, his family moved to Seoul, the capital city of Korea. Rhee's family was of the *yangban* class of Korea, the traditional Korean elite who often held bureaucratic positions in the government and came from a long tradition of scholarly pursuits. One of the principle yangban disciplines at the time of Rhee's youth was memorizing volumes of Korean genealogies: the family trees of Koreans. Yi Kyong-sun could sit and recite volumes of his family genealogy, going back seventeen generations to a time when the family was connected to royal blood. Rhee's family, though elite, was fairly poor.

Rhee's father wanted him to follow in the yangban tradition, so he spent his time as a boy studying Confucian classics. Confucianism is a moral and religious system from China that teaches proper human behavior, particularly in terms of relationships between people. Confucianism in many ways serves to preserve the status quo (the way things are at the time), since it advocates that everyone should know their place in society and not overstep their position. By the time Rhee was in his teens, he longed for more modern ideas. He cut off his topknot of hair (traditional for yangban youth) and began to read Western books. In 1894, he enrolled in the Paejae Haktang, a Methodist mission high school, where he was taught Western traditions and the English language. Upon graduation from Paejae, he was employed by the academy as an English instructor.

Involvement with the politics of reform

When Rhee began his studies at the Methodist academy, a large popular uprising, the Tonghak Rebellion, swept across Korea. The rebels, reacting to corruption within the Korean government and the influence of outsiders in their country, sought a return to the traditional cultures and religions of Asia. When the Tonghak rebels got out of control, the Korean government called upon China to help put down the uprising; without being asked, Japan also sent in troops. China and Japan went to war, and the Japanese won in 1895. The

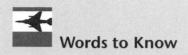

Words to Know

annex: to take over a nation that was independent, making it a dependent part of another nation.

armistice: talks between opposing forces in which they agree to a truce or suspension of hostilities.

autocrat: a person who rules with unlimited authority.

bureaucrat: a person working in the administration of a government or organization in a nonelective function.

coalition government: a temporary government formed by combining all the different parties and interests in order to take a joint action.

Communism: a system of government in which one party (usually the Communist Party) controls all property and goods and the means to produce and distribute them.

exile: forced or voluntary absence from one's home country.

martial law: suspension of civil rights during a time of state or national emergency.

multinational trusteeship: government by the joint rule of several countries that have

committed to act in what they deem to be the country's best interest.

protectorate: a dependent nation subject to the control of a more powerful nation, but not officially a part of the more powerful nation.

Provisional Korean Government: a government in exile, formed in Shanghai during Japanese rule of Korea (1910–45), that elected leaders and fought for the cause of an independent Korea, but had no actual power within occupied Korea.

puppet: someone who seems to be acting on his or her own, but is in fact controlled by someone or something else.

reunification: the process of bringing back together the separate parts of something that was once a single unit; in Korea, this usually refers to the dream of a single Korea ruled under one government, no longer divided into two nations at the demarcation line.

zealot: fanatic; someone who pursues his or her objectives with extreme passion and eagerness.

Japanese then began what would prove to be a long and forceful presence in Korea.

The Independence Club, a group seeking reform and Korean independence, was founded in 1896 by Philip Jaisohn, an American-educated reformer. The club published a newspaper, *The Independent.* Rhee, who was the editor of a school paper, was drawn to the club by his journalistic interests and by its Western ideas of reform. He became a member of the Independence Club and was one of its most impassioned speakers, demanding before crowds that the Japanese leave Korea and that Korea's monarchy (inherited rule by royalty) be reformed. He led a group of about eight thousand demonstrators who called for the removal of Russian advisers from Korea. The demand was carried out by the Korean government, but later the pro-Russian sector of the government regained its strength and went after the organization. The Korean king, too, came to believe that the Independence Club was against him and ordered it disbanded.

In 1898, Rhee was arrested, presumably for his involvement in the Independence Club. He was tortured for months, and at the end of the period of torture sentenced to life in prison. In prison, Rhee converted to Christianity. He believed that Christianity was a fitting set of beliefs for political reform, that helping others was the way to mend the world. His conversion to Christianity included a powerful belief that God had a plan for him to save his country. While in prison, Rhee wrote a book, *The Spirit of Independence,* in the hope of arousing public sentiment against the Japanese in Korea.

In 1904, six years after his arrest, Rhee was released from prison. According to him (and many have questioned this claim) some leaders of the Korean government asked him to go to the United States and plead for help against the Japanese. He arrived in Washington, D.C., on December 31, 1905. It took him another six months to get an appointment to see President Theodore Roosevelt (1887–1944) to ask for U.S. aid to help Korea rid itself of the Japanese. When he finally did get in to see the president, he was too late. The United States had already agreed to recognize Japan's interests in Korea. Soon after Rhee's visit with the president, Japan declared Korea a "protectorate." Within five years, Japan annexed Korea, making the peninsula, which had been an independent country for centuries, part of its expanding empire.

Education in the United States

After his frustrated attempt to save Korean independence, Rhee enrolled as a student in George Washington University, getting financial help from the Methodist Mission Board. Upon graduation in 1907, he was admitted to a master's program at Harvard University. He began to read extensively about international relations. He received his doctorate in political science from Princeton University in 1910, the year in which Japan formally annexed its Korean protectorate. During the last years of his schooling, he became friends with future U.S. President Woodrow Wilson (1856–1924), who was president of Princeton at the time.

Rhee returned to Korea in 1910 as a YMCA (Young Men's Christian Association) organizer, teacher, and evangelist among the youth of Korea, in effect paying back the Methodists for his education. He wasn't there long. He was disturbed by the strict rule of the Japanese and in danger of arrest. In 1912, while attending a conference in the United States, he decided to stay, accepting the head position at the Korean Compound School— later the Korean Institute—in Honolulu in 1913.

President of provisional government

On March 1, 1919, thirty-three leading Koreans signed a declaration of independence, which was then read to crowds in the streets of Seoul. A huge Korea-wide demonstration, which came to be known as the March First Movement, swept the country. The Japanese reaction to the massive uprising was swift and cruel, resulting in thousands of deaths, injuries, and arrests.

At that time, President Woodrow Wilson was at the Paris Peace Conference, negotiating peace after World War I (1914–18). He announced that he would champion "the right of self-determination of peoples." A group of independence leaders, still stirred by the March First Movement, met in Seoul in April 1919 and formed the Korean Provisional Government, naming Syngman Rhee as the first president, hoping that he could use his ties to Wilson to get help for Korea. Rhee asked for permission as the president in exile to attend the Paris Peace Conference, but Wilson was trying to gain Japanese cooperation and would not allow Rhee to attend.

The Korean Provisional Government was then moved to Shanghai, China, and Rhee continued to lead it from the United States, where he was best known. Even there, however, he could not find allies in his struggles against the Japanese. In

March 1925, Rhee was dismissed as the provisional government's president after conflicts arose with other members. When Korean leader Kim Ku became the president of the government in exile, Rhee simply ignored his dismissal and continued to claim the title of president.

In early 1933, while Rhee was in Geneva, Switzerland, attempting to make an appeal on behalf of Korea to the League of Nations (an international organization devoted to world peace), he first met Francesca Donner, the eldest daughter of a well-to-do iron merchant in Vienna, who was there as a secretary to the Austrian delegation to the League. They were married in October 1933, saying their vows in both Korean and English. He was then almost fifty-eight.

Rhee moved to Washington in 1940, as World War II (1939–45) was changing the relationship between the United States and Japan. He tried to put pressure on the Department of State to recognize the Korean Provisional Government. During this time he wrote another book, *Japan Inside Out*, that predicted Japan's aggression toward the United States. He was not very successful in his efforts, and many dismissed him as a nagging old man. By 1943, Rhee began blaming the Soviet Union for the many of the ills in Asia. His anticommunist stand won him some support. (The Soviet Union was the first communist country and was made up of fifteen republics, including Russia. It existed as a unified country from 1922 to 1991. Communism is a set of political beliefs that advances the elimination of private property. It is a system in which goods are owned by the community as a whole rather than by specific individuals and are available to all as needed.) During his years in the United States, Rhee became a very successful fundraiser, earning himself the money to live, travel, and publicize the Korean cause. His base benefactors were Koreans living in the United States and members of the Korean Christian Church in Hawaii, but he also received money from wealthy Americans in Christian church groups.

Return to Korea

When World War II came to an end in 1945, the Korean people were full of joy at their liberation, but their dreams of an independent Korea were short-lived. The United States and the Soviet Union agreed on a joint military occupation of Korea to accept the Japanese surrender, reasoning that the Koreans had been ruled by others for so long, they would not immediately have the resources to rule themselves. Once both powers had set up military governments in their sector of Korea, they found they could not agree to terms of a trusteeship. Neither occupier was willing to let the other take control of all of Korea, and so they remained there for three years, with the Soviets in the north above the 38th parallel helping to establish a communist government and the United States in the south trying to eliminate communist elements and establish a democratic government.

At the time of liberation, Syngman Rhee, sixty-nine years old, pressured the U.S. State Department to be allowed to return to Korea. He was initially ignored, but with help from his friends, Rhee was flown back to the country that he had not seen for some thirty-three years in General Douglas MacArthur's own plane. (**Douglas MacArthur** [1880–1964; see entry] at the time was the Allied supreme commander of U.S. forces in the southwest Pacific.) He was given a hero's reception by the American Military Government that was ruling the southern half of Korea and by the Korean people, who were overjoyed with the prospect of independence.

Rhee's name was known in Korea as a nationalist hero from the independence movement, but not much more was known of him. According to historian Joungwon Alexander Kim in *Divided Korea,* the elderly exile knew he had to prove his right to lead:

> Rhee was aware of the importance of proving his legitimacy, and kept in his possession a notebook that contained a tracing of his genealogy back to the Yi dynasty founder, the instructions from the members of the Korean cabinet in 1904 [telling him to seek help from Theodore Roosevelt against the Japanese], newspaper clippings about his activities on Korea's behalf at numerous international conferences, photographs of himself with Woodrow Wilson—indeed, every piece of evidence he could accumulate to demonstrate his claim to be the leader of the Korean people.

Political struggle in Korea, 1945–1948

At the time of liberation, the Korean people had quickly put together their own government, the Korean People's Republic. It had 145 branches throughout the country called People's Committees that governed locally. Rhee had been named its president before he returned to Korea, but he quickly distanced himself from the reform-oriented Korean People's Republic, which included large communist factions. His anticommunist stand made him very popular among the prosperous: the landholders and businessmen. Because the communists hated the national police, which was made up of a large majority of people who had been trained by the Japanese, the police as a group would also come to support Rhee. Rhee was a firm advocate of independence, and although he enjoyed the appearance of U.S. support, at times he fought to get the military government out of Korea. He made quite a few enemies in the American Military Government. For the first years of his return, his political position was far from secure.

By 1946, order in South Korea had given way. Political factions were dividing and fighting among each other. Violence and economic instability reigned. Political experience was nonexistent among the Koreans, because the Japanese had never allowed them to practice their own politics. At the same time, the American Military Government, with money and power, had surprisingly little knowledge of the Korean people and made many grave errors in policy. The leaders vying for power with Rhee within the Republic of Korea were Kim Koo, the leader of the Korean Provisional Government, a nationalist and anticommunist like himself; Kim Kyu-sik, another exile nationalist with a Ph.D. from Princeton; **Yö Un-hyöng** (Lyuh Woon Hyung; 1885–1947), the founder of the People's Republic and moderate leftist; and **Pak Hön-yöng** (1900–1955; see entries), the leader of the sizable group of Korean communists in the south. (Reform-seeking individuals, often communist, are referred to as leftists, or being on the political left wing. Conservatives, politically on the right, seek to maintain traditions and establish strong, authoritative governments. They tend to favor big business and power in the hands of the elite and are always anticommunist, since communists generally are concerned with the plight of the common people.) Among these men and their followers, a tremendous political struggle would take place.

In the meantime, the United States and the Soviet Union worked toward the trusteeship. While the general population was solidly against the trusteeship—the Korean people did not trust the Americans—the Korean Communist Party came out in favor of it. Thus, Yö Un-hyöng and Kim Kyu-sik worked with the Americans to form a coalition government. As the left gradually broke down into factions, Rhee, who had remained opposed to the trusteeship and to any coalition government, began to pick up support.

Rhee elected president

The Americans at first opposed the idea of the establishment of separate governments in Korea's Soviet-occupied north and American-occupied south. But they were also unwilling to agree to the Soviet's proposal that both occupiers withdraw from Korea at the same time and leave the Koreans to choose their government. In early 1948, at the urging of the United States, the United Nations (UN) agreed to sponsor elections in Korea, after which Korea would become independent. (The UN was founded in 1945 to maintain worldwide peace and to develop friendly relations among countries.) The Soviets and northern Koreans, believing that the UN did not have the authority to determine the government of Korea, would not allow its representatives into northern Korea to supervise the elections. So in the end, the United States supported elections in the south alone. Many Korean leaders, including Kim Koo and Kim Kyu-sik, opposed the elections, but Rhee, who had been arguing for elections in the south since 1946, knew that a one-sided election would be in his favor. And it was. In May 1948, Rhee was elected the first president of the new Republic of Korea. The northern Koreans soon held their own elections and established their own new government, the Democratic People's Republic of Korea.

Rhee was a charismatic leader and, by many accounts, a ruthless dictator. An interesting portrait of Rhee comes from a U.S. Central Intelligence Agency report, quoted in Joseph C. Goulden's *Korea: The Untold Story of the War,* written a year and a half after he became president:

> Rhee has devoted his life to the cause of an independent Korea with the ultimate objective of personally controlling the country. In pursuing this end he has shown few scruples [guiding principles about what is right and proper] about the elements which he has been willing to utilize for his personal advancement, with the important exception that he has always refused to deal with Communists. . . . He has also been

unscrupulous in his attempts to thrust aside any person or group he felt to be in his way. Rhee's vanity has made him highly susceptible to the contrived flattery of self-seeking interests. . . . His intellect is a shallow one, and his behavior is often irrational and literally childish. Yet Rhee, in the final analysis, has proved himself to be a remarkably astute politician. Although he has created for himself the combination role of Korean Moses and Messiah, he has very rarely permitted himself to forget the hard political realities of his position.

After he gained the office of president of Korea, Rhee went to work consolidating his power. In the six months that followed his inauguration, about 81,000 people were arrested, including a good number of elected members of the National Assembly. Rhee fired many of the officers of the ROK army and used the courts to keep any perceived enemies at bay. The economy was very bad and the public was unhappy. In the 1950 elections for National Assembly, only 47 of the 210 seats were held by Rhee supporters.

The Korean War

Rhee's dream was to reunify Korea under his own rule. He wanted to go to war with North Korea, but he knew he could not hope to win the war without the military backing of the United States. The United States did not want war and made it clear that it would not support South Korea in an unprovoked conflict. Even so, there were several border battles started by the South in 1949.

Then, on June 25, 1950, North Korean troops in huge numbers invaded the South, quickly occupying Seoul. This was the start of the Korean War, initially a civil war, with both sides desiring to reunify Korea under their own very different kinds of government. The civil war was quickly transformed into a superpower conflict, however, as United Nations forces, led by the United States, came to the aid of the South and then, later that year, soldiers from the new People's Republic of China joined on the side of the North. The war continued for three years, devastating both North and South Korea as cities were taken, abandoned, and retaken. A cease-fire was signed in the summer of 1953, but a formal peace treaty was never negotiated. A military demarcation line and demilitarized zone (with hundreds of thousands of troops ranged on either side) still divide the two countries.

Rhee spent the early days of the war fleeing from the invading North Koreans from one position to the next. Then, as the UN troops began to advance up into the North, he reclaimed Seoul and even Pyongyang, the capital of North Korea. Just as the North Koreans had come into South Korean cities and arrested and executed the people they thought to be part of Rhee's government, so, too, did Rhee have his troops arrest anyone suspected of having communist sympathies.

Many civilians were executed by his forces, and new evidence in the 1990s and 2000s indicates that there were more of these political killings than was ever recorded in history books. Although Rhee formally put his troops under UN command at the beginning of the war, he was quick to threaten to pull them out when he disagreed with the Americans. When the U.S. Joint Chiefs of Staff (the military advisors to the president and secretary of defense who established the U.S. forces' battle plans) were pondering the wisdom of crossing the 38th parallel into North Korea with the threat of Chinese intervention in the war, Rhee gave orders to the ROK (Republic of Korea) troops to proceed to the border regardless of UN orders.

Rhee had never allowed any opposition to his rule and as the war continued, he was losing support in his country. The end of his first four-year term came in 1952 and it was obvious that he would lose the election if it were carried out as the constitution directed, by a vote of the popularly elected National Assembly. Of course, his opponents on the National Assembly would not accept a constitutional change. Therefore, in May 1952, Rhee placed the area of Pusan, in southern Korea where his government was temporarily stationed, under martial law (a time when civil rights are suspended) and had some of the members of the National Assembly arrested. In July, he had the National Police gather the legislators, some of whom had been in hiding. They were brought to Assembly Hall along with those who had been arrested and were forced to vote on the changes to the constitution. The members of the National Assembly bowed to his will and changed the constitution. Rhee was elected for a second term, but there was little question that he had corrupted the democratic process.

Sabotaging the truce

When U.S. president **Harry S. Truman** (1884–1972) decided it was time to negotiate with the communists for an armistice, Rhee let it be known that he would never go along with a truce as long as the Korean nation was divided in two and there were still Chinese troops in the North. While the United Nations and the communists were trying to agree what to do with North Korean prisoners of war, Rhee was making his own plans to sabotage the truce. He gave orders to his troops in the prison camps to release the North Korean prisoners—twenty-five thousand of them—badly damaging relations at the negotiating table. **Dwight D. Eisenhower** (1890–1969; see entries), the new president, voiced his frustrations at Rhee in his diary: "It is almost hopeless to write about the Korea-Rhee situation. . . . It is impossible to attempt here to recite the long list of items in which Rhee has been completely uncooperative, even recalcitrant [defiant]. . . . There has been so much backing and filling, indecision, doubt, and frustration engendered by both Rhee and the communists that I am doubtful that an armistice even if achieved will have any great meaning. Certainly we must be extremely wary and watchful of both sides. Of course the fact remains that the probable enemy is the communists, but Rhee has been such an unsatisfactory ally that it is difficult indeed to avoid excoriating [severely criticizing] him in the strongest of terms." Rhee did finally go along with the armistice after obtaining promises of millions of dollars in U.S. aid, enough arms and equipment to enlarge the ROK Army from sixteen to twenty divisions, and the prolonged presence of U.S. troops in the Republic of Korea. The promise of massive economic aid he squeezed out of the Eisenhower administration, in fact, may have been one of his greatest accomplishments for his country. In the five weeks that his actions prolonged the fighting, however, there were more than one hundred thousand casualties on both sides.

After the war

As Rhee aged, he seemed to become less able to compromise and work with others, skills which had never been his particular strengths. He was determined to keep his hold on power, however, even if it meant intimidating opponents and rigging elections. In April 1960, following his fourth successful bid for the presidency, massive student protests and violence in several South Korean cities forced Rhee to resign the presidency and once again flee Korea. South Koreans had finally had enough: corruption in government, election rigging, police violence, and Rhee's emphasis on foreign affairs at the expense of economic development all combined to create a popular outrage against which even the stubborn but aging Rhee could no longer fight. Rhee quickly left the country for exile in Hawaii.

Rhee lived out the remainder of his life in Hawaii, where he died in 1965 at the age of ninety. His body was returned to South Korea and buried in the National Cemetery.

Where to Learn More

Allen, Richard C. *Korea's Syngman Rhee: An Unauthorized Portrait*. New York: Charles E. Tuttle, 1960.

Cumings, Bruce. *The Origins of the Korean War*. 2 vols. Princeton, NJ: Princeton University Press, 1981.

Eisenhower, Dwight D. *The Eisenhower Diaries*. Edited by Robert H. Ferrell. New York: W. W. Norton, 1981.

Gibney, Frank. "Syngman Rhee: The Free Man's Burden." In *Harper's,* February 1954, pp. 27–34.

Goulden, Joseph C. *Korea: The Untold Story*. New York: Times Books, 1982.

Kim, Joungwon Alexander. *Divided Korea: The Politics of Development, 1945–1972*. Cambridge, MA: East Asian Research Center, Harvard University, 1975.

Kim, Quee-Young. *The Fall of Syngman Rhee*. Berkeley, CA: Institute of East Asian Studies, University of California, 1983.

Oliver, Robert T. *Syngman Rhee: The Man Behind the Myth*. New York: Dodd, Mead, 1960.

Oliver, Robert T. *Syngman Rhee and American Involvement in Korea, 1942–1960: A Personal Narrative*. Seoul, South Korea: Panmun Book Company, 1978.

Simmons, Robert R. "The Korean Civil War." In *Without Parallel: The American-Korean Relationship since 1945,* edited by Frank Baldwin. New York: Pantheon Books, 1973.

Matthew B. Ridgway

Born March 3, 1895
Fortress Monroe, Virginia
Died July 1993
Fox Chapel, Pennsylvania

American military leader and business executive

"Every soldier learns in time that war is a lonely business. All your study, all your training, all your drill anticipates the moment when abruptly the responsibility rests solely on you to decide whether to stand or pull back, or to order an attack that will expose thousands of men to sudden death."

Portrait reproduced courtesy of the Library of Congress.

When Matthew B. Ridgway became the commanding general of the Eighth Army in Korea in December 1950, the morale of the United Nations (UN) soldiers was very low. With the entry of the powerful Chinese forces into the Korean War, panic and withdrawal in the face of enemy attack had become the norm among the discouraged army troops. Through some of the most effective leadership seen in the war, Ridgway transformed the UN forces. His presence on the battlefront encouraged the troops and stopped the "bug-outs" that had characterized the war. His strategy of counterattacking blocked the advances of what had seemed an unstoppable enemy. Ridgway's intelligent and level-headed response to the explosive political turmoil that arose between his commander, General **Douglas MacArthur** (1880–1964; see entry), and the Truman administration kept the UN command on a steady course when MacArthur was relieved of command.

Growing up on army posts

Matthew Bunker Ridgway was born into a well-to-do family on March 3, 1895, at Fortress Monroe, Virginia. His father, Thomas, was a West Point military academy graduate and full colonel in World War I (1914–18), and his mother, Ruth, was a concert pianist from Long Island, New York. Ridgway was a happy and charming youngster, who spent his childhood at various army posts. Even at an early age, he knew he wanted to be an army general, and after high school he went straight to West Point. He graduated in the class of 1917, two weeks after the United States entered World War I (1914–18). Ridgway itched to join his classmates in the trenches of France, but was forced to spend World War I on the Mexican border. After the war, in 1918, he returned to West Point to teach Romance languages. During the 1920s, as one of six officers in the regular army fluent in Spanish, he was awarded several high-level assignments in Latin America. During the 1930s, he was selected for the best military graduate schools, the Infantry School, the Command and General Staff School, and the Army War College.

In the years prior to World War II (1939–45), Ridgway rarely commanded troops. But when he did, he proved to be a master motivator. Commanding from the front, Ridgway exhorted his troops with his deep-pitched bellows. His perfectionist attitude and short temper led his men to joke: "There is a right way, a wrong way, and a Ridgway."

Words to Know

airborne unit: a military unit that moves the troops into a combat area by aircraft, often using parachutes.

bug-out: to panic and run away from a battle in confusion; a disorderly retreat without permission.

morale: the way that a person or a group of people feels about the job they are doing or the mission they are working on.

motivate: to give someone a desire or need to do something; to make a person or a group want to excel at something.

NATO: the acronym for the North Atlantic Treaty Organization, an alliance of nations in Europe and North America with shores on the Atlantic Ocean, formed in 1949 primarily to counter the threat of Soviet and communist expansion.

unilateral: acting alone, on one's own part and in one's own interests, without reference to others.

A mentor in George C. Marshall

Ridgway's peacetime ascendance was greatly assisted by the acclaimed general and statesman George C. Marshall (1880–1959), under whom he served on four separate occasions. Marshall became Ridgway's greatest supporter and after the start of World War II promoted him to brigadier general, assisting in command of General **Omar N. Bradley**'s (1893–1981; see entry) Eighty-second Infantry Division. In early 1942, Bradley was promoted and Ridgway was named commander of the Eighty-second. He transformed the division into one of the army's first airborne units, a unit trained to be transported to combat by air and by parachute.

In World War II, Ridgway and his command participated in the invasion of Sicily in 1943, and subsequent operations in Salerno, Normandy, Holland, and Germany, and in the Battle of the Bulge. Ridgway's paratroopers fought magnificently, and their exploits became legendary. After the Normandy invasion in June 1944, Ridgway was named to head the Eighteenth Airborne Corps. He commanded it through Germany, pushing across the Elbe before meeting advancing Soviet forces on May 3, 1945.

Ridgway came out of World War II much decorated and much admired. One commander called the now three-star general "undoubtedly the best combat corps commander in the American Army in WWII." His troops found his presence inspiring. In commanding his forces from the front, he often exposed himself to heavy fire that resulted in numerous close calls. Once, after being wounded by a German grenade, Ridgway refused treatment and thereafter carried a fragment in his shoulder.

Korea

When the Korean War broke out in 1950, Ridgway was in Washington, D.C., serving as the army's deputy chief of staff for administration. Lieutenant General **Walton H. "Johnnie" Walker** (1899–1950; see entry) had led the Eighth Army in Korea through the terrible first six months of war. On December 23, Walker was killed in a jeep accident near Seoul. That evening back in the United States, Ridgway was having a cocktail with some friends when he received a call from the Army Chief of Staff telling him that Walker was dead and that he had been preselected to replace him as commander of the Eighth Army in Korea. He was to get there at once.

The Korean War had at its heart an arrangement put into place at the end of World War II. In August 1945, when the Japanese, who were occupying Korea, were defeated, the general order for the Japanese surrender included a provision for Korea in which the Americans were to accept the Japanese surrender south of the 38th parallel (the dividing line between northern and southern Korea) and the Soviets, who were already on the Korean border, would receive the surrender north of it. Soon the United States requested that the United Nations sponsor elections in Korea, with the idea that Korea would become independent after a leader was elected. (The UN was founded in 1945 to maintain worldwide peace and to develop friendly relations among countries.) The Soviet Union and the northern Koreans, on the other hand, did not believe that the UN had the authority to decide the future of Korea, and they refused to take part in the elections. The vote was held in southern Korea anyway, without the northern Koreans, and a new government was formed to rule a united Republic of Korea (ROK). Not accepting that government, the Koreans in the north held their own elections and established the Democratic People's Republic of Korea (DPRK). In the summer of 1950, as North Korea invaded South Korea—both countries hoped to reunify Korea under their leadership—the United Nations, with the strong backing of the United States, entered the war to aid the South Koreans. After the North Koreans suffered massive losses in counterattacks by the South Koreans and their allies, the Chinese came to the aid of the North Koreans.

Ridgway's task in Korea was difficult. Chinese General **Peng Dehuai**'s (P'eng Teh-huai; 1898–1974; see entry) massive Chinese forces had crushed the UN troops that had advanced up toward the North Korea-China border at the Yalu River, forcing them into a massive retreat south below the 38th parallel. On their sweep from the north, the Chinese had mauled the First Cavalry Division, the Second Infantry Division, and the South Korean forces. The Eighth Army's morale had been drained. Some military experts doubted if the United States could maintain a foothold on the Korean peninsula.

It was the perfect job for Ridgway, who was noted for his motivational skills. On New Year's morning 1951, Ridgway was out at the front and, to his dismay, found many of his troops in retreat. Republic of Korea (ROK) soldiers "were streaming south, without order, without arms, without lead-

Matthew B. Ridgway
(center, with binoculars)
and his officers check
positions at the Korean
front, February 1951.
*Reproduced by permission
of AP/Wide World Photos.*

ers, in full retreat. . . . They had just one aim—to get as far away from the Chinese as possible." Some of the U.S. troops, too, were fleeing. Ridgway recalled in his book *The Korean War* interviewing the men, finding them "thoroughly dispirited, without the eagerness to rejoin the unit that American fighting men, when not too severely wounded, usually show. We were obviously a long way from building the will to fight that we needed."

Ridgway withdrew his troops south of Seoul, evacuating the capital city for the second time, and then proceeded with virtually rebuilding the Eighth Army. Finally attentive to the desperate need for troops and supplies in Korea, the U.S. military establishment was sending reinforcements in well-trained troops, weapons and ammunition, food rations, medical services, and high quality officers. Ridgway knew his task: "Before going on the offensive, we had work to do, weaknesses to shore up, mistakes to learn from, faulty procedures to correct, and a sense of pride to restore," he wrote in *The Korean*

War. This last task of restoring pride was perhaps the most fundamental and the one among many that Ridgway is best remembered for, because it was apparent to all concerned that he transformed his troops into courageous and loyal fighting men. Ridgway strapped a hand grenade into his vest as a symbol of the fight and toured the troops, shaking hands and learning people's names and what was bothering them. He built up the defense line and promised that no unit would be abandoned if the Chinese attacked. Ridgway then wrote a letter to all the troops, explaining why the UN forces were fighting in Korea in his view. His efforts were successful. Within a month the Chinese and North Koreans were facing a new enemy, one with the spirit to stand and fight when battles grew tough.

Operation Killer

Established south of Seoul, Ridgway began to suspect that the enemy was not always there. Although army intelligence systems reported that 178,000 Chinese troops faced the Eighth Army, Ridgway began to take low-flying scouting trips over enemy territory in an airplane, and could see no sign of them. He knew from recent history that the Chinese tended to attack very hard and then suddenly disappear, presumably to resupply. He decided to advance. With his troops in top form, organized by interlinked supporting units, he proceeded with his famous offensives.

On February 21, 1951, Ridgway launched Operation Killer (Killer and its extension Operation Ripper were later renamed Operation Courageous to connote a more benign [gentle] image, although Ridgway thought they should be named in accord with their objective, which was by no means benign). Operation Killer was enormous. Eight infantry divisions comprising more than one hundred thousand troops were backed by twenty-two artillery battalions, five tank battalions, and the Far East Air Force. Killer counterattacked the Chinese on the central front with the fresh First Marine Division as the focal point. The rejuvenated U.S. forces fought superbly, retaking Seoul and forcing the Chinese above the 38th parallel. "The Eighth Army soon proved itself to be what I knew already it could become: as fine a fighting field army as our country had yet produced," Ridgway described the troops in his memoirs. "They were fighting for themselves, with pride rekindled, and with a determination that they would never again take the sort of licking they had accepted a month before."

Taking over for MacArthur

After MacArthur was relieved of command for insubordination on April 11, 1951, Ridgway was appointed to serve simultaneously as commander in chief of the Far East command; commander in chief of the UN command; commander in chief of the U.S. Army forces Far East; and supreme commander of Allied forces occupying Japan. Ridgway relocated to Tokyo, where he would oversee the war for the remainder of the year. He was one of the central players in the early days of the peace talks at Panmunjom; it was Ridgway, for example, who insisted that the UN forces continue armed conflict during the truce negotiations because he did not trust the Chinese and North Koreans. The decision to fight while negotiating meant two years of high casualties and destruction for both sides.

Ridgway was by now an American hero. His charm made him a darling with the press, who described him in glowing terms. Ridgway's flowery articulation of his thoughts made him highly quotable for reporters, but evoked ridicule from some of the other officers, who saw him as artificial and humorless.

In May 1952, Ridgway replaced **Dwight D. Eisenhower** (1890–1969; see entry) as the supreme commander of Allied powers in Europe and as head of NATO. (NATO stands for North Atlantic Treaty Organization, an alliance of nations in Europe and North America formed in 1949 primarily to counter the threat of Soviet and communist expansion.) He left that position in October 1953 to become the army chief of staff. In that position he would play a major role in keeping the U.S. military from intervening in the French-Indochina (Vietnam) conflict. Ridgway retired from active duty to become director of Colt Industries in June 1955 after constant battles with the Eisenhower administration over relying too much on nuclear weapons (widely devastating atomic bombs) for America's defense.

Vietnam

During the 1960s, Ridgway advocated limiting U.S. involvement in Vietnam. He put forward a middle-ground approach between unilateral (one-sided) withdrawal and all-out war. He resisted air force general Curtis LeMay's suggestion that the United States bomb North Vietnam "back to the stone age." In March 1968, President Lyndon B. Johnson (1908–1973) invited Ridgway and several prominent former government officials and military men to form the Senior Advisory Group, which would help the president on his Vietnam strategy. The panel recommended the United States seek a negotiated settlement. Johnson concurred, announcing in March 1968 that the United States would deescalate and seek a peaceful resolution to the war.

Ridgway was married three times. His first two marriages, to Caroline Blount and Margaret Wilson, ended in divorce. In 1947, he married Marjory "Penny" Anthony Long and the marriage endured. He had two daughters, Constance and Shirley, and a son, Matthew B. Ridgway Jr., who died in train accident in 1971.

Ridgeway died at his home in Fox Chapel, Pennsylvania, in July 1993.

Where to Learn More

Clay, Blair. *The Forgotten War: America in Korea, 1950–1953*. New York: Times Books, 1987.

Clay, Blair. *Ridgway's Paratroopers*. New York: Dial Press, 1985.

Fleming, Thomas. "A Right Way, a Wrong Way, and a Ridgway." *Boys' Life*. November 2000, p. 40.

Ridgway, Matthew B. *The Korean War: How We Met the Challenge, How All-Out Asian War Was Averted, Why MacArthur Was Dismissed, Why Today's War Objectives Must Be Limited*. Garden City, NY: Doubleday, 1967.

Ridgway, Matthew B. *Soldier: The Memoirs of Matthew B. Ridgway*. New York: Harper, 1956.

Anna Rosenberg

Born June 19, 1902
Budapest, Hungary
Died May 9, 1983
New York, New York

Hungarian-born American public relations consultant, political appointee, and assistant secretary of defense

Even after "forty years of public and private business life, the situation—vis á vis women in careers— has not changed substantially."

Portrait reproduced by permission of AP/Wide World Photos.

When Anna Rosenberg came of age in the second decade of the twentieth century, women did not have the right to vote and segregation between the races was standard. From her childhood and throughout her life, Rosenberg served her country with a clear vision of equality and justice for all people. As assistant secretary of defense for manpower and personnel during the Korean War (1950–53), Anna Rosenberg achieved the highest position in the U.S. military ever held by a woman. Things were changing for women and minorities in the 1950s in the military as elsewhere, and there were many people in powerful positions in the military and in the government who were not comfortable with the changes. Rosenberg faced the male-dominated public world with grace and with power. In her capacity as assistant secretary of defense, she was responsible for bringing many women into the military, for helping to bring about the desegregation of African Americans and whites in the armed services, and for developing training programs and improving conditions for everyone in the service.

Anna Marie Lederer Rosenberg was born in 1902 in Budapest, Hungary, the daughter of Albert Lederer, a successful furniture manufacturer, and Charlotte Lederer, the author and illustrator of children's books. The family lived a comfortable life in Budapest until Rosenberg was ten years old. Albert Lederer's prosperous business was destroyed at that time, when Franz Joseph (1830–1916), the Austrian emperor and Hungarian king, canceled a large furniture order. Lederer, disgusted that the whim of a monarch could instantly ruin his life's work, moved with his family to the United States in 1912. They settled in the Bronx, New York.

An activist from age twelve

Anna Rosenberg became active in politics while attending New York City's Wadleigh High School. In 1914, at the age of twelve, she organized the Future Voters League, an association dedicated to woman's suffrage (the right to vote; women gained full voting rights in the United States in 1928). Next World War I (1914–18) took up her energy and attention. She volunteered at a military hospital in Manhattan and sold Liberty Bonds and Thrift Stamps, investments people could buy to help finance the war effort. In 1919, she married a soldier, Julius Rosenberg, and became a citizen of the United States. Two years later, at the age of 21, she gave birth to their son, Thomas, her only child.

In the 1920s, Rosenberg was active in Democratic politics in New York. After managing a successful campaign for a city elder, she opened her own business as a public relations, personnel, and labor consultant. The business was extremely successful, and one of her clients was the (then) governor of New York, Franklin D. Roosevelt (1882–1945), who wanted her help on important labor matters. In 1934, she became an assis-

Words to Know

cold war: the struggle for power, authority, and prestige between the communist Soviet Union and the capitalist Western powers of Europe and the United States from 1945 until 1991.

demobilization: bringing the soldiers home.

desegregation: eliminating separation of people because of race or other factors.

integration: the act of bringing all the groups of individuals within an organization into the whole as equals; the elimination of separate facilities and structures for different racial groups.

mobilization: assembling soldiers to serve in the war.

segregation: the separation of different groups of individuals within an organization or society.

suffrage: the right to vote.

tant to the regional director of the National Recovery Administration and then took over as regional director.

From 1936 to 1942, Rosenberg served as a regional commissioner for New York for the Social Security Board, the first woman to hold the position. At the same time, she served on many boards in New York City, working closely with New York City Mayor Fiorello H. LaGuardia (1882–1947). She also worked at the state level, and on vital national issues, performing an extensive study on labor relations for (now) President Roosevelt. She kept her consulting business running successfully through it all. In 1942, the U.S. House Appropriations Committee investigated the possible conflict of interest Rosenberg might have between her position in the Social Security administration and her own consulting firm. She convinced them that none of her other work conflicted with her government duties. Her tireless energy and interest enabled her to do several jobs and do them extremely well. La Guardia once said, as quoted in *Current Biography,* that she knew "more about labor relations and human relations than any man in the country."

The observer for presidents, World War II

During World War II (1939–45), Rosenberg became the first woman to hold the post of regional director of the War Manpower Commission, a position she held from 1942 to 1945. In 1944, she accepted a short-term position as the chief assistant to Brigadier General Frank T. Hines, director of retraining and re-employment. In 1944, she toured the theater of war operations in Europe at the request of Roosevelt to serve as his personal observer and especially to find out what the enlisted men wanted from the government when the war was over. After interviewing the troops in the field, Rosenberg concluded that they wanted access to the kind of education that had been too expensive for them to consider in the past. She came back a champion of the GI Bill, which provided funds for a college education as a benefit of joining the service, and saw the bill pass. In 1945, President **Harry S. Truman** (1884–1972; see entry) sent her on another mission to Europe, at the war's end, to oversee demobilization, bringing the soldiers home.

Rosenberg was by this time quite an expert on military personnel issues and was known for her progressive values regarding women and minorities. After leaving her position on

the War Manpower Commission, she returned to her consulting firm, but continued to serve on many boards and committees related to military personnel.

War in Korea

When the Korean War erupted on June 25, 1950, there were dire shortages of military personnel. Truman had, after World War II, reduced the military budget drastically and the number of troops available was desperately low. When it was decided that the United States was going to send ground troops into Korea, a twelve-member committee was formed to investigate and advise on mobilization (assembling soldiers to serve in the war). Rosenberg was one of the members. Later in 1950, Rosenberg was offered the position of assistant secretary of defense for manpower and personnel, serving under Secretary of Defense George C. Marshall (1880–1959). She was confirmed for the position by the Senate Arms Services Committee.

Anna Rosenberg touring the Twenty-fifth Division positions on the Korean front in October 1951, flanked by James A. Van Fleet (right) and Lieutenant General William Hoge.
Reproduced by permission of AP/Wide World Photos.

Just as she assumed her new position, Rosenberg temporarily became a victim of the cold war. Rumors began to spread that she was a communist, and her appointment as assistant secretary of defense was revoked. (The cold war was a period of political tension and military rivalry between the United States and the communist Soviet Union that began after World War II and persisted until the breakup of the Soviet Union in 1991. Communism is a set of political beliefs that advocates the elimination of private property, a system in which goods are owned by the community as a whole rather than by specific individuals and are available to all as needed. Communism is at odds with the American economic system, capitalism, in which individuals, rather than the state, own the property and businesses.) Senator **Joseph McCarthy** (1908–1957; see entry) of Wisconsin, who had stirred up the American public by accusing many government officials of being communists, had been involved in the accusations against Rosenberg, as was a member of the racist group the Ku Klux Klan. It was a time when rumors and false accusations ruined many careers, and observers felt that Rosenberg was being targeted because she was a woman, because she was Jewish, and because she held liberal values that would lead to change. In the investigation that followed she was quickly cleared of having communist affiliations and reinstated to her post.

As assistant secretary of defense, Rosenberg was responsible for coordinating all of the Defense Department's personnel activities, which had previously been carried out among a number of agencies. The first major project she undertook was to draft what later came to be known as the Universal Service and Training bill. The goal of the Defense Department was to keep the nation's labor resources equally distributed among farms, factories, and the military. The new bill provided for training enough eighteen-year-olds to maintain a force of more than three million troops by July 1951, which entailed lowering the draft age to eighteen.

New recruits, better conditions

In 1948, Congress had passed the Women's Armed Forces Integration Act, which aimed to open military career prospects to women. With the outbreak of war and shortage of personnel, Rosenberg sought ways to recruit more women into military service. She knew from personal experience that women entering what had always been a man's world were going to encounter obstacles to advancement and social snubbing. In August 1951, she established the Defense Advisory Committee on Women in the Services (DACOWITS). This group of fifty accomplished women from a wide range of professions led a drive to recruit women into military service. They also investigated ways to improve the conditions under which women would serve, such as providing women with access to prestigious career paths and educating the public to accept women in important professional roles.

Before the war in Korea, most of the American military was still racially segregated (African Americans were separated from whites). Coming into the war, it had some all-black units. The men in those units were not always treated well by the rest of the army and the training and leadership were often inferior. President Truman had signed Executive Order 9981 in 1948, which provided for "equality of treatment and opportunity for all persons in the Armed Forces," but only the air force had actually integrated its troops, with African Americans and other minorities living and working in the same facilities. The army had dragged its feet on the issue. Rosenberg, always an advocate of civil rights, oversaw the racial integration of the services. During the war, the last of the segregated units were deactivated and the men from the all-black units were absorbed into other, integrated units.

In 1953, when the Republican **Dwight D. Eisenhower** (1890–1969; see entry) came into office as president, the Democratic Rosenberg was replaced as assistant secretary of defense. The 1950s were a tough time for women and minorities, but Rosenberg had done a great deal to change the make-up of the military personnel during the war, and more to keep it progressing in the years to come.

Private citizen Rosenberg

Rosenberg was never exempt from the prejudices of the day. Most of the press coverage of her in the 1950s and 1960s reported more on her bracelets and hats than on her exceptional public service. However, she won the respect of so many of the nation's leaders that it is clear she was highly skilled in negotiating in a men's world, and, according to most sources, she did it with dignity, humor, and intelligence.

After the war, Rosenberg returned to her public relations firm, where she worked for thirty more years. She remained active on boards and committees, earning the nickname "Seven Job Anna." In 1968, President Lyndon B. Johnson (1908–1973) appointed her to serve on the Commission on Income Maintenance, a committee formed to study welfare programs. She received many awards in her lifetime, including being the first civilian to receive the Medal of Freedom (1945) and the first woman to receive the Medal for Merit (1947). She was also honored with a Horatio Alger Award (1949); Department of Defense Exceptional Civilian Award (1953); Medallion of the City of New York (1966); and a Congressional Certificate of Appreciation (1972). From the age of twelve, when she started organizing for woman suffrage, to the day she died from complications of cancer in 1983, Rosenberg had skillfully and tirelessly served her country.

Where to Learn More

Tananbaum, Susan L. "Anna Lederer Rosenberg." In *Jewish Women in America: A Historical Encyclopedia,* Vol. II, edited by Paula E. Hyman and Deborah Dash Moore. New York: Routledge, 1997.

Thurston, Christy. "Anna Marie Lederer Rosenberg." In *American National Biography,* Vol. 18, edited by John A. Garraty and Mark C. Carnes. New York: Oxford University Press, 1999.

Web sites

United States Army. "Women in the Korean War." Fiftieth Anniversary of the Korean War Commemoration Site. [Online] http://korea50.army.mil/history/factsheets/women.html (accessed on August 14, 2001).

Oliver P. Smith

Born October 26, 1893
Menard, Texas
Died December 25, 1977
Los Altos, California

American military leader

A s the commander of the First Division of the U.S. Marines, Oliver P. Smith led the highly acclaimed division in its renowned battles in the first year of the Korean War: the successful amphibious landing at Inchon and the grueling battles against the Chinese in the Chosin (Changjin) Reservoir. Smith was a thoughtful, cautious military leader who preferred strategy and planning to rash actions. Known for being soft-spoken and polite, when it came to risking the lives of the men in his command, Smith objected loudly and strongly to the orders from his superiors, General Edward M. Almond (1892–1979), the commander of the X Corps, and General **Douglas MacArthur** (1880–1964; see entry), the commander of the United Nations forces in Korea. Very few military leaders, including his superiors, had dared stand up to MacArthur, even when they knew he was making rash and dangerous decisions. Many historians credit Smith's heroic leadership in Chosin for saving the lives of large numbers of his troops and avoiding a total massacre.

Becoming a marine

Oliver Prince Smith was born in 1893 in Texas but grew up in California. He attended the University of California at

"We've been looking for the enemy for several days now. We've finally found them. We're surrounded. That simplifies our problem of getting to these people and killing them."

Portrait reproduced by permission of AP/Wide World Photos.

Berkeley, graduating in 1916. In 1917, he was commissioned a second lieutenant in the U.S. Marine Corps Reserve. When the United States entered World War I (1914–18), he was stationed at Guam in the western Pacific, where he joined the regular Marine Corps.

After World War I ended, Smith held a number of positions in the Marine Corps, including commanding a marine unit aboard a ship for two years and being attached to the *gendarmerie,* a combined army and police force, in Haiti for three years. He graduated from the army's infantry school and from the école Supérieure de Guerre in Paris, France, and became an instructor in operations and training, specializing in amphibious warfare (carried out on land, sea, and air), at the marine corps school in Quantico, Virginia.

In June 1940, Smith became commanding officer of the First Battalion of the Sixth Marine Regiment and in May 1941, took the regiment to Iceland, where he remained until March 1942.

World War II

Smith spent the first years of U.S. involvement in World War II (1939–45) in Washington D.C. In May 1942, he became the executive officer of the Division of Plans and spent two years on the staff at the Marine Corps Headquarters. He was given a combat assignment in January 1944 as the commander of the Fifth Marine Regiment, First Division. He successfully led the regiment through a campaign in New Britain, an island in the South Pacific that is part of New Guinea. After the campaign he was promoted to brigadier general and became the assistant commander of the First Marine Division. In that position, Smith commanded the operations on the beaches of the Peleliu and Ngesebus Islands in the September and October 1944 campaign.

Smith was quickly earning the respect of his superiors for his carefully planned strategies and his intelligent assessment of situations. For his action in the South Pacific islands he received a Legion of Merit Award, which read, in part (as quoted in the Marine Corps Research Center, Marine Corps University, O. P. Smith Collection):

> Brigadier General Smith displayed marked professional skill
> in supervision of the training of the division in landing opera-

tions, greatly enhancing its efficiency in the technique of reef landing to a point where successful landings on both islands were made under the most difficult of conditions. Although the initial beachhead was under intense enemy fire, Brigadier General Smith coolly coordinated the three assault regimental combat teams so that the division was able to advance to its initial objectives, repel several intense counterattacks, and launch an attack which gained the Peleliu airdrome.

After the action at Peleliu, Smith served as the Marine Corps deputy chief of staff to the commander of the Tenth Army, to which the First Marines Division was attached. With the Tenth Army he saw action in the Okinawa, Japan, campaign just prior to the end of the war. After World War II, Smith returned to the United States to become the commandant of the Marine Corps School at Quantico.

The Korean War begins

Though the Korean War began in 1950, it was rooted in an arrangement established at the end of World War II. In August 1945, when the Japanese, who were occupying Korea, were defeated, the general order for their surrender included a provision for Korea that had the U.S. troops accepting the Japanese surrender south of the 38th parallel (the dividing line between northern and southern Korea) and the Soviets, who were already on the Korean border, receiving the surrender north of it. Soon the United Nations, and the U.S. government's request, sponsored elections in Korea, with the idea that Korea would become independent after a leader was chosen. (The UN was founded in 1945 to maintain worldwide peace and to develop friendly relations among countries.) The Soviet Union and the northern Koreans did not accept the United Nations' authority to decide the future of Korea, and they refused to take part in the elections. The vote was nonetheless held in southern Korea, without the northern Koreans, and a new government was formed to rule a united Republic of Korea (ROK). Not accepting that government, the Koreans in the north held their own elections and established the Democratic People's Republic of Korea (DPRK). In the summer of 1950, as North Korea invaded South Korea—both countries hoped to reunify Korea under their leadership—the United Nations, with the strong backing of the United States, entered the war to aid the South Koreans. After the North Koreans suffered massive

Troops of the First Cavalry Division splash ashore at Pohang on the east coast of Korea, July 19, 1950, in the first combat amphibious operation since World War II. Oliver P. Smith, an expert in amphibious attacks, would soon lead the landing at Inchon.
Reproduced by permission of AP/Wide World Photos.

losses in counterattacks by the South Koreans and their allies, the Chinese came to the aid of the North Koreans.

By 1950, Smith had been promoted to major general. He took command of the First Marine Division at around the time the North Koreans invaded South Korea on June 25, 1950. In the early days of the war, the better trained and equipped North Korean People's Army relentlessly drove the South Koreans as well as U.S. Army troops steadily southward in one disorganized retreat after another. By the end of July, U.S. and South Korean forces were concentrated in an area called the Pusan Perimeter, in southeast South Korea. By the end of July, it was clear that the training and experience of the marines was desperately needed.

Meanwhile, General Douglas MacArthur had a plan. He formed a new corps separate from General **Walton H. "Johnnie" Walker**'s (1889–1950; see entry) Eighth Army, then penned in at the Pusan Perimeter. MacArthur's new X Corps, under the command of General Almond, would carry out an amphibious invasion (a coordinated attack using land, sea, and air) at the port of Inchon, thirty miles from Seoul and well to the north of the defense line. Knowing that the First Marines were on their way to Asia, he asked the Joint Chiefs of Staff to send them to him for deployment at Inchon. (The Joint Chiefs are the advisors to the president and the secretary of defense on matters of war and are responsible for developing battle plans and directing unified combat actions.) After heated debate, the Joint Chiefs reluctantly agreed. Between August 14 and 18, 1950, Smith sent a hastily pulled-together division by ship to Asia.

Inchon

MacArthur's plans to land at Inchon caused a great deal of concern among military and defense leaders. The tides at Inchon are among the most dangerous in the world, the islands surrounding it were held by the enemy, and there were many other ports that made more sense. Smith, an expert on amphibious warfare, was among those who argued for another point of attack. He tried to discuss the matter with Almond, but Almond was insulting and dismissive to Smith, starting ill will between the two that lasted into other battles. Smith said of his conference with Almond, as quoted in Joseph C. Goulden's *Korea: The Untold Story of the War:* "I tried to tell him a few of the facts of life, and he was rather supercilious [patronizing or haughty], and he called me 'son,' which kind of annoyed me."

Smith and his division went ahead with the plans for Inchon. In one of the most famous battles of the war, a huge fleet of ships, well supported by aircraft, landed at the port city without much difficulty. The marines were the first to hit the beaches and secure the city, incurring few casualties. Inchon was a smashing success and the months of retreat were over.

On from Inchon

The X Corps drove on from Inchon to liberate the capital city of Seoul from the North Koreans. Almond told Smith that MacArthur wanted the capture of the city by September 25, to mark the three-month anniversary of the initial invasion of the South on June 25. Smith viewed the order with some disgust, not wanting to rush the operation and risk hundreds of his troops' lives for a publicity gesture. Smith's own strategy for invasion would have cut off the enemy from aid, ensuring the safety of his men, but it would have taken longer. Almond wanted a direct attack immediately. The arguments persisted. In the end Smith obeyed Almond's orders, but ordered his units to move slowly and with great caution. They fought a desperate battle against the well-armed North Koreans. Even after the main battle, there were several more days of vicious fighting inside the city before the UN forces held the capital. Smith later learned that Almond told the press that Seoul had been recaptured before the first battle had even started.

After the capture of Seoul, the North Korean army was exhausted, and the Eighth Army and X Corps pushed on up to the 38th parallel and beyond. MacArthur split the two armies, with the Eighth Army going by ground north from the 38th parallel and X Corps going by boat to the port city of Wonsan. Smith grimly obeyed orders that cost the Marines two weeks at sea when they could have been in hot pursuit by land. When the Marines finally reached Wonsan, the South Korean soldiers had already liberated it.

The Battle at the Chosin Reservoir

After great delay, the First Marines moved on, again under the command of Almond, up into North Korea toward its border with China at the Yalu River. The X Corps was still split from the Eighth Army. Having heard that Chinese troops had attacked the South Korean soldiers, Smith was very apprehensive about following the orders to send his division into the Chosin (Changjin) Reservoir in North Korea. If an attack of any power occurred, they were without standard support and there were too few of them to safely cover such a large territory.

Smith was in a difficult position. Known as the "intellectual" Marine—soft-spoken, thoughtful, polite, and very intelligent—he reacted strongly against the rashness of MacArthur's plan to race up through North Korea without adequate support for his units. While the Joint Chiefs and the Truman administration were very concerned about MacArthur's plans to use UN forces near the Chinese border and especially about his splitting the Eighth Army from the X Corps, no one had the nerve to stand up to the charismatic and dramatic commanding general. Smith had the nerve. He argued fiercely with the commander up until the day the order came through to proceed. Then he had no alternative but to obey. He ordered an airstrip to be built in the city of Hagaru, so that casualties—of which he thought there would be many—could be taken out. He ordered his units to move north from the port of Hungnam very slowly, taking time to continuously restock ammunition and supplies. His precautions were to save many lives in the brutal days ahead.

On the night of November 27, 1950, as the Marines of the Fifth and Seventh regiments set up positions in the frozen hills of the Chosin Reservoir, three Chinese divisions attacked. The Chinese had heard of the First Marine Division and knew it was a formidable enemy, so they sent a powerful force out to annihilate them. The marines were outnumbered by more than three to one and the casualties were tremendous. The Chinese cut off their road of exit and surrounded them.

That night, an anguished Smith listened by radio to the reports of what was happening to his marines in Chosin. The Eighth Army had already been defeated and there was no longer any point to the offensive. His men were being slaughtered for a doomed mission. He desperately tried to reach Almond to get new orders. He did not hear back from Almond for nearly two days. Unable to order a retreat without permission, Smith ordered the Fifth and Seventh Marine regiments to forget their offensive, but to continue to defend their positions.

"When you break out, you attack"

In the late hours of November 28, Smith finally received orders to retreat. Under the very extreme circumstances, he staged a remarkably orderly withdrawal of the First Division while it was being assaulted by eight enemy divisions. Under his skillful leadership his troops were able to inflict great damage on the attacking Chinese units and remain in position as they worked their way out of the trap. The marines had no history of retreating and the breaking story caused a sensation worldwide. When war correspondents questioned Smith about the retreat, he snapped back at them, "Retreat, hell, we are simply attacking in another direction." The quote became famous. Donald Knox's oral history *The Korean War: Pusan to Chosin* provides Smith's explanation of this quote from a later interview: "You can't retreat or withdraw when you are surrounded. The only thing you can do is break out. When you break out, you attack. That's what we were doing." In fact, the retreat to Hagaru from November 28 through December 5 presented some of the most brutal fighting in the Korean War.

When they had completed one of the most fierce ordeals in U.S. Marine history, the marines had not been able to carry out their mission, but they had defied the Chinese efforts to annihilate them. The Chinese had sent twelve divisions to face three American and two South Korean divisions and they had focused most of their manpower on the First Marines. By managing to survive at such odds, in brutal sub-zero temperatures, the First Marines had a true victory. But of the approximately twenty-five thousand troops from the UN forces in the Chosin campaign, there were six thousand casualties: one in every four men had been killed, wounded, or was missing in action.

By the new year, the X Corps was incorporated into the Eighth Army. Smith returned to the United States in the spring of 1951, where he took command of the Marine base Camp Pendleton in southern California. He was promoted to lieutenant general in 1953 and took command of the Fleet Marine Force, Atlantic. He retired from the military in 1955 to live a private life for the next twelve years. Smith was married to Esther King and the couple had two daughters. He died in Los Altos, California, in 1977.

Where to Learn More

Alexander, Bevin. *Korea: The First War We Lost*. New York: Hippocrene Books, 1986, revised edition, 2000.

Goulden, Joseph C. *Korea: The Untold Story of the War*. New York: Times Books, 1982.

Knox, Donald. *The Korean War: Pusan to Chosin: An Oral History*. New York: Harcourt Brace Jovanovich, 1988.

Ohl, John Kennedy. "Oliver P. Smith." In *The Korean War: An Encyclopedia,* edited by Stanley Sandler. New York: Garland Publishing, 1999.

Webster's American Military Biographies. Springfield, MA: G. & C. Merriam Company, 1978.

Web sites

"O. P. Smith Collection." Marine Corps Research Center, Marine Corps University. [Online] http://www.mcu.usmc.mil/MCRCweb/archive5smith.html (accessed on August 14, 2001).

Joseph Stalin

Born December 21, 1879
Gori, Russia
Died March 5, 1953
Union of Soviet Socialist Republics

Soviet revolutionary and political leader

"One feature of the history of old Russia was the continual beatings she suffered because of her backwardness. . . . We are fifty or one hundred years behind the advanced countries. . . . We must make good this distance in ten years. Either we do it, or we shall go under."

Portrait reproduced by permission of AP/Wide World Photos.

Joseph Stalin took control of the Soviet Union after the death of Vladimir Lenin (1870–1924), the force behind the October revolutions of 1917 that established the Soviet regime. During Stalin's thirty-year dictatorial rule, the Soviet Union greatly enlarged its territory and transformed itself from a relatively backward country into the second most important industrial nation in the world. These achievements came at a heavy price, which included the loss of millions of lives, political repression, an untold waste of resources, and the establishment of an inflexible and dictatorial system of rule.

Childhood

Joseph Stalin was born Iosif Vissarionovich Dzhugashvili on December 21, 1879, in Gori, Georgia, a part of czarist Russia's empire in western Asia. (A czar is a ruler who exercises unlimited power over the people.) His father, a former serf (member of a servant class who works the soil), was a shoemaker, and his mother was a domestic servant.

Iosif, or Joseph, better known as Soso, grew up speaking Georgian and only learned Russian at the age of eight or nine. In 1888 he began attending the church school at Gori. He did well in his classes, especially in religious studies, geography, and Georgian. He also studied Greek and Russian. When he left the school in 1894, he was near the top of his class.

Seminary student

Stalin won a scholarship to study at the Tbilisi Theological Seminary, Georgia's leading educational institution. During his first year there, he received high marks; the next year, however, he began to rebel against the institution's stern religious rules. He smuggled banned books into school, and joined secret study groups opposed to the Russian czarist government. At one point he was sent to a punishment cell for five hours for not bowing to a school official. In 1899, the seminary directors expelled him for spreading subversive views (extremist ideas, often against the government). Stalin's mother wanted him to become a priest and was disappointed when he pursued another course in life. Years later, even after he had become leader of the Soviet Union, she considered him a failure for not having completed his religious studies.

Discovery of Marx

Stalin had begun reading Marxist works while still at the seminary, focusing especially on the writings of Russian Marxist Vladimir Lenin. Marxism—the belief that a revolution by the working class would eventually lead to a classless society—would furnish the basis of Stalin's worldview for the rest of his life.

In 1899, Stalin was hired as an accountant at the Tbilisi observatory. Russia's Social Democrats, members of a communist party opposed by the czar, had been using the observatory as a hideout, and Stalin ultimately joined them. (Communism is a set of political beliefs that advocates the elimination of private property. It is a system in which goods are owned by the community as a whole rather than by specific individuals and are available to all as needed.) A police raid exposed this association, and Stalin was fired from his accounting job. From this point on, Stalin was a professional revolutionary.

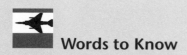

Words to Know

atomic bomb: a powerful bomb created by splitting the nuclei of a heavy chemical, such as plutonium or uranium, in a rapid chain reaction, resulting in a violent and destructive shock wave as well as radiation.

collective farm: a farm under government control, in which the government dictates what will be grown, how much of it, and what the farmworkers will be paid for their work.

Communism: a system of government in which one party (usually the Communist Party) controls all property and goods and the means to produce and distribute them.

czar: a Russian ruler who exercises unlimited power over the people.

Gulag: a network of labor camps in Russia for people accused of committing crimes against the state.

industrialization: causing a place to become more devoted to industry, the manufacture or refinement of products in a systemized manner and usually by many people in one place, as a factory or plant.

Marxism: the belief, originating with German political philosopher Karl Marx that a revolution by the working class would eventually lead to a classless society.

paranoia: a condition in which someone feels obsessive suspicion and has delusions that others are bent on doing him or her harm.

purges: a method of removing or eliminating unwanted elements or members from an organization.

sabotage: deliberate destructive acts designed to undermine a person, organization, or army.

serf: member of a servant class who works the soil.

subversive: tending toward the destruction or overthrow of an institution or government from within.

Western nations: the noncommunist nations of Europe and America.

Early days as a revolutionary

At the turn of the twentieth century, Stalin became active in the militant wing of the Russian Social Democratic Party. He was arrested in 1902 and deported to Siberia, a frozen wasteland in eastern Russia, but he escaped and was back in Georgia two years later. He first met Lenin, the leader of the radical Bolshevik faction of the Social Democratic Party, in 1905, and became a devoted follower. *Bolsheviki* in Russian means "majority," though the Bolsheviks didn't have greater numbers in the party. The Bolsheviks thought the party would be more effective if it were small, limited to professional revolutionaries whose actions were coordinated. Their opponents in the party, the Mensheviks (minority), believed in a mass party that was loosely organized. Lenin secretly approved of bank robberies, which he called "expropriations," to finance the Bolsheviks. In 1907, Stalin was involved in several bank heists in Georgia. To avoid connection with any illegal activities, the local party expelled him, and he disappeared. He spent the next few years organizing Bolshevik factions and spending time in exile.

In 1912, Lenin broke from the Social Democratic Party and formed a new party. That year Stalin spent some time with Lenin and his wife in Krakow, in present-day Poland, and then went to Vienna, Austria, to study Marxist literature. Lenin saw in Stalin a dependable—and ruthless—enforcer of the Bolsheviks' will and nominated him to the party's Central Committee. However, Stalin was arrested shortly thereafter and exiled once again to Siberia, where he remained until the czar was overthrown in 1917. He adopted the name Stalin ("man of steel") about 1913.

The new Soviet government

After the fall of czarism, Stalin made his way at once to Petrograd (St. Petersburg). The October Revolution of 1917 placed the Bolsheviks in power and Lenin became the new ruler of Russia. Lenin had come to admire Stalin for his loyalty and his organizational talents, particularly the way he could get things done, and he named Stalin to his cabinet as Commissar of Nationalities. In his book, *Stalin: Breaker of Nations,* Robert Conquest quotes an insight into Stalin's particular set of strengths made by American communist John Reed, who observed that Stalin was "not an intellectual. . . . He's not even well informed, but he knows what he wants. He's got the willpower, and he's going to be at the top of the pile some day."

ment of industries through systemized manufacturing or refinement of products by many people in one place, usually a factory or plant. Stalin's Five-Year Plan for industrialization officially began in 1928. Factories, dams, and other enterprises were constructed all across the Soviet Union. By late 1932, Soviet factories were producing basic industrial products such as steel, machine tools, and tractors. However, these achievements had a high cost and caused much suffering for the Russian people. Workers were paid low wages, sometimes only enough to buy the basic necessities of life. Consumer goods and food were often scarce. Changing jobs without permission became illegal, and interior passports were issued to restrict free movement among citizens. Much of the construction work on canals, mines, and other enterprises was performed by political prisoners who were sent by the millions into the Gulag, a network of labor camps for people accused of committing crimes against the state. Anyone accused of sabotage (deliberate destructive acts by a discontented employee against an employer) or wrecking could be shot.

Collectivization of agriculture

Meanwhile, in late 1929, Stalin instigated the collectivization of agriculture, in which farmers would be forced to abandon their individual farms and move onto state-owned collective farms. His extreme policy included executing or deporting the more prosperous peasants, who were called *kulaks* (tightwads). The rest of the peasants were to be placed on state-controlled communal farms. This program met with massive resistance from the farmers, who resented being driven from their land, but the government was ruthless. Millions of kulaks were shot or sent to labor camps. In Ukraine, southern Russia, and Khazakstan, millions more died in artificial famines created when Soviet officials confiscated the farmers' grain. By 1939, most of Soviet agriculture had been collectivized. In all, twenty-six million farmers were placed on 250,000 collective farms, but it had cost more than ten million lives.

Power gone astray: The purges

Stalin developed a so-called cult of personality around himself, meaning that his rule was to be perceived as that of an almost godlike father, beloved and obeyed without question by his people. Dozens of cities, towns, and villages were named after him, as was the tallest mountain in the Soviet Union. In books and movies, he was compared to the sun, moon, and stars. In one famous poem of the 1930s, as quoted in the *Houston Chronicle*, he was called the "Genius of all mankind" who "didst give birth to man . . . who didst make fertile the earth."

Behind Stalin's power lay a monstrous policy of terror. It reached its height between 1934 and 1939, when Stalin and his secret police carried out mass arrests, executions, and deportations. Stalin claimed that throughout the country traitors were masking as loyal citizens. Countless millions of innocent people perished or spent long years in forced labor camps. Victims included top party and government elites, army officers, artists, writers, scientists, and even children. From the party's Central Committee elected in 1934, 98 out of 139 members were shot.

Stalin had an irrational fear of his enemies. In December 1934, Sergey Kirov (1886–1934), one of his old supporters, was murdered. Kirov's popularity among some Communist Party leaders may have angered Stalin and prompted him to arrange his death, although it has never been proven. Stalin blamed the death on his old enemies Kamenev and Zinovyev. Using the murder as his reason to go after traitors, he then launched a series of purges to eliminate unwanted individuals in which millions of people were eventually shot or sent to the Gulag. Stalin personally signed orders for the execution of thousands of Soviet citizens.

In a move that seriously impaired the Soviet Union's ability to defend itself, Stalin ordered a purge of the armed forces in 1937 that took the lives of most of the country's marshals, generals, and admirals. When World War II broke out a few years later, the Soviet Union would suffer severely for its lack of trained military leaders.

Germany violates its agreement

In 1939, Stalin worked out a nonaggression treaty with German leader Adolf Hitler (1889–1945). Despite the treaty, Germany invaded the Soviet Union in 1941, forcing it into World War II on the side of the Allies (which included Great Britain and the United States). The initial Soviet losses were devastating, for Stalin had ignored warnings that an attack was coming. For nearly two weeks after the attack, Stalin secluded himself, apparently suffering a nervous breakdown. He reemerged to take personal command of the war effort, and in October 1941, with German troops at the gates of Moscow, he refused to leave the city.

By the end of the war in 1945, Stalin stood at the height of his power and fully shared in the glory of the victory. During the war, he had insisted on conducting diplomacy himself. At the wartime conferences, he won the respect of the Allied leaders U.S. President Franklin D. Roosevelt (1882–1945) and British Prime Minister Winston Churchill (1874–1965). The Soviets, having secured the status of a major world power, demanded and received control over much of Eastern Europe.

Postwar relations with Allied leaders

In February 1945, Churchill, Stalin, and Roosevelt met at Yalta in Ukraine, in the Crimea, where they sealed the fate of Poland. Churchill and Roosevelt accepted the provisional Polish government supported by Moscow in return for the promise of free elections for the Polish people. At the Potsdam Conference in July 1945, the three leaders divided Germany into occupation zones. Stalin wanted to cart off as much of Germany's industry as he could, both to help rebuild the Soviet economy and to prevent Germany's recovery. The other Allied powers sought to rehabilitate Germany economically, knowing that not to do so would mean costly Western aid in the future. Stalin was not interested in rehabilitating Germany.

The Soviet bloc

Stalin's postwar foreign policy was a continuation of his wartime goals. In Eastern Europe, he wanted to gain political control over the areas the Soviet army was occupying to form a Soviet bloc of nations. He supported the rise of communist regimes in Poland, Bulgaria, Albania, Rumania, Yugoslavia, Hungary, and Czechoslovakia. In the end, the Soviets maneuvered themselves into control in these nations and began transforming the various economies and societies into copies of the Soviet model.

Stalin had trouble with the Chinese Communists. After World War II, Stalin, underestimating the Communists' power, urged **Mao Zedong** (Mao Tse-tung; 1893–1976), the Chinese Communist leader, to join the Nationalist government of **Chiang Kai-shek** (1887–1975; see entries). The Russians were drawn to the larger and better organized Nationalist group, which had been founded by revolutionary leader Sun Yat-sen (1866–1925). Although a Nationalist, Sun Yat-sen

An overhead view during the "Big Three" meeting in Potsdam, between Joseph Stalin, Harry S. Truman, and British Prime Minister Clement Attlee, July 1945. *Reproduced by permission of Archive Photos, Inc.*

had welcomed help from the Soviets. With their assistance, he had built the Kuomintang party along Soviet lines. In 1921, the Chinese Communist Party was founded in Shanghai, and the Soviets immediately requested that the new Chinese Communist Party cooperate with the Kuomintang. For several years they did. In 1927, however, Chiang, who succeeded Sun as leader of the Nationalists, turned his army on the Communists, slaughtering thousands, and beginning the long and bloody war between the two groups. Mao continued to fight the Nationalists, and the Communists eventually came to power on October 1, 1949. Stalin continued to provide economic assistance to the Chinese in the hope of ensuring Chinese dependency, but the relationship continued to be marked by mistrust.

The Berlin Blockade

By 1948, the British and Americans had merged their occupation zones in Germany in anticipation of German statehood, a merger to which Stalin strenuously objected. On June 18 of that year, the Soviets stopped all surface traffic between the West and the capital city of Berlin, also divided, citing technical problems with the routes. This was followed by a cutoff of electricity, coal, and food to the city: the Berlin Blockade was in place. The Anglo-American powers immediately began an airlift of essential supplies to Berlin, which held out until Stalin called off the blockade in May 1949. The failure of Stalin's eleven-month blockade was an acute embarrassment to the Soviet government.

Soviet atomic weaponry

On August 29, 1949, the Soviets detonated their first atomic device, finally achieving one of Stalin's primary postwar goals: acquisition of the weapon that would allow the Soviets to attain military equality with the United States. (The United States had detonated two atomic bombs over Japan in August 1945 to speed the end of the war.) When he was first informed of the bomb's existence in 1945, Stalin had appeared quite unimpressed by it, but he had immediately ordered his scientists and those captured from Germany to increase their efforts to develop nuclear weapons for the Soviet Union.

The Korean War

At the end of World War II, the general order for Japan's surrender included a provision for Korea, which Japan had occupied for decades, that had the U.S. troops accepting the Japanese surrender south of the 38th parallel (the dividing line between northern and southern Korea) and the Soviets, who were already on the Korean border, receiving the surrender north of it. The Soviets were soon helping the northern Koreans develop a communist government and economic system. In negotiating with the United States, which was bolstering anticommunist forces in the south, the Soviets continually asked that the foreign powers withdraw and leave the Koreans to govern themselves. This was primarily because it appeared that, left on their own, the Koreans would choose some kind of communist government. The United Nations (UN), at the request of the United States, was called in to set up elections across Korea, after which the country would be independent. Claiming the UN lacked the authority to determine the future of Korea, the Soviets and northern Koreans refused to take part in the elections. They were held nonetheless, only in the south, and a new country, the Republic of Korea (ROK; South Korea), was established. The northern Koreans then held elections of their own, and established the communist Democratic People's Republic of Korea (North Korea). Both Koreas sought to reunite the country, but only under its own government.

There is still some controversy over the role played by Stalin in the invasion of South Korea by the well-trained and Soviet-equipped North Korean army that sparked the war. Evidence indicates that North Korean leader **Kim Il Sung** (1912–1994; see entry) pressed Stalin for help in the invasion, but did not receive much more than a reluctant approval and the option to purchase Soviet weapons and equipment. It seems that Stalin had no desire to become engaged in a confrontation with the United States in Asia. Stalin did gain some advantages from the Korean War: the United States had to commit a large number of troops to the peninsula, troops that otherwise could have been used to hinder Soviet moves in Eastern Europe. Further, the Chinese became more dependent on Soviet military equipment and on the Soviet Union itself, thereby delaying the eventual split between the two countries.

But the Korean War fundamentally transformed American opinion towards the U.S.-Soviet rivalry. The cold war was on, with a tense political climate and deep suspicions on both sides. Stalin saw the Soviet system as continuously imperiled by the Western capitalist states—in which individuals, rather than the state, own the property and businesses—and reportedly said to one of his lieutenants, "You'll see, when I'm gone the imperialist powers will wring your necks like chickens."

The later years

During Stalin's last years, he launched several waves of repression. He sent returning prisoners of war directly into forced labor camps, calling them traitors for having surrendered. Whole nationalities, which he accused of treason, were deported. He even came to believe that his own inner circle was plotting against him. Before his death, Stalin seems to have been planning to execute them and purge a substantial portion of the party. Nikita Khrushchev (1894–1971), his successor as general secretary, wrote in his memoirs that Stalin told him in 1951: "I'm finished. I do not trust anyone, not even myself."

On the night of March 1, 1953, Stalin unexpectedly suffered a stroke and died three days later. The nation was stunned, and the Russian people initially mourned. But over the next few years, the memory of the dictator became shadowed. For all that Stalin had accomplished in making a world power out of the once backward Soviet Union, he had ruled through terror and was responsible for perhaps as many as forty million deaths. In a speech in 1956, Khrushchev denounced Stalin as a murderer and a criminal against the state and its people.

Where to Learn More

Abram, Lynwood. "Bright Days for Darkness." *Houston Chronicle,* December 14, 2000.

Caulkins, Janet. *Joseph Stalin.* New York: Franklin Watts, 1990.

Conquest, Robert. *Stalin: Breaker of Nations.* New York: Viking Penguin, 1991.

Deutscher, Isaac. *Stalin: A Political Biography.* New York: Oxford University Press, 1966.

Hoobler, Dorothy, and Thomas Hoobler. *Joseph Stalin*. New York: Chelsea House, 1985.

Johnson, Paul. *Modern Times*. New York: St. Martin's, 1983.

Kallen, Stuart A. *The Stalin Era: 1925–1953*. Edina, MN: Abdo & Daughters, 1992.

Khrushchev, Nikita. *The Crimes of the Stalin Era*. The New Leader, 1962.

Malia, Martin. *The Soviet Tragedy: A History of Socialism in Russia, 1917–1991*. New York: Free Press, 1994.

Marrin, Albert. *Stalin*. New York: Viking Kestrel, 1988.

Otfinoski, Steven. *Joseph Stalin: Russia's Last Czar*. Brookfield, CT: Millbrook Press, 1993.

Spielvogel, Jackson J. *Western Civilization,* 2nd ed. St. Paul, MN: West, 1994.

Whitelaw, Nancy. *Joseph Stalin: From Peasant to Premier*. New York: Dillon Press, 1992.

Web sites

Lenin, Vladimire Illyich. "Testament, 1922." Modern History Sourcebook. [Online] http://www.fordham.edu/halsall/mod/lenin-testament.html (accessed on August 14, 2001).

Harry S. Truman

Born May 8, 1884
Lamar, Missouri
Died December 26, 1972
Kansas City, Missouri

American president and judge

"I could see that history had some extremely valuable lessons to teach. I learned from it that a leader is a man who has the ability to get other people to do what they don't want to do, and like it."

Harry S. Truman became the thirty-third president of the United States when his predecessor, Franklin D. Roosevelt, died in 1945. Truman stepped into office at a time when the world was changing and the conflicts were red hot. Among his many acts as president were the decision to use atomic weapons to bring an end to World War II (1939–45); programs that helped to restructure Europe after the war; help in founding the United Nations (UN) and the North Atlantic Treaty Organization (NATO); and leading the United States through the Korean War (1950–53) and the cold war, a period of political anxiety and military rivalry between the United States and the Soviet Union that stopped short of full-scale war. Because Truman came from a humble rural background and did not have a college education, he gained an image as the "common man." He was proud of this image, founded on the hard work, common sense, and practical wisdom he learned early in life, and combined it effectively with his uncommon abilities, ethics, and determination.

Family life in Missouri

Harry S. Truman was born May 8, 1884, in Lamar, Missouri, the son of John Anderson and Martha Ellen Truman. John Truman had been running a horse and mule business in Lamar, but soon after Harry's birth he turned to farming the family farm in Grandview in 1887. The family moved in 1890 to Independence, Missouri, where John Truman returned to the animal trading business. He made a comfortable living for his family, and from childhood Harry Truman was called on to perform daily chores and to help on the farm.

Truman's childhood was marked by a loving and devoted family. He was very close to his mother, who was college-educated and taught him to read and to value the arts. His father was a politically active Democrat, who brought his son with him to political meetings. His grandfather on his mother's side, Solomon Young, was another great influence. (His grandfather on his father's side was Anderson Shippe Truman. Harry received the middle initial "S," which did not stand for anything, to recognize both grandfathers. That is why his middle initial often appears without the usual period after it.) The family was regular in its church attendance, and Truman is said to have read the Bible twice through by the time he was twelve.

The young Truman was an excellent student, the favorite of many teachers. He was an avid reader, and loved to read biographies of great men. His eyesight was very poor, however, and he had to start wearing glasses at an early age, making him unable to participate in sports (glasses in those days were very fragile). At the age of ten, Truman and his brother both developed a disease called diptheria. There was no cure for the disease at that time, and Truman's case became so severe that he was paralyzed for months. He was left terribly thin and weak after his illness, but when he recovered he managed to catch up in school and then went on to skip a grade. Truman worked very hard preparing to fulfill his dream of going to one of the military academies, West Point or Annapolis. But when he graduated from high school in 1901 at the age of seventeen, the academies rejected him because his eyesight was so poor. At the time, his family's finances were in poor shape. There was no way to pay for college, so Truman began looking for work.

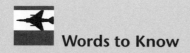

Words to Know

atomic bomb: a powerful bomb created by splitting the nuclei of a heavy chemical, such as plutonium or uranium, in a rapid chain reaction, resulting in a violent and destructive shock wave as well as radiation.

cold war: the struggle for power, authority, and prestige between the communist Soviet Union and the capitalist Western powers of Europe and the United States from 1945 until 1991.

communism: an economic system that does not include the concept of private property. Instead, the public (usually represented by the government) owns the goods and the means to produce them in common.

containment: a policy or process of keeping an enemy power, such as the Soviet Union, from expanding its empire outside its own borders.

isolationism: the view that a country should take care of its problems at home and not interfere in conflicts in other countries.

limited warfare: warfare with an objective other than the enemy's complete destruction, as in holding a defensive line during negotiations

National Guard: a military defense force recruited by the states, but equipped by the federal government.

NATO: the acronym for the North Atlantic Treaty Organization, an alliance of nations in Europe and North America with shores on the Atlantic Ocean, formed in 1949 primarily to counter the threat of Soviet and communist expansion.

Work and war

Truman worked briefly as timekeeper for a railroad construction contractor and then moved to nearby Kansas City. He worked as a clerk in banks in the city for five years. During that time he joined the Missouri National Guard, which he served from 1905 to 1911. After that, he returned to the family farm, where he worked for the next ten years. He managed the six-hundred-acre spread largely by himself. It was difficult work that required intense scheduling to juggle the tasks and many long hours. The habits Truman acquired on the farm—rising at 5 A.M. daily and handling all the details of administration by himself—stood him well for the rest of his life.

At the outbreak of World War I (1914–18), Truman enlisted in the army almost immediately. He helped organize his National Guard battery into a regiment, and it was soon called into service as the 129th Field Artillery. In France, he was promoted to captain and given command of Battery D, the most unruly battery in the regiment, which had already gone through four commanders. Truman proved to have a strong talent for managing men. He successfully brought his unit through several major actions in the war. His troops idolized him, calling him Captain Harry. Years later, at Truman's presidential inauguration, they marched on each side of his car in the parade. After the war, he joined the reserves and was commissioned a major. He was promoted to colonel on June 17, 1932.

Upon his return to the United States, Truman married his childhood sweetheart, Bess Wallace, on June 28, 1919. He and an army associate, Eddie Jacobson, set up a haberdashery in Kansas City. The store, Truman & Jacobson, failed in 1922. Saddled with debts totaling about $20,000, Truman stubbornly refused to file bankruptcy proceedings and insisted upon repaying his creditors, which took him more than fifteen years to accomplish.

The Pendergast machine and an entry to politics

During this period, Thomas J. "Tom" Pendergast, boss of the Kansas City Democratic machine, appointed Truman to a Jackson County position as an overseer of highways, a post that he held for a year. (The Pendergast machine was a very organized political unit, with some of its powers arising from corrupt practices, that acted under Pendergast's leadership to rule Kansas City, and later Missouri, politics.) Next Pendergast chose Truman to run for the position of county judge for Jackson County. Truman served as judge from 1922 to 1924 but was defeated when he ran for a second term. Around this time, Truman's only child, his daughter Margaret, was born, and the family was without income. They managed to hold on until 1926, when he ran for, and was elected, presiding judge, a post he held for eight years. Truman was determined to measure up to his new title and, although Missouri law did not require that a county judge be a qualified lawyer, he studied law in a Kansas City night school from 1923 to 1925.

Truman ran for the Senate in 1934 and easily won the election. Despite his association with the Pendergast political machine, with its dishonesty and corruption a matter of public record, Truman had established a reputation for personal honesty. In 1940, when he came up for reelection, the Pendergast machine had collapsed. More than two hundred persons associated with the machine had been convicted of vote fraud and Pendergast himself had been convicted of income tax evasion and was sentenced to serve a prison term. Despite his association with the discredited machine, Truman won the primary and the regular election; his own record won him the votes he needed.

Truman never tried to conceal the fact that it was with Pendergast's help that he got his political start. His views on the ethics of machine politics were frank and very practical. After he was nominated for the vice presidency, fellow Democrats urged him to disown his political mentor. He refused, and when Pendergast died in January 1945, Truman attended the funeral.

Senator Harry Truman

Truman made his big splash as senator by attacking military spending. Having learned of wasteful spending from his constituents, he persuaded the Senate to establish an investigating committee, which he chaired. At first, the Roosevelt administration paid little attention; his committee was only allotted $15,000 to investigate billions in possible waste. But Truman was determined; he brought together senators who conducted thirty investigations of major aspects of defense and war spending. It was estimated that the Truman Committee saved the nation $15 billion. Truman had proved his leadership abilities in the Senate and many top Democrats began to view him as presidential material.

The moon, the stars, and all the planets fall

In the July 1944 Democratic National Convention, Truman was nominated as the vice presidential candidate to run with Franklin D. Roosevelt (1882–1945). He had served as vice president only eighty-three days when Roosevelt died on April 12, 1945. The next day Truman told a group of newspaper reporters he felt as if "the moon, the stars, and all the planets" had fallen upon him, and he asked them to pray for him. Roosevelt had been secretive and provided him with no preparation for his post as president. Wisely, he asked the members of Roosevelt's cabinet and his advisers to stay in their posts. Most agreed Truman was off to a good start as president, his personality contributing greatly to his success. He listened well to his advisers. He was ready and willing to act on urgent matters after getting the advice of the right people.

And at the time Truman took office there were many urgent matters before him. World War II, although winding to an end in Europe, was still being fought with Japan in the Pacific. Almost at once, Truman found himself trying to deal with the leaders of England and the Soviet Union, who had made their agreements with Roosevelt. By July 6, 1945, he was participating in a conference dealing with the major issues of the war with Soviet Premier **Joseph Stalin** (1879–1953; see entry) and British Prime Minister Winston Churchill (1874–1965) at Potsdam in Germany.

The Allies and Japan

In the summer of 1945, Japan continued to fight, although exhausted from the war. Military leaders of the Allied powers (the United States, the British Commonwealth, the Soviet Union, and other European nations) estimated that it might take another eighteen months to subdue Japan and that invading her borders would be necessary. There was a new development to consider, too. The United States had successfully formed an atom bomb. Whether or not to use this new weapon was part of the Potsdam discussion. Another eighteen months of war would cost numerous lives on both sides. Already, air raids had claimed countless lives: seventy-eight thousand in Tokyo alone. Invading Japan, if the bomb wasn't used, would probably kill more than one million people on both sides. The three Allied leaders agreed to bring the war to an end quickly and warned Japan to surrender or be destroyed. Finally, Truman chose the path he felt would result in the fewest casualties: he ordered the atom bomb to be used to bring Japan to the peace table, but requested that it not be dropped on the most heavily populated areas near Tokyo and Kyoto.

Did You Know?

- Harry S. Truman was the first president of the United States to have a television in the White House.

- When Truman ran for president in 1948, a *Newsweek* poll of the top fifty newspapers and magazines found that not even one of them predicted him to win; all had bet on his opponent, Thomas Dewey.

- On November 1, 1950, three members of the revolutionary Puerto Rican Nationalist Party broke into Blair House and attempted to assassinate Truman, who was napping. One of them was sentenced to die in the electric chair, but Truman had the sentence commuted to a life sentence.

- Truman kept a now-famous plaque on his desk that read: "The buck stops here."

- When Truman was dying in the hospital in 1972, twenty-seven years after ordering atomic bombs to be dropped upon Japan, the bombing was still deeply troubling to him. Weak and ill, he nevertheless spent forty-five minutes discussing and defending that act with former Supreme Court Justice Tom Clark (1899–1977), who had just dropped by to visit.

Dropping the bomb

On August 6, 1945, the atom bomb was dropped at Hiroshima. Some seventy-five thousand people in this military city were killed and nearly one hundred thousand injured or declared missing. On August 8, Russia declared war on Japan per a prior agreement among the Allies. The next day an American plane dropped a second atom bomb on the naval base at Nagasaki; eighty thousand people were killed or injured. On August 14, Japan agreed to surrender and to accept an initial military rule under the commander of the U.S. forces in the Far East, U.S. General **Douglas MacArthur** (1880–1964; see entry).

Peace and the division of Korea

A problem arose, however, in the agreements that were made prior to the dropping of the atomic bomb in regard to the Soviet Union's position in Korea. When, at the Potsdam conference, the Allies had asked the Soviets to join the war in the Pacific at such time as the war in Europe was over, they had thought that the Japanese troops in Manchuria, China, were likely to give them trouble if they invaded the Japanese homelands. They hoped that Soviet soldiers would contend with them in China. Once the atomic bombs stopped the war, however, this was no longer an issue. But the Soviets, according to earlier plan, were already in Manchuria and marching into Korea when the atom bombs fell. The U.S. troops could not immediately get to Korea, and it was feared that the

Soviet Union would take over the whole peninsula. MacArthur quickly announced a plan for the Japanese surrender. In the plan he proposed a line across Korea at the 38th parallel; Soviet military leaders would accept the surrender of Japanese forces north of the 38th parallel, while the United States would accept the surrender south of that line. The Soviets did not object, and thus the land of Korea was split into two zones. By 1948, both North and South Korea had established their own governments; Soviet and American troops then withdrew. North Korea was firmly communistic, with support coming in from China as well as the Soviet Union. (Communism is a a set of political beliefs that advocates the elimination of private property. It is a system in which goods are owned by the community as a whole rather than by specific individuals and are available to all as needed.) South Korea had set up a democratic government that drew support from the United States.

Monumental changes in foreign policy

Truman had become president at the end of a world war. With no prior foreign affairs experience, he faced international issues of huge proportions. It was in this capacity that he made significant historical changes, with the help of an able staff that included **Dean Acheson** (1893–1971; see entry), at first undersecretary of state and later full secretary of state. Truman and his team reversed the U.S. foreign policy that had included years of isolationism (not getting involved in external conflicts) and initiated cold war logic. Observing that the Soviet Union was working to expand its empire worldwide—the Soviet Union was composed of fifteen communist republics—they believed that the goal of all foreign policy had to be the containment of communism to its existing borders. With that end in mind, the Truman administration announced its far-reaching cold war programs: the Truman Doctrine on March 12, 1947, which promised United States support to countries threatened by communism; the Marshall Plan on June 5, 1947, which provided billions in financial aid to struggling Western European countries; and the North Atlantic Treaty Organization (NATO) on April 4, 1949, which assured military assistance among the allied Western European nations.

As Truman was taking these steps, the world was changing. Berlin, Germany, had been divided between the

Soviet Union and the Western allies. In June 1948, the Soviets began a land blockade of the western sectors of the city and the United States had to begin airlifting supplies to Germans behind the blockade. On May 14, 1948, the new State of Israel was born in Palestine, and at the same time Arab armies attacked, hoping to eliminate the new nation before it was settled. In 1947, Greece and Turkey lost the support of the British and, threatened by Soviet expansionism, began to receive U.S. aid via the Truman Doctrine.

Declining popularity and reelection

By the time he came up for election, Truman's popularity had begun to decline. Fewer than 25 percent of the voters felt that he was doing a good job. Many did not understand his foreign policies. In the presidential election of 1948, his Republican opponent was Thomas Dewey (1902–1971), the poised and intelligent governor of New York. The American press predicted that Truman would lose by a landslide. But Truman was a fighter. Once he had decided to run, he put his whole heart into the battle, making hundreds of speeches and traveling thousands of miles in a vigorous campaign. Still, on election eve, the American newspapers were predicting a landslide defeat. One magazine felt so sure of this it prepared an issue to be released after the election with the headline "Dewey Defeats Truman." (The magazine went out of business after the election.) There was no landslide. Truman was elected president.

Korean War

In his second term, Truman faced a new problem when North Korea's army invaded South Korea, quickly capturing the capital city of Seoul and threatening to push the South Korean army south and into the sea. Although Korea was not uppermost on the list of importance in Washington, D.C., it was assumed almost immediately that the Soviets were behind the invasion. At first Truman moved cautiously, providing only air and naval support for the security of evacuation efforts, but emotions rapidly rose. At the strong urging of MacArthur, the commanding general in the Far East, Truman committed ground troops. He did not go to Congress or declare war, calling the operation in Korea a "police action." The recently created United Nations, established to promote

peace among nations, joined the American initiative and MacArthur was made commander of all UN forces.

The war went very badly in its first month. Truman had greatly reduced the military after World War II and the limited troops available were not prepared for combat. The North Koreans drove them south at an alarming pace in retreat after retreat. By August 1950, the UN forces were penned in at the Pusan Perimeter, the southern part of the Korean peninsula. In September, MacArthur turned the situation around when he launched an amphibious attack (using land, sea, and air forces) at the port city of Inchon, near Seoul, the South Korean capital. The attack was completely successful and the North Korean troops were forced to retreat. UN forces then crossed the 38th parallel and advanced up to the Yalu River border with China. The Chinese had issued several warnings that they would enter the war if U.S. soldiers came too close to their borders, but their warnings went unheeded. In November 1950, the Communist Chinese army entered the war in

Women at a communist peace demonstration in London, England, in 1950, protesting U.S. involvement in the Korean War. *Portrait reproduced by permission of Archive Photos, Inc.*

massive strength, rushing to the support of North Korea. The UN forces, after grueling combat, were forced back below the 38th parallel. After this, the enemies held their positions, more or less, for two-and-a-half more years. For the last two years, truce negotiations proceeded at a snail's pace. In the end, both sides agreed to establish a buffer zone along the 38th parallel and to hold their positions north and south. Truman had worked within the policy of containment to stop a communist takeover of South Korea and had done so through limited warfare without risking a third world war.

Firing an idol

In the course of the war, MacArthur had publicly contradicted the president on many occasions. The general did not merely argue with the president and his staff that the Far East was a more important theater of cold war concern than Western Europe; he also talked to newspaper reporters, delivered a message to the Veterans of Foreign Wars, and made public announcements of a diplomatic kind. After six months of the war, Truman issued a directive that military and diplomatic officials clear their public statements with Washington before going public with them. He did this specifically to stop MacArthur from undercutting his administration's positions. MacArthur did not stop, and went so far as to issue an inflammatory statement to the enemy that directly contradicted what the Truman administration had planned. After intense consideration and the agreement of his staff, Truman fired him. MacArthur had a big following as a war hero from World War I and the Philippines. He was a staunch Republican and had the sympathy of many Republican congressmen. Politically, Truman took a terrible beating.

Retirement

In early 1952, Truman announced that he would not run for another term. With some misgivings, he supported Adlai Stevenson as the Democratic candidate. When nominated, Stevenson began immediately to distance himself from the unpopular Truman. Truman was offended, but gave Stevenson his strong support in the losing race against **Dwight D. Eisenhower** (1890–1969; see entry). As soon as the election was over, Truman quietly packed his bags and went home to Independence. He left in the same condition that he had entered the presidency: not much richer and as humble as before. When reporters asked what he did as soon as he and Bess arrived home, his answer was that he carried their bags up to the attic.

Truman lived quietly with Bess in their old Independence home until his death on December 26, 1972. His headstone merely lists in order the government positions in which he served.

Where to Learn More

Donovan, Robert J. *Tumultuous Years: The Presidency of Harry S Truman, 1949–53*. New York: Norton, 1982.

Feinberg, Barbara Silberdick. *Harry S Truman*. New York: Franklin Watts, 1994.

Ferrell, Robert H. *Harry S Truman: A Life*. Columbia: University of Missouri Press, 1994.

Ferrell, Robert H. *Harry S Truman and the Modern American Presidency*. Boston: Little, Brown, 1983.

Ferrell, Robert H. *Dear Bess: The Letters from Harry to Bess Truman, 1910–1959*. New York: Norton, 1983.

Gosnell, Harold F. *Truman's Crises*. Westport, CT: Greenwood Press, 1980.

Hudson, Wilma J. *Harry S Truman: Missouri Farm Boy*. New York: Maxwell Macmillan International, 1992.

Jenkins, Roy. *Truman*. New York: Harper and Row, 1986.

Kirkendall, Richard S., ed. *The Harry S Truman Encyclopedia*. New York: G. K. Hall, 1989.

McCoy, Donald R. *The Presidency of Harry S Truman*. Lawrence: University Press of Kansas, 1984.

McCullough, David. *Truman*. New York: Simon & Schuster, 1992.

Miller, Merle. *Plain Speaking, an Oral Biography of Harry S Truman*. New York: G. P. Putnam, 1950.

Morris, Jeffrey Brandon. *The Truman Way*. Minneapolis, MN: Lerner, 1995.

Schuman, Michael A. *Harry S Truman*. Berkeley Heights, NJ: Enslow, 1997.

Truman, Margaret. *Harry S Truman*. New York: William Morrow, 1973.

Web sites

Project Whistlestop: The Truman Digital Archive Project. [Online] http://www.whistlestop.org (accessed on August 14, 2001).

James A. Van Fleet

Born March 19, 1892
Coytesville, New Jersey
Died September 23, 1992
Polk City, Florida

American military leader and diplomat

"I have looked the Chinese Red in the eye and this is my verdict: If ever I should be called back to fight him again I would go with a confident heart. . . . If we retreat from the Communists in Asia, we are lost anyway. What are we afraid of?"

James A. Van Fleet left Korea four months before the end of the Korean War and retired from the U.S. Army, embittered by his experiences with the limited warfare that was favored there. The highly respected four-star general was a man who saw the world in black and white. He believed his mission as the commander of the Eighth Army in Korea was to try to defeat the enemy and win the war. Fearing a third world war, neither the Truman administration nor the later Eisenhower administration allowed him to launch any of the all-out offensives he drew up. Van Fleet became a harsh critic of the two-year truce negotiations in Korea, and a firm supporter of the Republic of Korea (ROK) president **Syngman Rhee** (1875–1965; see entry) in his desire to unify Korea by military force. When he returned to the United States from Korea in 1953, Van Fleet blasted the politicians who had impeded military offensives for fear of large-scale war. His frustration was heightened by his grief over the loss of his son, a U.S. Air Force pilot, who had been lost in a bombing mission in Korea. Despite his bitterness, Van Fleet was responsible for some outstanding military efforts in Korea, most notably his restructuring and retraining of the ROK army. Always a man who got things done effectively and efficiently, he held solid defense lines in the trench warfare during the truce period and led the troops to victories in the desperate battles at Heartbreak Ridge and Bloody Ridge.

Early life

James Alward Van Fleet was born in New Jersey, but only because his mother had traveled there during her pregnancy to escape a flu epidemic in their home in Florida. Van Fleet was raised in Florida from the time of infancy and was known for his southern accent and manners throughout his life. Van Fleet came from a military family. His grandfather had been in the New York militia during the American Revolution (1775–83). His parents were friends of U.S. President Abraham Lincoln (1809–1865), and his father, William, served in the Union Army during the Civil War (1861–65). William then went on to establish the first railroad in Florida, where the family remained.

Van Fleet graduated from the Summerlin Institute in Bartow, Florida, and was nominated to the military academy at West Point in 1911. At West Point he had as classmates **Dwight D. Eisenhower** (1890–1969), the future general and U.S. president, and **Omar N. Bradley** (1893–1981; see entries), the future general and chairman of the Joint Chiefs of Staff. Van Fleet was tall, graceful, and athletic. He was a fullback on the successful West Point football team, but he was always something of a loner. John Toland, in his history of the Korean War *In Mortal Combat*, quotes the West Point year book, in which Van Fleet was described as "a brusque, outspoken individual and not much of a mixer. He finds pleasure in the society of magazines and

Words to Know

bug-out: to panic and run away from a battle in confusion; a disorderly retreat without permission.

limited warfare: warfare with an objective other than the enemy's complete destruction, as in holding a defensive line during negotiations.

morale: the way that a person or a group of people feels about the job they are doing or the mission they are working on.

trench warfare: combat in which enemies dig into ditches facing each other across the battlefield; the ditches then serve as defensive positions. Trench warfare is usually associated with World War I (1914–18).

unlimited war: a military conflict in which a combatant nation uses every means within its power to pursue the goal of completely defeating the enemy.

books, and is a frequenter of the gym. Perhaps this reticent [quiet] attitude has kept some of us from knowing him as well as we should."

Military life begins

After graduating from West Point, Van Fleet fought with the U.S. Army in the Mexican border campaign, participating in the pursuit of the famous rebel bandit Pancho Villa (1878–1923) from 1916 to 1917. During that time he was promoted to captain. World War I (1914–18) then brought him to France as the commander of a machine gun battalion. He was wounded in action in 1918 and received two Silver Stars for bravery in his World War I service.

During the period between the world wars, Van Fleet spent many years teaching military science and Reserve Officers' Training Corps (ROTC) training at several colleges. From 1921 to 1924, and again from 1932 to 1933, he was a winning football coach at the University of Florida.

World War II

When the United States entered World War II in December 1941, Van Fleet was a colonel commanding the Eighth Infantry Regiment. Unlike many of his peers, he did not rise quickly in the ranks. This was due to a mix-up. George C. Marshall (1880–1959), later a great general and secretary of state, had mistaken him for another man who was an alcoholic. According the John Kennedy Ohl in *The Korean War: An Encyclopedia:* "As Marshall's importance in the Army grew in the 1930s, culminating in his appointment as chief of staff in 1939, Van Fleet's career progression suffered."

Leading his regiment as a colonel, Van Fleet quickly put any doubts about his leadership abilities to rest. He participated in some of the fierce battles in France and in the Battle of the Bulge. By March 1945, he had been promoted to major general and placed in command of the III Corps. He led the corps into Germany and then in its drive to Austria, gaining the reputation of one of the great fighting generals of World War II for his efforts.

Greek battle against communists

In 1948, Greece was experiencing a strong uprising of communist rebels that threatened the standing government. Van Fleet was named the director of the joint U.S. Military Advisory and Planning Group, with the mission to advise the Greek government in its fight against the communists. (Communism is a set of political beliefs that advocates the elimination of private property. It is a system in which goods are owned by the community as a whole rather than by specific individuals and are available to all as needed.) He set to work reshaping the Greek army, with a rigorous program of training and discipline and an overall reorganization. After two years of Van Fleet's direction, the Greek army was able to eliminate the communist rebel force entirely.

Taking over in Korea

In August 1945, when the Japanese, who were occupying Korea, were defeated, the general order for their surrender included an arrangement for Korea in which the Americans were to accept the Japanese surrender south of the 38th parallel (the dividing line between northern and southern Korea) and the Soviets, who were already on the Korean border, would receive the surrender north of it. The Soviets did not object, and thus the land of Korea was split into two zones. By 1948, both North and South Korea had established their own governments; Soviet and American troops then withdrew. North Korea was firmly communistic, with support coming in from China as well as the Soviet Union. South Korea had set up a democratic government that drew support from the United States. The governments of both communist North Korea and nationalist South Korea hoped to reunify Korea under their leadership. Thus, in the summer of 1950, North Korea invaded South Korea. The United States and the United Nations forces soon entered the war on the side of the South Koreans while the Chinese came to the defense of the North Koreans. (The UN was founded following World War II to maintain worldwide peace and to develop friendly relations among countries.)

In April 1951, President **Harry S. Truman** (1884–1972) relieved General **Douglas MacArthur** (1880–1964; see entries), the supreme commander of the UN forces in Korea

James A. Van Fleet (left) at the front in Korea, June 1951. *Reproduced by permission of AP/Wide World Photos.*

and U.S. forces in the Far East, of his command. MacArthur had on several occasions publicly misrepresented the intentions of the president and his administration in the Korean conflict. MacArthur sought an unlimited war in Korea in which he could go after the enemies in North Korea and China with all the force the allies could muster. Truman worried about a third world war being ignited by an all-out defense against China and set his staff on a mission to negotiate an end to the war at the truce table.

General **Matthew B. Ridgway** (1895–1993; see entry), the commander of the Eighth Army in Korea, was appointed to replace MacArthur, and Van Fleet was sent to Korea to take over Ridgway's post as Eighth Army commander. He arrived in April 1951, ready to command. Van Fleet found the Eighth Army in a face-off with the Chinese and North Korean armies, with both sides digging in for sustained trench warfare at the 38th parallel. Almost immediately after his arrival the Chinese launched a powerful offensive against the UN forces. Van Fleet quickly engineered a highly skillful defense, killing tens of thousands of enemy soldiers and barring them from breaking through the UN lines to recapture the capital city of Seoul.

A month later, Van Fleet ordered his forces to drive north to North Korea's Iron Triangle area. Although his drive was successful, Ridgway ordered the troops to go back to the defense lines held before Van Fleet's offensive, the Kansas and Wyoming lines. Later in the summer of 1951, Van Fleet launched several other, smaller offensives, capturing Heartbreak Ridge and Bloody Ridge after bitter and bloody fighting. By late fall, though, Ridgway ordered Van Fleet to stop all offensives. The truce talks, which had been stalled, were once again in motion.

From that point on, Van Fleet's forces were allowed to engage only in small, limited attacks. Van Fleet grew increasingly discouraged, saying that the limited warfare was lowering the morale among his men and that he was not receiving enough ammunition to maintain security for his troops.

Retraining the ROKs

Throughout the war, the American military and the American press had been scornful about the Republic of Korea (ROK) Army. Although the South Koreans had lost many times the number of soldiers that the UN forces had lost, they had frequently broken ranks and scattered when the enemy was fierce. The Chinese knew to hit the defense lines of the Eighth Army at the ROK positions, where there was often weakness. The ROKs never had sufficient equipment or arms and ammunition and they had little training when the war began. The leadership was also inconsistent. Despite all this, they had proven repeatedly to be dedicated fighters.

Not long after he took command, Van Fleet decided to take all the ROK divisions out of the line and retrain them. In July 1951, he established the Field Training Command. The training program took nine weeks and was done division by division. According to ROK General **Paik Sun Yup** (1920–; see entry) in his memoirs, *From Pusan to Panmunjom*:

The center started from scratch, assuming nobody knew anything. Every man in a division, with the exception of its commander, was required to undergo the training, and when the training was over, a unit had to pass a test before being assigned to the front. . . . By the end of 1952, all ten ROK Army divisions had completed the training. Units that completed the course lost 50 percent fewer men and equipment in combat than did units that had not had the training. Furthermore, divisions that completed the course and returned to the front revealed an élan [spirit] and confidence quite superior to what they had shown before going through the training.

After their training, the ROKs were finally provided with a more reasonable supply of arms and ammunition. When they went back to the line, the South Korean army was strong and skilled and had no more "bug-outs," or disorganized retreats. By December 1952, three out of four Eighth Army soldiers at the battle front were ROKs. Today in South Korea, there is a statue of Van Fleet at the site of the military academy there.

The loss of a son

Van Fleet and his wife Helen had two daughters and a son. Their son, James A. Van Fleet Jr., had followed his father's footsteps into the military as a U.S. Air Force B-26 pilot. He was a captain at the time of the Korean War. In April 1952, he was on a night bombing mission in North Korea when he was shot down. He was reported missing in action; two years later his status changed to "presumed dead."

Grieving over his son and eager to go after the enemy, Van Fleet repeatedly prepared plans for large-scale offensives against the Chinese and North Koreans. He suggested using the Chinese Nationalist troops in Taiwan (formerly Formosa) and also wanted to bomb mainland China. (Chinese Communists had driven the American-backed Chinese Nationalist leader **Chiang Kai-shek** [1887–1975; see entry] and his forces to the island of Taiwan in October 1949 following a bloody civil war.) Van Fleet believed that his successes on the battlefields proved that the UN forces could win the war and forcibly unite Korea under ROK president Syngman Rhee. And he became increasingly bitter when his views were rejected by Ridgway and the Truman administration. "Though we could readily have followed up our success, that was not the intention in Washington," he later wrote in an article in *Life* magazine. "Our State Department had already let the Reds [communists] know that we were willing to settle on the 38th Parallel. Instead of getting directives for offensive action, we found our activities more and more proscribed |prohibited| as the time went on." When Eisenhower became president, Van Fleet found, once again, that his plans to defeat the enemy through military force were not even considered. The Eisenhower administration was just as anxious to settle the war through negotiation as the Truman administration had been.

Going home

In disgust, Van Fleet gave up his command of the Eighth Army in February 1953 and returned to the United States, where he promptly retired from military service. He wrote two articles for *Life* in which he claimed that the United States could easily win the war in Korea if politicians and policy-makers would stop restraining the forces. For a short time the articles raised controversy about the U.S. position in Korea, but Van Fleet's claims were convincingly disputed by many military leaders in Korea, particularly Ridgway and Van Fleet's successor, Maxwell Taylor. Van Fleet, the fighting general, would never accept the idea that war could be limited or that an enemy could be swayed by words rather than arms.

After retiring, Van Fleet served as an ambassador to the Far East under Eisenhower in 1954 and as a consultant on the National Guard and Special Service Forces to President John F. Kennedy (1917–1963) in 1961. He lived a long life, making his last public appearance at his one-hundredth birthday party in March 1992. He died six months later in his sleep.

Where to Learn More

Graebner, Norman A. "Van Fleet, James A." In *Historical Dictionary of the Korean War,* edited by James I. Matray. New York: Greenwood Press, 1991.

Life, May 11, 1953.

Ohl, John Kennedy. "Van Fleet, James A." In *The Korean War: An Encyclopedia,* edited by Stanley Sandler. New York: Garland, 1995.

Paik Sun Yup. *From Pusan to Panmunjom: Wartime Memoirs of the Republic of Korea's First Four-Star General.* Dulles, VA: Brassey's, 1992.

Toland, John. *In Mortal Combat: Korea, 1950–1953.* New York: William Morrow, 1991.

Web sites

"James Alward Van Fleet." Arlington National Cemetery Website. [Online] http://www.arlingtoncemetery.com/vanfleet.htm (accessed on August 14, 2001).

Walton H. "Johnnie" Walker

Born December 3, 1889
Belton, Texas
Died December 23, 1950
Near Seoul, South Korea

American military commander

W alton H. "Johnnie" Walker, one of the great generals of World War II (1939–45), commanded the Eighth Army in the Korean War from early July 1950, when the first U.S. troops arrived on the peninsula, until his sudden death on December 23, 1950. Few would envy him those five months of command. With the odds all in the enemy's favor, he led raw, untrained troops through vicious combat and constant defeat. The terrain and enemy were unknown, his troops had little experience or training and were short on equipment, and he did not get along well with his superior, General **Douglas MacArthur** (1880–1964; see entry). But "Bulldog" Walker was a professional soldier. Short of stature and short on words, he was tough and fearless in combat. When the North Koreans penned in the Eighth Army at the southern end of the Korean peninsula, Walker staged a concentrated defense of a large area known as the Pusan Perimeter. Although his forces did not have the strength to stop the enemy from penetrating the perimeter, Walker's dogged persistence in keeping his units moving to the holes in the defense line thwarted the efforts of the North Korean Army to push the United Nations forces out

"A retreat to Pusan would be one of the greatest butcheries in history. We must fight until the end. . . . Any man who gives ground may be personally responsible for the death of thousands of his comrades. . . . We are going to hold this line. We are going to win."

Portrait reproduced by permission of AP/Wide World Photos.

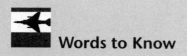

Words to Know

division (or infantry division): a self-sufficient unit, usually about 15,000 to 16,000 strong, under the command of a major general.

infiltrate: to enter into enemy lines by passing through gaps in its defense.

stalemate: deadlock; the state in which the efforts of each party in a conflict cancels out the efforts of the other party so that no one makes any headway.

of Korea. Walker's defense of the Pusan Perimeter is considered one of history's great military feats.

Background

Walton Harris Walker was born on December 3, 1889, in Belton, Texas. He entered the Victoria Military Institute in 1907 and then entered the U.S. Military Academy at West Point, where he graduated in 1912. He received a commission in the infantry and put in garrison duty (time at a military post) in several locations. Just before World War I (1914–18), he took part in the occupation of Vera Cruz, Mexico, and served on the border patrol near Mexico. In 1917, he was promoted to captain and went to France as a company commander. He was then promoted to major and led his troops in the Saint-Mihiel and Meuse-Argonne offensives. His skill leading troops in combat was noticed: he was awarded two Silver Stars for bravery and was promoted to lieutenant colonel.

In the years between World War I and World War II, Walker served in many positions involving the training of troops. He also met and married Caroline Victoria Emerson in 1924. They had a son Sam.

"A fighter in every sense of the word"

At the beginning of World War II, Walker (by that time called "Johnnie Walker," after the scotch whiskey he drank), took command of the Third Armored Division. In 1941, he took over as the commander of the IV Armored Corps, which later became known as the XX Corps. In 1944, Walker led his division in the famous invasion of Normandy under the command of General George S. Patton (1885–1945) and his Third Army. Walker and the XX Corps saw very difficult and bloody combat and were central in the drive across northern France and the capture of key positions. By 1945, Walker's XX Corps had entered Austria and liberated Buchenwald, the German death camp. At the war's end, Walker was promoted to lieu-

the future of Korea, the Soviets and northern Koreans refused to take part in the elections. They were held nonetheless, only in the south, and a new country, the Republic of Korea (ROK), was established. The northern Koreans then held elections of their own, and established the communist Democratic People's Republic of Korea. Both Korean governments sought to reunite the country, but only under its own control. In the summer of 1950, North Korea invaded South Korea to begin the war.

Once MacArthur had cleared sending U.S. ground troops to help the ROK Army in its efforts to stop the advancing North Korean People's Army (NKPA), he put Walker in charge of all ground units in Korea on June 30, 1950. General **William F. Dean** (1899–1981; see entry) and his Twenty-fourth Division had been the first American units in the war. On July 7, Walker flew to the current defensive position near the city of Taejon to find Dean and his troops in a desperate position after multiple retreats and heavy casualties. He made up his mind to bring the entire Eighth Army to Korea. Walker was officially in command of U.S. troops in Korea on July 13 and took command of the ROK troops as well on July 17.

Walker created a headquarters for the Eighth Army at the city of Taegu in the south of the peninsula. Soon he learned that the Twenty-fourth Division had been defeated at their position on the Kum River. As he would do at every crucial battle throughout the war, he had his private pilot, Captain Eugene Michael Lynch, fly him to the scene to get a bird's eye view. The flights were often hair-raising: flying low to observe the battlefields closely inevitably drew enemy fire. Walker was more concerned about the vulnerability of the troops below, knowing they were unprepared for battle. His orders were to delay the NKPA forces in their southward advance. MacArthur and the Joint Chiefs of Staff (the president's and secretary of defense's war advisors) believed the North Koreans to be a weak force that the United States could scare off just by appearing. Walker saw for himself that this assessment was very far from true, but, always a good soldier, steeled himself to carry out the orders.

"There will be no more retreating"

By the end of July, MacArthur and the Defense Department understood how strong an enemy the NKPA was.

Enough UN forces were shipped to Korea that the North Koreans no longer outnumbered the Eighth Army forces. Tanks, guns, ammunition, and other military equipment were arriving daily. Even so, the Eighth Army was defeated time and again. After the city of Taejon fell to the North Koreans, the city of Taegu, temporarily serving as the ROK capital and Eighth Army headquarters, was in jeopardy. Walker knew his troops were being ravaged by the enemy and that they were more likely to panic and run than to hold their ground. As the divisions continued to withdraw, he told the commanders that retreat was unacceptable. On July 29, after receiving word from MacArthur's headquarters that there would be no more retreats, Walker delivered his famous "stand or die" speech to the Twenty-fifth Division staff, as quoted in John Toland's *In Mortal Combat: Korea 1950–1953:* "We are fighting a battle against time. There will be no more retreating, withdrawal, or readjustment of the lines. . . . There is no line behind us to which we can retreat."

Oddly, at the time Walker delivered this speech, he had a well-developed plan to retreat with all Eighth Army forces to the Naktong River, where they would set up a strategic defense line. He wanted to set up a solid front from which standard U.S. military methods, including artillery and air power from interlocking units, provided a tight and secure defense line. He had mapped out the Pusan Perimeter, a one-hundred-mile long, fifty-mile wide rectangle with the Naktong River serving as its western boundary. His pilot, Mike Lynch, was busy flying Walker all over the Naktong River area during late July and early August. He described the general's activity, as quoted in Joseph C. Goulden's book, *Korea: The Untold Story of the War:* "General Walker got to know every nook and cranny of the river. When the fighting began, and Hill So-and-so was the scene, Walker could immediately envision the terrain. This helped him immensely in his defense."

The Pusan Perimeter

The withdrawal to the Pusan Perimeter took place between August 1 and 3, 1950. Walker carefully planned the positions of every unit assigned to Korea for the defense of the huge area. The first order of business was to stop the North

Walton H. "Johnnie" Walker (sitting in jeep) confers with Brigadier General F. W. Farrell at Walker's headquarters as ROK and U.S. soldiers look on, August 1950. *Reproduced by permission of the Corbis Corporation.*

Korean drive down the western roads leading to Masan. Walker sent the Twenty-fifth Division. This counterattack ultimately failed. The marines, in their first highly publicized fight in Korea, bailed out the Twenty-fifth Division twice. But even their support was not enough. From the hills, the North Koreans achieved the advantage, engaging the Americans in a vicious battle later known as Bloody Gulch. At the end of August, the Masan front was in a stalemate.

The North Koreans began an attack on August 5 in an area called the Naktong Bulge. They crossed the river during the night on underwater bridges (made up of sandbags, rocks, logs, and barrels built up from the river bottom to about a foot below the river's surface) and then infiltrated and, despite fierce combat, continued on their drive into the perimeter. On August 17, the marines struck the ridge line within the Naktong Bulge called Obnong-ni and shattered the North Koreans.

The battle for Taegu

In mid-August, the North Koreans made two unsuccessful attacks on the city of Taegu, but they kept attacking. By August 15, the NKPA was only fifteen miles north of Taegu. Walker, unwilling to allow any kind of withdrawal, sent in the highly successful Twenty-seventh Regiment, called the Wolfhounds, led by Lieutenant Colonel John "Mike" Michaelis to join ROK First Commander General **Paik Sun Yup** (1920–; see entry). A seven-night battle raged in a place called the "Bowling Alley," a two-mile stretch of road with mountains rising on either side. During this battle, the North Korean tanks would begin the attack each night by firing down the road at the Americans. The Twenty-seventh's bazookas would destroy the first couple of tanks in line, and the rest would eventually turn around, only to come back the next night. As the North Koreans fired, red balls flew down the road. By day, the air support strafed the enemy, firing upon them with machine guns from low-flying aircraft. Unable to penetrate the UN positions, the North Koreans traveled around them in the hills, but the air support again bombed them relentlessly, stopping their drive for Taegu.

In the last few days of August, MacArthur was finalizing his plans for an amphibious (using land, sea, and air forces) attack at the port city of Inchon, near Seoul. He was creating a new X Corps, combining marines and army infantry divisions and a huge naval fleet for the attack. His boasts to the media made the plan common knowledge, and the North Koreans knew they had to capture the Pusan Perimeter soon. In the first days of September, they struck savagely on five different fronts, penetrating the Naktong Bulge and moving in force into the mountains just north of Taegu.

Walker was worried about the Naktong Bulge, where the penetration was deepest. Although he was aware that the marines were preparing for the attack at Inchon, in desperation he asked for their help. MacArthur allowed him the use of the marines, but only for three days. In those three days, the marines counterattacked, but just after midnight on September 6, they pulled out, under orders from MacArthur. As the marines got ready for the attack at Inchon, Walker was faced with a continuing North Korean penetration at the Pusan Perimeter. The loss of the marines was devastating, as they were the only force that had been able to stop the NKPA so far. He knew that another withdrawal was the only way to ensure the safety of his troops. But he held the line.

After Inchon

The X Corps' attack at Inchon was a complete success, but the NKPA soldiers fighting at the Pusan were not informed of it right away and kept up a vicious battle. As Walker's army fought to break out of the perimeter, they incurred heavy casualties. Finally, on September 23, the North Korean troops got word that the UN forces had invaded behind them and they began their retreat. The Eighth Army then raced up the peninsula to meet with the X Corps.

The Eighth Army advanced north, recapturing the capital city of Seoul after a difficult battle. They crossed the 38th parallel that divided North and South Korea and captured, with less difficulty, the North Korean capital of Pyongyang on October 20. By late October, Walker had set himself up with a headquarters in North Korean Premier **Kim Il Sung's** (1912–1994; see entry) former headquarters. His troops were at the Chongchon River in North Korea, and he received orders from MacArthur to advance as rapidly as possible to the north. The X Corps would also advance, but separated from the Eighth Army by mountains and under the command of General Edward M. Almond (1892–1979). As the troops were beginning their advance, word came in that the ROK divisions were being attacked in strength by Chinese troops, which had entered the war to aid the North Koreans. Walker believed the reports, and expressed grave concerns to MacArthur. MacArthur did not believe the reports, and ordered a rapid advance to the north, promising a prompt end to the war.

The Eighth Army was hit all around by the Chinese as it advanced, but MacArthur ordered Walker to press on. Walker did not get along well with MacArthur, but was too professional to argue with his commander. He was faced with brutally cold weather, a shortage of supplies, and a vicious enemy. Without the support of the X Corps, the Eighth Army was completely exposed on its mountainous side, where the Chinese were already known to have infiltrated. While MacArthur was telling the press the army might be "home by Christmas," Walker cautiously stalled his army's advance to the north, waiting for supplies and personnel. When he did launch the offensive, heading up to the Chinese border, the Chinese attacked powerfully. The attack took place on November 25; by November 26, three ROK divisions had been destroyed and the entire Eighth Army was threatened with annihilation. Walker promptly flew to MacArthur's headquarters in Tokyo, Japan, to get permission from the general to retreat. The Eighth Army then retreated in several stages to the 38th parallel. Not long after Walker's retreat, the X Corps began its bloody retreat from the Chosin (Changjin) Reservoir.

Taking the heat

From the perspective of most military historians, Walker acted prudently and correctly in delaying what he could see was a dangerous and ill-conceived mission. In fact, he almost certainly saved thousands of lives. But at the command headquarters in Tokyo, his actions were criticized. Even if he had been right to question the risk, his doing so made MacArthur and his staff, who admitted no risk, look bad. There was talk of replacing Walker as commander of the Eighth Army in Korea. Walker had never been a man of words and did not attempt to defend himself. He was not a particularly charming or popular man, and could not compete with MacArthur's theatrics.

At the end of December 1950, the Eighth Army was preparing to back up the ROK forces at the 38th parallel. On December 23, Walker went to inspect some units at the front near Seoul. His son, Lieutenant Sam Walker, was a battalion commander in the Nineteenth Division in Korea, and he was being awarded a Silver Star that day. Walker was going to present it to him as a surprise during this trip. He never got there. Traveling at high speeds was typical for the busy general, and he ordered his driver to go fast. When an ROK truck unexpectedly pulled out in front of them, Walker's jeep turned over on the icy road. The general was killed immediately.

At the time of Walker's death, the Eighth Army troops were demoralized from the onslaught of the Chinese invasion. They had lost the ground that they had worked so hard to gain. General **Matthew B. Ridgway** (1895–1993; see entry) replaced Walker as commander of the Eighth Army in Korea. After one more Chinese offensive and more losses, he built up the morale of the soldiers and began a successful program of counteroffensives. For all that Walker had achieved during his months of fighting in Korea, he would be remembered more for the defeats that occurred in the first months of the war than his skillful strategies and iron determination under fire. He had borne the brunt of the worst that war had to offer and shouldered the responsibilities, never calling attention to his own achievements. John Toland quotes British author Callum MacDonald on the legacy of Walker: "As for Walker, his crime was to be associated with an embarrassing defeat in an army with a cult of winning. It is difficult to believe that any other general could have done any better."

Walker was brought home by his son Sam and buried in Arlington National Cemetery. Sam Walker was a combat veteran of both the Korean and Vietnam Wars and was twice awarded the Silver Star for gallantry in action. He and his father are the only father and son to achieve the rank of four-star general in U.S. Army history.

Where to Learn More

Alexander, Bevin. *Korea: The First War We Lost.* New York: Hippocrene Books, 1986, revised edition, 2000.

Fredriksen, John C. *American Military Leaders: From Colonial Times to the Present.* Santa Barbara, CA: ABC-CLIO, 1991.

Goulden, Joseph C. *Korea: The Untold Story of the War.* New York: Times Books, 1982.

Kangas, David. "Walton H. Walker." In *The Korean War: An Encyclopedia,* edited by Stanley Sandler. New York: Garland, 1995.

Toland, John. *In Mortal Combat: Korea, 1950–1953.* New York: William Morrow, 1991.

Webster's American Military Biographies. Springfield, MA: G. & C. Merriam Company, 1978.

Yö Un-hyöng

Born 1885
Yanp'yong, Kyönggi Province, Korea
Died July 19, 1947
Seoul, Korea

Korean statesman and educator

When World War II was drawing to a close in 1945 and the Koreans understood that they were finally to be freed after forty years of Japanese colonial rule, they immediately developed plans to govern their country independently. This was no easy task, since the Japanese had not allowed any form of political organization among Koreans. At the time of liberation, a man named Yö Un-hyöng emerged as one of the important leaders in Korea. Known for being moderate, he was interested in active reform and self-rule, but he was not a member of the Communist Party. He was an attractive and charming man with silver hair who dressed smartly in Western clothes, but took his political philosophy from a wide range of Asian and Western sources, which was particularly befitting the Korean experience at the time.

In the tumultuous days at the close of World War II, Yö was a main force in leading his people to an orderly and non-violent transition to independent rule and constructing a new government, the Korean People's Republic. He worked hard to bring together the many political factions, from the right (the conservative establishment made up of the wealthy and pow-

"We believed that we must construct a country which, though standing for true and progressive democracy, would receive without hesitation recognition from the rest of the nations of the world . . . and we thought of course the [American] Military Government would wholly aid in setting up such a government and follow the path to independence."

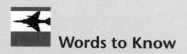
Words to Know

coalition government: a temporary government formed by combining all the different parties and interests in order to take a joint action.

collaborator: someone who cooperates with, or helps out, enemies to his or her own nation.

concessions: things that are given up and granted to the other side in an argument or conflict.

leftists: people who advocate change and reform, usually in the interest of gaining greater freedoms and equality for average citizens and the poor; some leftist groups aspire to overthrow the government; others seek to change from within.

moderate: of neither one extreme nor the other; having political beliefs that are not extreme.

multinational trusteeship: government by the joint rule of several countries that have committed to act in what they deem to be the country's best interest.

Provisional Korean Government: a government in exile, formed in Shanghai during Japanese rule of Korea (1910–45), that elected leaders and fought for the cause of an independent Korea, but had no actual power within occupied Korea.

reprisal: violence or other use of force by one side in a conflict in retaliation for something bad that was done by the other side; a system of getting even for harm done.

rightist: a person who advocates maintaining tradition and the status quo and generally supports a strong and authoritarian government by the elite.

erful) and the left (those leaning toward reform, redistribution of wealth, and equality). In the first years after the war, Yö seemed a likely leader of a unified Korea. While it is impossible to know what may have occurred had he survived, Yö's life offers useful insight into the Korean experience of the war in Korea, a side often overlooked in American history books.

Early life

Yö Un-hyöng (often called Lyuh Woon Hyung by Americans) was born in 1885 in Yanp'yong, in the Kyönggi Province of Korea. Yö's family was of the *yangban* class of Korea, the traditional Korean elite who often held bureaucratic positions in the government and came from a long tradition of scholarly pursuits. His family was, however, quite poor. When Yö was fourteen years old, he entered the Christian missionary high school, Paejae Haktang, where he was introduced to Christianity and Western learning. When he had graduated from school, he founded some private schools, but they were soon closed, in 1910, by the Japanese when they annexed Korea. (Japan incorporated Korea as a part of Japan with the help of a very weak Korean monarch whom they had helped to the throne.) In 1910, Yö entered the Presbyterian Theological Seminary in Pyongyang (later the capital of North Korea). In 1914, frustrated by the harsh rule of the Japanese, he set out for China to fight for Korean independence. He attended college in Nanjing, China, and in 1918 organized the New Korean Youth Party there. In 1919, he took part in the founding of the Korean Provisional Government in Shanghai, China.

Return to Korea

In Shanghai, Yö became involved with the Korean Communist Party, which was founded in China in 1919. (Communism is a set of political beliefs that advocates the elimination of private property. It is a system in which goods are owned by the community as a whole rather than by specific individuals and are available to all as needed.) In 1921, he went to Moscow, Russia, to attend the Congress of the Toilers of the Far East. At the conference, he met Russian communist leaders Vladimir Lenin (1870–1924) and Leon Trotsky (1879–1940). Also during this time he worked for the Chinese revolutionary Sun Yat-sen (1866–1925) and probably met the future Communist Chinese leader **Mao Zedong** (Mao Tsetung; 1893–1976; see entry).

While he was in Shanghai in 1929 or 1930, Yö was arrested by Japanese agents and returned to Korea. There, he was imprisoned in Taejon for three years. When he got out of prison in 1933, he became the editor of the *Central Daily* newspaper in Seoul, which the Japanese closed down in 1938. The Japanese never stopped pressuring him to work with them, but Yö held out steadfastly. (His brother, however, yielded to the pressure and collaborated with the Japanese, and Yö is often associated with his brother's deeds.)

Yö was very active politically, and his presence was increasingly appreciated in the underground (secret) Korean political world. He worked from a wide range of political ideals. He was not a member of the Korean Communist Party in Shanghai, but had been involved with it and found many socialist ideas useful and valid. (Socialism is an economic system in which there is no private property, and business and industry are owned by the workers. Communism is a political ideology based on socialism.) He believed in a Western form of democracy in which everyone was represented in government. He was Christian in his religious beliefs. One historian in Korea at the time of liberation is quoted in Bruce Cumings's history *The Origins of the Korean War* for his description of Yö: "What an amazing Korean he was . . . grey fedora, grey tweed overcoat, grey flannel trousers, well-tailored tweed coat, blue shirt with clean collar and neatly tied foreinhand [necktie] looking for all the world as though he were off for a date at the Greenwich Country Club." Yö was also very involved in Korean sports.

By 1943, Yö felt certain that the Japanese would be defeated in World War II (1939–45) and knew that the Koreans needed to prepare to rule themselves. Although it was illegal and very dangerous to organize any kind of Korean political party, he secretly founded the Korean Independence League in 1944, which remained one of the main political bases of Korea after the war.

Transition from Japanese rule

In August 1945, with the war all but over, the Japanese in Korea grew fearful of reprisals (attacks to get even) against them by the Korean people, and sought help among Korean leaders. They made several unsuccessful attempts to work with conservative leaders, who refused to collaborate with the Japanese even as their rule was ending. The Japanese then approached Yö, knowing that he was an activist popular among students and reformers. He met with the Japanese Governor General's secretary on August 15, the day the Japanese surrendered in World War II, prepared to negotiate. In return for his promise to help restrain the Korean people from violent retaliation against the Japanese, he demanded concessions from the Japanese: to release all political prisoners in Korea; to guarantee food provisions for three months after their departure; and to promise not to interfere with Korean programs for independence. Yö received these promises from the reluctant Japanese official, and the power to maintain law and order was turned over to him. He called a meeting of Korean leaders that same day, August 15. The group, selected by Yö from all political sectors, formed the Committee for the Preparation of Korean Independence (CPKI), organized to function as a temporary governing body. Yö had prepared for the meeting with two documents: one, a statement to incoming Allied forces, thanking them for their part in liberating Korea, but stating the thought foremost on Koreans' minds: that Korea must be governed by Koreans; and the other, a Korean Declaration of Independence, which included a provision for getting rid of the Koreans in government who had collaborated with the Japanese.

The next day, August 16, Yö fulfilled his promise to the Japanese by urging a gathering of five thousand Koreans to refrain from violence against their colonial rulers during the transition of power. He called for Koreans of all political beliefs to join together and work for the independent rule of Korea. Political prisoners were released that day, sending thousands of Korean communists whom the Japanese had arrested back into the population. The next day, the Korean public learned that the CPKI was effectively ruling Korea. By radio and other media, the committee instructed the people of Korea to form committees to govern locally until a new government could be put in place. Within two weeks, there were 145 branches of this government. The branches were called People's Committees and they ruled in the cities and villages throughout the country, assuming the function of government on the local level.

The Korean People's Republic
In Seoul, the CPKI leaders separated into two factions: the communists and those who followed Yö's lead, seeking the unity of Korean people, elimination of the Japanese and Koreans who had collaborated with them, and most of all, Korean independence. Yö's stand wasn't well accepted by the Japanese, however, who continued to represent themselves as rulers and demanded that the CPKI serve only as a peacekeeping organization. On August 18, Yö was attacked by terrorists—in the first of many such attacks on him—and had to take some time out to recover.

On September 6, the Americans were on their way to Korea, in theory to accept the surrender of the Japanese. Most Koreans understood that it was essential that they have a functioning government in place if they wished to remain independent when the large powers arrived. From the Kyŏnggi Girl's High School, the CPKI announced the formation of the Korean People's Republic (KPR). Fifty-five Korean leaders were selected to serve in an interim (temporary) government until elections could put a democratic administration in place. The leaders of the KPR included people from all of the political factions. In fact, the future president of South Korea, **Syngman Rhee** (1875–1965; see entry), in exile at the time, was named president of the interim group, since his name was associated with the independence movement of earlier days. Some other right-wing (conservative) leaders were also selected as leaders of the interim government, but the majority were more left-wing (reform-oriented). Yŏ became vice-chairman of the cabinet, and it is believed that he took the lead in selecting the diverse group of leaders, and had in fact been the undeclared leader of Korea since the Japanese defeat.

The arrival of the American Military Government

The Americans landed at the port city of Inchon on September 8, 1945, under the command of Major General John Reed Hodge, armed with money and power but little understanding of the Korean people and the tangled political situation. Completely ignoring the new government of the new Korean People's Republic (KPR), they initially allied themselves as rulers with the Japanese—the former occupiers who were defeated in the world war—rather than the Koreans. When they did begin to work with Koreans, they conferred with the most right-wing faction, the Korean Democratic Party (KDP). Representatives from the KDP told the Americans that the KPR and Yŏ were both pro-Japanese and communist, which, had it been true, would have made a very unlikely combination, since the Japanese were staunchly anticommunist. Yŏ was labeled a communist by the army's intelligence almost immediately, and he could not even get in to talk to Hodge until October 5. At that time, the Americans treated Yŏ rudely, accusing him of collaborating with the Japanese.

The American Military Government probably did not acknowledge the Korean People's Republic because it sought reforms they disapproved of and because it included communists at a time when the United States was fiercely anticommunist. (Communism, with its theory of "sharing the wealth" among the community, was fundamentally at odds with the American economic system, capitalism, in which individuals can amass personal wealth.) But after a time, the American Military Government decided to create an advisory council of Koreans to help rule the country. They asked Yö to join. He initially agreed to be part of the council, but when he found that the other members were all from the conservative KDP, he quickly resigned. When he did this, the Military Government published a condemnation of the Korean People's Republic in the newspapers, insulting most Koreans by calling the KPR's leaders foolish to think that they could take on the task of successfully running the government of Korea.

In October, the Military Government was involved in the return to Korea of the exiled Syngman Rhee from the United States and Kim Koo, the president of the Korean Provisional Government in Shanghai. In November, the Americans demanded that the Korean People's Republic change its name, to give up any claim to being a government. (It eventually became known as the People's Party.) In December, General Hodge called the KPR a "public enemy" and declared its activities to be illegal. Even so, in February 1946, an American intelligence report found that the majority of Koreans wished to be represented by the KPR.

In February 1946, Yö's party joined the Korean National Democratic Front, an alliance with many of the communist and moderate left-leaning groups that replaced the Seoul Central People's Committee. Speaking to a large crowd in mid-February, Yö received an enthusiastic standing ovation. With the branches of the left working together in a coalition, the Americans feared losing their stronghold and foresaw a possible communist takeover. Seeing that Yö continued to have a very strong following among the Korean people, Hodge tried to recruit him into a new leadership coalition that would be more representative of the Korean people. The coalition of Korean political factions that the Americans envisioned, however, was equal parts conservative and reform-oriented, when, in truth, the conservative elements were a tiny minority of landlords and business-men. The vast majority of the Korean population was intent on reform after so many years of abuse by the Japanese.

The Americans urged Yö to break with the communists. Yö and Korean communist leader **Pak Hön-yöng** (1900–1955; see entry) had been rigorously competing for leadership of the Democratic Front. At around this time, the Korean communists decided to back the American and Soviet plan for a five-year, multi-country trusteeship to govern Korea. The trusteeship was very unpopular with the Korean people, and many were breaking with the Communist Party over this. For his part, Yö was interested in the idea of a coalition and listened to the Americans. He hoped to use the American support to help him in his fight with the communists and he also hoped to influence the Americans in their policies toward Korea. He cut ties with the Korean Communist Party altogether and joined the Coalition Committee for Cooperation between the rightists and the leftists. Yö, of course, was criticized by many for joining with the Americans.

Police state

By 1947, South Korea was in an economic tailspin, with widespread famine and unemployment. A new and stronger right wing was forming, supported by the national police and youth gangs that terrorized leftists. Conflicts among the Koreans were becoming more violent and more frequent. In May, Roger Baldwin, the head of the American Civil Liberties Union, traveled to Korea to see for himself what was happening there. He reported in the *New York Times* on June 23, 1947, that southern Korea was in a "state of undeclared war . . . . in the grip of a police regime and a private terror." He spent some time interviewing Yö about the problems in the divided country. Yö told him, as he had expressed many other times, that the national police were at the heart of the chaos. The police force was made up mainly of people who had been trained by the Japanese during colonial rule. There was a lot of ill will between the police and the population. In the city of Taegu in late 1946, fifty-three policemen were killed by angry mobs. The police were overzealous, often brutal, and politically motivated. In fact, Yö repeatedly complained that the police were following him everywhere.

In early 1947, the Korean population was violently rebelling against the American government in their country. Yö resigned from the Coalition Committee after being attacked several times. At this time, most of his followers had split into factions. Hope for an independent Korean government was fading. The Americans saw, as the other factions dissolved into fragments, that Syngman Rhee and his nationalist forces were gaining momentum. The Americans feared Rhee's dictatorial power, based on the backing of the national police and some violent youth gangs, as well as his unwillingness to go along with them. They decided to try one more time to create a middle-of-the-road leadership and once again contacted Yö.

The death of a leader

The American civil administrator in Korea, E. A. J. Johnson, described the chain of events on the day of Yö's death, July 19, 1947, as quoted in Cumings:

> Our instructions were to try to form a government of the center. We decided to try to offset the rightism of the administration with the leftism of Lyuh Woon Hyung [Yö]. It was finally decided that I would speak to Lyuh about joining the government. It was decided that the meeting must be very quiet and that it wouldn't do for Lyuh to come to the government building to meet me, so we arranged for him to come to meet me at my house. Lyuh was contacted, and he was willing. . . . Lyuh was to come to my house at 4 o'clock. I waited past 4, 4:30. . . . And then finally at 4:35 the interpreter arrived panting and alarmed at my door. . . . He looked terrified. And then he told me. Just one block before he reached my house, Lyuh had been shot. That of course ended our attempts at forming a centrist government.

Yö had been the victim of nine murder attempts in two years. He had repeatedly asked the American Military Government for permission to carry a weapon, but had never received it. On that day in July 1947, while Yö was riding in a car, a young man had jumped onto the running board and pumped three bullets into his head, killing him instantly. Evidence indicates that the killer was a nineteen-year-old member of the Black Tiger Gang, which operated secretly alongside the Seoul police force. He may have been a follower of Kim Koo.

Although terrorism was common in Korea at this time, the Korean people were stunned and greatly saddened by the death of this popular leader. For two weeks after his death his body was laid out in state and thousands of people came to pay their respects, many pledging to carry on his fight for the People's Republic of Korea. A National Salvation Committee was formed almost immediately as a coalition among the left and the moderates of both sides to carry on Yö's work, but it was quickly outlawed by the police. On the day of Yö's funeral, the police prohibited any of the trappings of a public ceremony, but there was no stopping the huge procession of thousands of people from many different factions who had come out to honor the man many felt represented Korea. Three years later, when Yö's admirers tried to hold a memorial service for him, Syngman Rhee had ninety-seven of them arrested.

Where to Learn More

Cumings, Bruce. *The Origins of the Korean War.* 2 vols. Princeton, NJ: Princeton University Press, 1981.

Deane, Hugh. *The Korean War, 1945–1953.* San Francisco: China Books, 1999.

Kim, Joungwon Alexander. *Divided Korea: The Politics of Development, 1945–1972.* Cambridge, MA: East Asian Research Center, Harvard University, 1975.

Nahm, Andrew C. *Historical Dictionary of the Republic of Korea.* Metuchen, NJ: Scarecrow Press, 1993.

New York Times, June 23, 1947.

Index

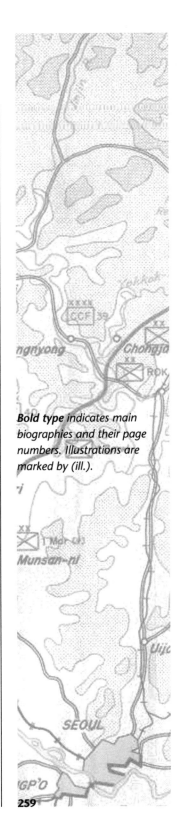

Bold type indicates main biographies and their page numbers. Illustrations are marked by (ill.).

Berlin Airlift and Blockade, 65, 214, 226
Bigart, Homer, 67, 69
Black Tiger Gang, 257
Blair, Clay, 35
Blevin, Alexander, 58
Bloody Gulch, 244
Bloody Ridge, 235
Bolshevik Revolution. *See* Russian Revolution of 1917
Bradley, John S., 66 (ill.)
Bradley, Omar N., 13–19, 13 (ill.), 17 (ill.), 182, 231
Brandeis, Louis D., 3–4
Brooke, Alan, 54
Buchenwald concentration camp, 63, 240
Bukharin, Nikolay, 208–209
Burchett, Wilfred, 47
Byrnes, James F., 4, 121

C

Calculated Risk (Clark), 35
Capitalism, 79, 99
Carter, James E., 80
Carter, Jimmy. *See* Carter, James E.
Cease-fire. *See* Armistice
Chang Chi-chung, 111 (ill.)
Chang Hsueh-liang. *See* Zhang Xueliang
Changjin Reservoir. *See* Chosin Reservoir
Chiang Kai-shek, 20–27, 20 (ill.), 26 (ill.)
　Acheson, Dean, 7–8, 11
　Clark, Mark W., 34, 57
　MacArthur, Douglas, 92–93
　Malik, Jacob A., 99
　Mao Zedong, 110–111, 113
　Peng Duhuai, 155, 159, 163–164
　Stalin, Joseph, 213–214
　Van Fleet, James A., 236
Chicago Daily News, 65, 69
China Lobby, 11
China (Mainland). *See also* Taiwan
　Acheson, Dean, 10
　Chiang Kai-shek, 20, 23–25
　Japanese invasion, 24–25, 110, 157–158
　MacArthur, Douglas, 92–93

Malik, Jacob A., 97, 99, 100
Mao Zedong, 107–116, 158
Paik Sun Yup, 141–143
Peng Dehuai, 156–164
Quemoy-Matsu Crisis, 164
relations with United States, 101, 104, 116
Ridgway, Matthew B., 183–186
Smith, Oliver P., 201–202
Stalin, Joseph, 213–214
Truman, Harry S., 227–228
United Nations and, 97, 99–100, 111–112
Van Fleet, James A., 234–235
Walker, Walton H. "Johnnie," 246–247
Chinese Civil War, 7–8, 25, 158
Chinese Nationalists, 22–23. *See also* Taiwan
Chinese People's Volunteers (CPV), 159, 162–163
Chosin Reservoir, 160–162, 161 (ill.), 195, 200–202, 247
Chu Teh, 111 (ill.)
Church, John H., 132
Churchill, Winston, 31, 54, 63, 212, 223
Clark, Mark W., 28–36, 28 (ill.), 35 (ill.), 57–58
Clark, Tom, 224
Coalition Committee for Cooperation, 256, 257
Cohn, Roy, 123
Cold War. *See also* Communism
　Acheson, Dean, 3–10
　Bradley, Omar N., 13
　Dean, William F., 40, 47
　Eisenhower, Dwight D., 49
　Higgins, Marguerite, 64–65
　Kennan, George F., 102–103
　Malik, Jacob A., 97, 99
　Rosenberg, Anna, 192
　Stalin, Joseph, 216
　Truman, Harry S., 218
Collective farming, 115, 210
Collins, J. Lawton, 16, 88
Committee for the Preparation of Korean Independence (CPKI), 149–151, 253. *See also* People's Committees
Communism. *See also* Anticommunism
　Acheson, Dean, 1–3, 5, 7–9, 11, 121

Chiang Kai-shek, 22
in China, 7, 22, 115–116
cult of personality, 71, 76–77, 210–211
Dean, William F., 46–47
in Greece, 233
Higgins, Marguerite, 64
Kennan, George F., 102–103
Kim Il Sung, 72–73, 75–77
in Korea, 173–174, 255–256
Malik, Jacob A., 99
Mao Zedong, 109–113
Marxism, 205
McCarthy, Joseph, 118
Pak Hön-yöng, 148–152
Peng Dehuai, 155–165
in Soviet Union, 205–216, 225–226
Communist China. *See* China (Mainland)
Communist Group. *See* Communist Party (Korea)
Communist Party (Korea), 148–149, 174, 251, 256
Communist Party (Soviet Union), 205–216
Concentration camps, 56, 63–64, 240
Confucianism, 167
Conner, Fox, 52
Conquest, Robert, 207
Containment, 9
CPKI (Committee for the Preparation of Korean Independence), 149–151, 253
CPV. *See* Chinese People's Volunteers
Cult of personality, 71, 76–77, 210–211
Cultural Revolution (China), 116
Cumings, Bruce, 252, 257
Current Biography (LaGuardia), 190
Current Biography (Marshall), 48

DeGaulle, Charles, 31
Democratic People's Republic of Korea (DPRK). *See* North Korea
Department of Defense (U.S.), 16
Desegregation, military, 188, 193
Dewey, Thomas, 226
Dissidence, political. *See* Political protests
Divided Korea (Joungwon), 172
DPRK. *See* North Korea
Draft, 10
Dulles, John Foster, 164
Dzhugashvili, Iosif Vissarionovich. *See* Stalin, Joseph

E

East Germany, 7
Economic aid, 5, 178
Eisenhower, Dwight D., 10, **49–59**, 49 (ill.), 57 (ill.)
Bradley, Omar N., 14
Clark, Mark W., 29, 34, 56–57
MacArthur, Douglas, 85, 88
McCarthy, Joseph, 118, 123, 124
Paik Sun Yup, 145–146
Rhee, Syngman, 178
Ridgway, Matthew B., 186
Rosenberg, Anna, 193
Truman, Harry S., 228
Van Fleet, James A., 230–231, 237
Elections, Korean, 114, 128–129, 174, 183, 197, 215, 241–242
Dean, William F., 41–42
Kim Il Sung, 73–74
Rhee, Syngman, 41–42, 128, 174
Embassy at War (Noble), 128
Executive Order 9981, 193

D

Dachen Islands, 163
DACOWITS, 193
Dauchau concentration camp, 64
Dean, William F., **37–48**, 37 (ill.), 46 (ill.), 132, 242
Defense Advisory Committee on Women in the Services (DACOWITS), 193

F

Farming, collective, 115, 210
Farrell, F. W., 244 (ill.)
Fechteler, William M., 16
Federal Republic of West Germany, 6–7
First, Peter, 63–64
Five Year Plan (Soviet Union), 210

Flanders, Ralph, 124
Foreign policy
    Acheson, Dean, 1, 3, 6, 9–11
    Kennan, George F., 103
    Stalin, Joseph, 212–214
    Truman, Harry S., 225–226
*The Forgotten War: America in
    Korea, 1950–1953,* (Blair), 35
Formosa. *See* Taiwan
Fredericksen, John C., 241
*From Pusan to Panmunjom:
    Wartime Memoirs of the
    Republic of Korea's First
    Four-Star General* (Paik),
    135, 235–236
From the Danube to the Yalu
    (Clark), 32, 35

G

General Dean's Story (Dean), 37,
    45–46, 48
German Democratic Republic, 7
Germany, 6–7
GI Bill, 190
Goulden, Joseph C., 18, 94, 174,
    199, 243
Great Depression, 84
Great Leap Forward, 115,
    164–165
Gromyko, Andrei A., 105
Guerilla warfare, 87, 145, 153

H

Hall, William, 65, 69
Hardy, Mary Pinkney, 82–83
Harriman, W. Averell, 102
Heartbreak Ridge, 145, 235
Hersey, John, 85
Hess, Jerry N., 89, 129, 131
Higgins, Marguerite, 60–70,
    60 (ill.), 66 (ill.)
Higgins and Beech (Movie), 70
Hines, Frank T., 190
Hiss, Alger, 121
Hitler, Adolph, 211
Ho Chi Minh, 10
Hodge, John Reed, 254–255
Hoge, William, 191 (ill.)
Hoover, Herbert, 84
Hu Han-min, 22

Hu Tsungnan, 158
Hunan Provincial Soviet
    Government, 156
Hydrogen bombs, 7, 10. *See also*
    Atomic bombs

I

*In Mortal Combat: Korea,
    1950–1953* (Toland), 130,
    231–232, 243
Inchon, South Korea, 88, 141,
    195, 199, 227, 245
Independence, Korean
    Kim Il Sung, 72–73
    Pak Hön-yöng, 148
    Rhee, Syngman, 168–172, 257
    Yö Un-hyöng, 249,
        252–254, 257
Independence Club, 168–169
International Bank for
    Reconstruction and
    Development, 4, 102
International Monetary Fund,
    4, 102
International trusteeship,
    173–174, 256
Isolationism, U.S., 4

J

Jaisohn, Philip, 168
Japan
    Constitution of 1947, 89
    government of, 87–90, 252–253
    invasion of China, 24–25, 110,
        157–158
    MacArthur, Douglas, 87–90
    relations with U.S., 10, 169,
        223–224
    surrender of, 183, 224
    Walker, Walton H.
        "Johnnie," 241
    World War II, 85–87
    Yö Un-hyöng, 252–253
Japan Inside Out (Rhee), 171
Japanese constitution of 1947, 89
Japanese occupation, 167–171
Jessup, Philip C., 122
Johnson, E. A. J., 257
Johnson, Louis Arthur, 16